Living on the Diagonal

and Other Selected Writings

by William G. Durden

President of Dickinson College
From 1999 to 2013

Published by Dickinson College
P.O. Box 1773
Carlisle, Pa. 17103

ISBN-13: 978-1484167182

Cover photo by A. Pierce Bounds

"Liberal Arts for All, Not Just the Rich," "The Liberal Arts as a Bulwark of
Business Education" and "A Liberal-Arts Home for the Military" appeared
originally in *The Chronicle of Higher Education*. "Complaints About
Corporatization in Academe Are Overstated and Polemical" appeared
originally in *Trusteeship Magazine*. "No God Left Behind—Why Not?,"
"Let Us Disarm!," "Vertigo Years," "The Real Tsunami" and "A Useful
Liberal Arts" appeared originally in *Inside Higher Ed*. "Helping Students
Govern Themselves" appeared originally in *The Philadelphia Inquirer*.
"The Silence Is Broken" appeared originally in *The Huffington Post*.

Acknowledgements

I want to thank especially my wife, Elke, and colleagues Karen Faryniak and Stephanie Balmer for the time they took to read and talk with me about this publication and to provide critical edits. For editing, design and production, I would like to thank Matt Getty, Tony Moore and Pat Pohlman.

Contents

Living on the Diagonal

Notes to a 21st-Century Student
From a Retiring College President

Preface

As I set off after a 14-year tenure as president of Dickinson College, I feel compelled to share what I have learned about how to live a life in the 21st century with both current and future students. I suppose this is my final teaching gesture. I wish to do so not from abstract theory but rather from personal experience. And I write from a perspective that is not the ordinary within the educational establishment of higher education. Yes, I am a college president. But I did not pursue the typical path to a college presidency—far from it. I never sought tenure, and I have not experienced the academic progression of assistant to associate to full professor. I am an outsider masquerading as an insider. Perhaps I am best characterized as an academic entrepreneur. I delight in taking knowledge and connecting it to other knowledge wherever it exists and out of that building something new—either within the academy or beyond it. And it is perhaps my "distance" from and uneasiness within the traditional academy that permit me to see what those squarely inside the educational circle never see or appreciate.

Chapter 1

Lessons to Share

I am a graduate of Dickinson College. I was a double major—German and philosophy. On the face of it, what could be more useless? And yet, my professional life has proven such a conclusion wrong.

I have been—sometimes simultaneously—a military officer, a precollegiate teacher, an administrator and a coach. I have founded an athletic team, developed a major center at a prestigious research university and have been a senior consultant to the U.S. Department of State with diplomatic status, a senior executive in two publicly traded companies and, most recently, president of Dickinson College. Most of these jobs involved leadership. Notably, for none of the areas of professional activity for which I am known nationally and internationally did I ever study formally. I never took a course in gifted and talented education or in business development and marketing. I am not necessarily proud of that, but what I have realized is that the breadth of knowledge and the depth of cognitive skill that my core college courses and all the courses in art, political science, science and social science I took at Dickinson prepared me to master independently and rather rapidly any field of professional pursuit with which I was confronted.

I was prepared for professional chance. I knew regardless of area of job activity how to ask the right questions, how to gather information to make things work, how to make informed decisions, how to see connections among disparate areas of knowledge and activity, how to see what others never see, how to learn quickly the basics of a profession, where to go for more information, how to discern pertinent information from that which is false or misleading, how to judge good, helpful people from those who wish you ill. All of this I gathered in a useful liberal education in and out of the classroom—in my formal course of study: courses in the humanities, arts, sciences and social sciences—and in an intense residential setting, where experimentation with citizenship and social responsibility were guiding principles. However, there were no formal, discrete courses to learn these habits of mind and action, no courses devoted exclusively to brain exercises, critical-thinking skills, leadership as a skill and citizenship; rather, professors and staff were united in all interactions to impress upon students day after day, year after year, a liberal-arts learning environment that was intellectually rigorous and defining. This was contextual learning at its fullest deployment. I absorbed and displayed ultimately useful knowledge and skill not in a studied manner but discretely and naturally. At that time, however, in the late 1960s and early 1970s, if anyone claimed that what I was experiencing was a "useful" liberal-arts education, he or she would have been derided. For a liberal-arts education in America to be in any way associated with usefulness was to compromise it by linking it to the industrial complex—to corporate America and crass materialism.

But the most prevailing example of the power of the usefulness of my liberal-arts education to the wider world originates decades ago with my Ph.D. dissertation from Johns Hopkins University's Department of German Language and Literature. I treasure my graduate education at Hopkins. It was rigorous, intellectually exciting, liberal-arts focused and interdisciplinary. In fact, I chose Hopkins over the University of Chicago because the latter would not let me take courses in departments other than German, and Hopkins celebrated such interdisciplinarity. I believe the vocational ambition of the graduate division was to yield young scholars, not necessarily teachers, who would model their professor—that is, pursue a career within the academy and, most specifically, a research university. Anything less was a disappointment.

My dissertation established a new genre—the 18th-century German literary advisory letter. The literary letter shares characteristics with other kinds of letters as well as with closely related genres such as the treatise and the essay, but it is distinguished by a proprietary form and function. The work is either a fictional or semifictional prose letter, and it has a characteristic configuration: an older or more experienced poet (a mentor) addresses a younger or less mature poet (a pupil). The letter's purpose is, at least on one level, an informal presentation of literary advice from the fictional or semifictional writer to his reader. However, the letter also functions on another more extensive level. The empirical author—German, in the case of those studied in my dissertation—expects the letter to be read by a larger audience of empirical readers, many of them young or aspiring poets, and thus intends it to influence this public with opinions about literature and the responsibilities of a poet.

The literary advisory letter did not only enjoy popularity in the 18th century. Although the epistle is absent for most of the 19th century, it was used by many 20th-century German authors to accomplish purposes similar to those for which it was applied nearly 200 years earlier. Rainer Maria Rilke's "Letters to a Young Poet" is the most prominent 20th-century example. However, the advisory letter was not restricted to Germany. For example, the 20th-century American author and physician William Carlos Williams published in the October 1942 issue of *The View* "Advice to a Young Poet."

While I enjoyed immensely writing my dissertation, there was never mention of this liberal-arts document serving anyone or anything beyond the academic field itself. It was at once an important intellectual milestone and a required step on the way to its objective—to secure a professorship at a research university. It was sufficient in and of itself.

But now I know that this early engagement in the literary genre of an older, experienced person sharing personally gained insight into life and sharing that with younger persons is the model that defines how I chose to leave academia. I am now the "older poet" and future students are the "young poets." I have lessons to share.

Chapter 2

Usefulness at Dickinson College

When I came back to Dickinson as president in 1999, I immediately recognized that students had absolutely no idea what it meant to be a Dickinsonian. They could provide no larger purpose for attending the college other than it was what society demanded. For them it was merely a box to check on the way to something else. It was merely transactional. My discovery of our students' lack of greater vision and purpose is well documented in a chapter devoted to Dickinson College in David Kirp's 2003 book *Shakespeare, Einstein and the Bottom Line: The Marketing of Higher Education.* Citing me, Kirp writes:

> "Soon after I got here, I hiked part of the Appalachian Trail with some students," he [Durden] recalls, retelling a story that he has made part of the new Dickinson folklore. "A senior who'd done very well told me that she didn't really know what it meant to be a Dickinsonian. In retrospect, that became a defining moment of my administration."

I needed as soon as possible to help our students appreciate the greater reasons for attending Dickinson and in turn a liberal-arts college. I intuitively knew that the purpose and the value of the education lay in not only the acquisition of knowledge but also in citizenship. I had gained this appreciation from a year I had spent after my Ph.D. at Columbia University Teachers College on a Klingenstein Fellowship. A good part of my time at Columbia was devoted to independent readings in the history of American education—particularly the writings of Lawrence Cremin, a Pulitzer Prize-winning historian of education and president of Teachers College at the time. I just didn't know how I would make the connection between citizenship and Dickinson most vivid and dramatic—it had to be a compelling connection that provided the students distinctive ownership.

The breakthrough came within the first few months of my administration. My wife, who also had earned a Ph.D. from the Johns Hopkins Department of German Language and Literature, asked me if I had ever heard of Dr. Benjamin Rush and his possible relationship to Dickinson College. Embarrassingly, I had no idea who he was, much less his relationship to the college. She had read something about him and thought I would want to look into his life and times. To that end, she bought me a copy of his complete letters. Well, after just a few pages of the letters, I realized that I had found precisely what I was seeking.

I am a devotee of Harvard professor Howard Gardner's perspective on leadership. Leadership is all about crafting a narrative that people want to inhabit; they want to be a character in the narrative with you, and in that way they are brought with you to new levels of accomplishment. For Professor Gardner, a leadership narrative has three components—a protagonist, goals and a foil. In Dr. Benjamin Rush I had the protagonist I needed to move our students to a new level of appreciation for the purpose of Dickinson College and the values that they might embrace through our education as inherited from him. I could also link their education directly with citizenship.

Dr. Rush was a signer of the Declaration of Independence and one of the most outspoken advocates of separation of the colonies from England, even if it meant revolution. He was clearly a person defined by the prejudices of the 18th century, and yet amidst all his contradictory statements, you can perceive a progressive thinker and actor moving into a new, more enlightened era. He was an early abolitionist and was president of the first society dedicated to abolition in the United States; he funded and attended the first African American church in America and advanced the serious education of women; he advocated for the humane treatment of the mentally challenged and fought for the reform of prisons; and he was against the death penalty. A temperamental and outspoken personality, Rush was arguably the first army officer to challenge the commander in chief during war. He questioned General Washington's oversight of the medical condition of his troops and attributed the Continental Army's many early defeats not to soldiers' battle wounds but to their sorry state through medical treatment. After registering his concern, he resigned as surgeon general of the Middle Army. Gen. Washington, however, heeded Dr. Rush's admonitions and suggestions and made many of the recommended changes.

But perhaps most important for my purposes, Dr. Rush wrote extensively about the reform of American education to accommodate the new democracy that was the United States. He wanted a useful liberal education that matched learning with the responsibilities of college graduates to participate fully in the new nation. Dickinson College in particular was to be the model institution for a new national network of colleges and universities devoted to educating students for democratic commitment. He called for an engaged student who was globally aware and equipped with the knowledge and skill to confront America's opportunities. As a scientist and physician, he espoused an interest in and a caring for the natural environment and the human body. Mindful eating, drinking and exercise were espoused. This was a rousing, youthful call to revolution in education to match that in government, and Dickinsonians were by definition committed to positive social change. His coconspirators were John Adams and Thomas Jefferson, and while they did not agree with all his vision in its entirety, they enthusiastically became his sounding board.

While I was a student at Dickinson in the late 1960s and early 1970s, absolutely no mention was made of Dr. Rush by the administration. Had anyone mentioned his name, we would have been clueless. I would hazard to say that my fellow students and I thought John Dickinson was the founder of the college, as it bore his name! And while there were periods in Dickinson's long history when Dr. Rush was discussed, this was in the confines of academic pursuits and was never translated into a leadership narrative for the college to provide it identity and to motivate its students to see themselves as part of something of value larger than themselves. Dr. Rush was never used, in modern parlance, to "brand" the college.

In 2000, I began to incorporate Dr. Rush—his thoughts, reforms, calls for action by Dickinson College—in all my speeches and writings. Students were exposed year after year to a litany of Rush references. I was unrelenting. Catchphrases were copyrighted that reflected

Dr. Rush's urgings—"Engage the World," "Distinctively Dickinson," "Walking on the Diagonal," "First in America." Students, faculty and alumni were invoked to join with me in fulfilling the dream of a signer of the Declaration of Independence—a dream for a progressive and ultimately useful liberal-arts education for America. They were made aware of how rare it is to be able to participate in the ambitions of a signer and that they, as Dickinsonians, could not only do this, but the privilege was their inherited obligation—even into the 20th and then 21st centuries. The founder of their college expected they would engage his dream and fulfill it through their education at the college. I invited our community to join me and participate in continuing to write our distinctive leadership narrative by our individual and collective actions.

My colleagues and I also introduced during this period "A 21st Century Skill Set: The Dickinson Dimensions." This was an initial attempt to introduce students to habits of thought and action that potentially lead to the values that the college holds precious. With the exception of military academies and deeply religiously affiliated institutions, most colleges and universities rarely attempt to impart values to students. There is the notion that doing so can lead to controversy. Dickinson, however, sees such values and the actions needed to secure them as inextricably wedded to our historic mission. The Dimensions are extrapolated from the writings of our founder, Dr. Rush, and reflect our ambitions for students through participation in our academic and residential programs. This was our initial campuswide attempt to counter what Arthur Levine described as contemporary college students' obsession with the training needed to get a job and the neglect of those values that permit them to transcend themselves and commit to leadership and responsibility in a broader society.

The Dickinson Dimensions are referred to in all my speeches and those of my colleagues. They are listed on posters displayed prominently throughout campus, and posters of alumni who embody the Dimensions are also displayed throughout campus. The Dimensions are first introduced to students during first-year Orientation and are as follows:

- Write and communicate clearly, persuasively and logically in more than one language.

- Possess a global sensibility that permits you to be comfortable in the world and engage it without hesitation or anxiety.

- Listen well to others, and possess the judgment that not all good ideas issue from you alone or from those who speak only English.

- Appreciate the quantitative dimension in human knowledge while simultaneously comprehending that it is highly dangerous to believe that all truth can be incorporated in a single digit.

- Appreciate that we live in a world with potentially dwindling natural resources. There is no need to consume more than is necessary.

- Value the entrepreneurial capacity of human beings, and cultivate it to purposeful and beneficial ends.

- Gain a comfort level with uncertainty and ambiguity, as these qualities will define much of the professional and personal life you will encounter.

- Appreciate that change is inevitable and can be engaged productively. Remember that today's novelty is inevitably tomorrow's tradition.

- Recognize that all that is "different" is not necessarily good or virtuous. Some historical differences within cultures conflict with our global society's contemporary understanding of ethics and morals.

- Gain the ability to distinguish fact from rumor, both in direct human contact and on the Internet.

- Internalize a sense of civility and respect for other peoples that considers the interactive protocols of a variety of cultures—in more old-fashioned terms, employ good manners.

* Develop a personal voice, and use it to speak out confidently, yet civilly, on issues that matter.

* Appreciate the key moments of understanding and misunderstanding that have occurred through the ages in the humanities, the sciences, the arts and the social sciences and apply them to grasp contemporary challenges and opportunities.

* Appreciate that the liberal-arts education you gain at Dickinson is ultimately pragmatic and commits you to engage democracy in all its manifestations—from citizenship (both historically informed and entrepreneurial) to employment to public service. This commitment defines a distinctively "useful" American education as intended by the college's founder, Dr. Benjamin Rush, and his friend and fellow revolutionary Thomas Jefferson.

The practical results of this invitation to participate in a narrative are evident, and once again, the link between a liberal-arts notion and utility in the wider word is underscored. Without doubt, the Benjamin Rush narrative contributes directly to the flourishing of the college's business model from 1999 to 2013. Alumni, parents and friends engaged the narrative and in so doing supported the college financially and emotionally as never before in its history, and the college in general improved greatly in many key dimensions during this period. A June 2, 2006, article in the *Chronicle of Higher Education* tracks the advancement of the college to that point:

> If Dickinson College were a corporation, Wall Street would view it as a classic turnaround story. Less than a decade ago, the liberal-arts institution was struggling. Applications were down. Enrollment was declining. Net tuition revenue—the amount a college is able to keep after subtracting money spent

on financial aid—was plummeting, as was the college's bond rating.

To make matters worse, Dickinson's endowment was dribbling away. "We were spending 6 percent of the endowment on running the college, and that was not sustainable," says Annette S. Parker, the college's vice president and treasurer. Yet the college was doing relatively little to build the endowment, which was a modest $150 million.

Dickinson was not in danger of going under. But if these trends were not reversed, the venerable institution, founded in 1783 by Benjamin Rush, a signer of the Declaration of Independence, was heading for a major crisis.

Flash forward to this year, and the picture is vastly different. Applications are at a record high, topping 5,000 for the first time. Enrollment is up by more than 350 students and now exceeds 2,260. Net tuition revenue is rising, and the discount rate—the proportion of tuition revenue the college gives back to students in the form of grants—has plummeted from 52 percent to 34 percent. Some of the grants were merit awards designed to lure certain students to the college and were not necessarily based on need.

For Dickinson the future now looks promising, thanks in large part to the college's rapidly growing endowment. It rose by almost 30 percent from fiscal 2004 to 2005, placing Dickinson 16th in rate of growth among 746 institutions, according to a survey by the National Association of College and University Business Officers, done in conjunction with the pension funds TIAA-CREF. The survey puts Dickinson's endowment at $206 million, a figure that excludes pledges and deferred gifts. The college calculates that its endowment at the end of

June 2005 was almost $251 million and now stands at $283 million.

A substantial increase in alumni contributions has played a major role in the endowment's growth. Equally important has been the college's impressive return on its investments. For the past two years, Dickinson has significantly outperformed its peers. In fiscal 2005, its return on invested endowment funds was 12.6 percent, compared to a national average of 9.3 percent, according to the NACUBO study. The previous year, its return was 19.3 percent, topping the national average of 15.1 percent.

As a result of the turnaround, Standard & Poor's has upgraded Dickinson's bond rating by two notches to A, the highest rating in the college's history. "It is difficult for an institution of higher education to accomplish the kind of financial progress Dickinson has made," says Mary Peloquin-Dodd, a credit analyst at Standard & Poor's. "That type of improvement is not common." (p. B15)

A comparison of key performance indicators from the period before the introduction of the leadership narrative (1998) to the near end of the tenure of the current administration (2012) speaks for itself:

- First-year applications rose from 3,030 to 5,844 (with an all-time high in 2011 of 6,067).

- The average SAT scores for incoming students went from 1189 to 1293.

- The percentage of domestic students of color increased from 5.4 percent to 13.8 percent.

- The amount of gifted scholarship/institutional grant monies offered rose from $18.5 million to $39.2 million.

- Total endowment monies increased from $151.7 million to $355.8 million.

- Campus wireless infrastructure grew from a single connection in 1998 to a completely wired campus with close to 900 connections.

- Likewise, we started with one technology-equipped classroom and now have 114 across campus.

- Prior to 1999 the college received only three gifts of $1 million or more from individuals; during the past 14 years, the college received 33 such gifts.

- Prior to 1999 there were no faculty positions supported by gifts of $1 million or more; today, 17 faculty positions are supported by gifts at this level.

- Last, the college's visibility through the media grew exponentially, with the number of news stories rising from 56 to 3,584 and a corresponding increase in impressions from 10.3 million to 904.9 million.

Chapter 3

Notes to a 21st-Century Student

Although the Benjamin Rush-based leadership narrative and the related Dickinson Dimensions were institutionally successful at Dickinson, I nevertheless did not believe that the values forwarded by the college were affecting our current students to any great degree. I did not perceive a sufficient dialogue among students about what these values were and how embracing them would advance their lives beyond Dickinson—in the working world as well as in their personal affairs.

It was at this point that I made a switch to the protagonist of the narrative. I did not do away with the BR narrative—it remains strong—but I added myself as yet another protagonist. I reached back and brought forth my own version of a literary advisory letter titled "Notes to a 21st-Century Student." I thought that students might engage the topic more intimately if the habits of mind and action presented to them came from a contemporary figure they knew rather than a historical figure. I also believed that a "note" directly to them rather than a list of values on a poster was more accessible. To enforce further the immediacy of my advisory letter, I made it clear to students that the advice I was giving them for living and succeeding in the 21st century originated quite personally, as it was given to me by a series of mentors. In other words, I was once who those students are now.

The items in the "Notes to a 21st-Century Student" reflect what I have valued for habits of mind and action over a professional lifetime, but they also reflect completely the spirit of advice in the Dickinson Dimensions:

* Attempt to meet and speak with the great people of your time—approach them civilly and in an informed manner.

Ask them to share their advice about how to live an engaged life professionally and personally. Ask them about their passion and motivation for what they do.

- Be out in the world—engage it safely and vigorously, as it is only in this way that things happen.

- Live intensely during your first 25 years, because during that period you will essentially establish the patterns of your life.

- Never underestimate or belittle any experience you have had in your life. Think about the knowledge and skills you have gained. You never know what might come in handy in another context.

- Develop the ability to anticipate events. Visualize the end-point—various possible endpoints—before it occurs, as it is good to have "already been there."

- Work hard, but mask the effort in the end product, just as a fine literary work looks effortless but stands upon hours of hard work.

- Approach a subject or task from many perspectives—connect disparate areas where others just see a blank.

- Live on the "diagonal." Look for answers where others have not already tread.

- Don't worry about having a life plan—rather be prepared for chance and when it occurs, and then recognize and engage it.

- Seek a tough mentor—not a "yes person" who artificially builds up your self-esteem. And in general, beware of sycophants offering you unearned praise.

- Leadership is often narrative—storytelling—with a protagonist, a plot and a foil.

* Boredom and repetition are essential parts of leadership, as leadership consists primarily of telling a story again and again and in such a compelling manner that others want to be a part of it. Each repetition must sound as if it is being delivered for the first time with passion and urgency.

* Do not underestimate the role of passion in your profession—you must believe strongly in what you pursue, and it must be far bigger than yourself.

* Look at objects and people straight on, and seek to know precisely what defines them singularly and collectively.

* Remember that nothing is more mysterious than a fact closely examined.

* Just because something is allowed legally does not mean that that option should be exercised. Good judgment is the arbiter.

* Know that rights are linked to responsibilities. People often unproductively proclaim their rights but do nothing to either guarantee those rights or assume the personal responsibilities that uphold them.

* Question the simplicity of an either/or approach to life. Find meaning in the gray area, and see it as substantive—an active force.

* Live in the connective tissue as well as in the bone—that is, appreciate the qualitative and associative as well as the quantitative and orderly dimensions of life.

* Find meaning in contradictory ideas as a step to maturity and pragmatic action.

To ensure further that students will leave the college having thought about these habits of mind and action, during my final year at the college I invited all seniors to come to my office and chat one-on-one or in self-selected small groups about the "Notes" and their futures. Seniors have responded vigorously to this invitation.

In the personal meetings, I reveal to the students my life experiences that have informed the individual items of the "Notes." I detail four of those points in the next chapters.

Chapter 4

Meet the Great People of Your Time

Soon after my wife and I received our doctorates from Johns Hopkins, we were invited to the home of a distinguished professor of English, Hugh Kenner. Neither of us had taken a course with Professor Kenner while graduate students, so I believe this came about because I was teaching his son, Rob, at a local Baltimore independent school. The evening was delightful with Professor Kenner and his wife, but what soon became apparent was that he wanted to bestow upon us advice. He told us stories about his own professional life, linked to recommendations about how we might conduct ours.

As I recall after all these years, he began talking about his time as a graduate student and his need to talk to a certain rather prominent person in Paris—a person who was essential to his dissertation. While not a person of means, he put together enough money for boat passage and a cheap hotel. Once there he sent a gracious note every evening to the person he wished to meet. He simply stated that he was a graduate student and that he would value greatly time to chat with this person and understand why he did certain things as he did. Ten evenings went by and he was running out of money. While packing to go back to the States, there was a knock on his hotel room door and a messenger gave him a note, which read as follows:

Dear Mr. Kenner,

Of course, I would be delighted to chat with you. Sorry I did not respond earlier. I am out of the city. Please bring some wine or bread and we can talk.

Samuel Beckett

Beckett not only spoke to the young Hugh Kenner, but he introduced him to Ezra Pound, W.H. Auden and T.S. Eliot, and a brilliant career as a literary critic was established. Professor Kenner's advice to my wife and me was never to hesitate contacting those thought too famous for acquaintance. A polite approach with serious intent will open doors. Further, most famous people are actually lonely and appreciate a chance to talk about their own lives and to give advice to younger people based on what they have seen and done.

I have tried to follow Professor Kenner's advice throughout my professional career. And it has yielded benefits. For example, when I was first working at the Center for Talented Youth at Johns Hopkins, I noticed an op-ed piece in *The New York Times* about education written by Admiral Hyman Rickover, the founder of the U.S. nuclear navy. Heeding Professor Kenner's advice, I wrote the admiral a polite letter in which I both praised aspects of his argument and respectfully criticized several points. I asked for his opinion on my contrary perspective. I heard nothing for months. I thought that was that and I would receive no answer. While I was on a business trip to Arizona, my secretary called me and said that I had an unusual letter from Admiral Rickover. It was an invitation for my wife and me to attend the admiral's 80th birthday party, hosted by presidents Carter, Ford and Nixon (Ronald Reagan was president at that time), and indicating a rather hefty contribution. The then-astronomical numerical figure was crossed out and replaced by the words "Compliments of the Admiral." I was, perhaps needless to say, astounded.

My wife and I attended the birthday party and had an incredible experience. There was an opportunity to chat with the three former presidents and to end the evening with President Nixon at the piano leading everybody in a "Happy Birthday" salute to the admiral. Admiral Rickover had quite a reputation as a hard driver and a stubborn man with very demanding standards. President Carter, formerly an officer in the U.S. nuclear navy, remembered his experience as a nuclear naval officer interacting with a determined and opinionated Rickover, and during the course of the evening, he recounted a story from when he was the sitting president: He was on the phone in the Oval Office, calmly talking to Leonid Brezhnev, the leader of the Soviet Union, about some sensitive international issues, and he broke out in a cold sweat when his secretary came in to the room and placed under his eyes a note stating "The admiral is on the line."

Following the gala, I sent the admiral a thank-you note and a copy of a draft about education I was preparing for the journal of the American Academy of Arts and Sciences, *Daedalus*. (The article later appeared in the summer 1983 issue titled "Lessons for Excellence in Education.") Following Professor Kenner's advice, I asked for the admiral's critique. I boldly invited him to engage me in dialogue about an issue that mattered—he the distinguished admiral, and I a beginning academic and administrator. Two weeks later, I was on the phone in my Center for Talented Youth office and my secretary came in and placed a note under my eyes with explosive words: "Admiral Rickover is calling." I, of course, immediately remembered President Carter's reflections on precisely the same scene, but I also recalled President Carter's advice about how to deal with the admiral. I came on the line and at first heard nothing. Then I heard a rather sharp and harsh voice say, "Who is this? Whoever you are, you are dumb! Do you even have a high school diploma? You are simply an embarrassment. You know nothing." After pausing to absorb what I heard, I did what was advised. I said calmly yet emphatically, "With all due respect, Admiral, you do not know what you are talking about. You are totally misguided." Quite a risky statement for a young man to make! Then there was a long pause on his end. He grunted and said, "This is what we are going to do. I'm coming to your office next week, and we are going to talk. And I want you to arrange a lunch with the current president of Johns Hopkins, Steve Muller; my dear old friend, the former president of Hopkins, Dr. Milton Eisenhower; and you and me. Dr. Eisenhower's brother [U.S. President Dwight D. Eisenhower] sent us together to figure out the Soviet Union after the war, and I have not seen him for a long time."

Well, the lunch happened, and as a young man in my early 30s I could simply not believe what was occurring by just heeding the advice of Professor Kenner. Not only did I have a close relationship with Admiral Rickover from that point forward, but Dr. Eisenhower took me under his wing and mentored me in the art of university administration. Some of my fondest memories are going to Dr. Eisenhower's apartment when he was quite advanced in age and chatting with him about university life and American politics—with particular reference to his brother's likes and dislikes. I had an inside view of a world I previously could only but imagine. My professional career has been defined by these early meetings.

Chapter 5

Belittle No Experience

I grew up in a rural area of upstate New York. As a child I was an 11-year member of a 4-H Club—the Happy Clovers. As part of my 4-H engagement, I raised chickens and ducks. In fact, I had a chicken business and delivered eggs to families in the surrounding region. While other students in the independent school I attended in Albany for junior high and high school went to summer camps in New England, I worked a large garden and tended to my poultry.

One might think that with a growing sophistication in my life, I would want to deny this rather humble and mundane personal history. After all, I was operating in circles that never got closer to farms than the food served on their plates at fine restaurants. But I don't hide where I came from or what I did. That said, it took me a while to fully appreciate what this early rural experience meant to my life and professional career. For a few decades I was extremely cautious about revealing this farming past. How utterly foolish this was in retrospect.

I can think of at least three instances where my farming background helped me prepare for a successful professional career.

My ability to raise money for colleges, universities and other community organizations during my career is, I believe, directly tied to my egg business. As an 11-year-old, my parents would drive me about our part of the country and I would get out of the car with a model dozen eggs and approach a house I had never before visited. I would somewhat timidly knock and, when the door was opened, try to tell my story and close a deal on delivering fresh eggs weekly for an agreed-upon price. In contemporary development jargon, I had a short window of opportunity to present my case—my "elevator speech"—and close the deal on what was a "cold call." And I found out that I was pretty good at it. Proceeds from my egg business helped pay for my tuition at Dickinson College.

Part of my engagement with chickens through 4-H was to accept from the local Kiwanis Club a baby chick and raise it for market under the mentorship of a club member. I did this with Mr. Maxwell. As a reward for the accomplishment of the project, I was invited to a restaurant to present my experience to club members. Part of the deal was that while I was speaking, I had to have the bird with me. I had to take the fully-grown chicken out of a cage and hold it down at my side. Well, as can be imagined, the bird would have none of my oratory. While I was speaking and holding the bird next to me, it vigorously flapped it wings, tried to attack me and "screamed" quite loudly. But what happened was that I discovered a concentration and focus that permitted me to communicate with the audience despite the disruption. I kept my audience and did not lose my composure. To this day, I attribute my ability to speak to any crowd in any venue to that chicken, which I had fondly named Mabel. If I could talk through and over a frustrated, angry chicken held at my side, I could deliver to any audience.

And last, I remember a fundraising situation in Los Angeles while I was working for Johns Hopkins that turned out quite positively because of my 4-H experience. I was asked by Dr. Richard Longaker, the provost of the university at the time, to accompany the medical school's development officer and assist in raising money from a foundation president. I was to go along, I assumed, because I had had some success in raising money in California.

When we entered the president's office I knew that this was going to be a strenuous visit. There was absolutely nothing on the desk before us—not one pencil, pen or piece of paper. My very formal and proper colleague started to speak about the excellence of medicine at Hopkins and covered some of the great new accomplishments that would issue from funding provided by this foundation. I was the invited colleague and was not all that sure I was that welcome. I just sat there and watched. I noticed two things: The foundation president was absolutely bored, and my colleague just kept going without sensitivity to the situation. This was going absolutely nowhere. I also spotted but one item on the wall—a bronze relief of a chicken! So what to do? Do I break my silence and start talking about chickens in this austere yet prestigious office high over downtown Los Angeles, or do

I remain silent? I made my decision. I spoke. "Excuse me, sir. Is that a chicken I see on the wall?" The look on my colleagues face was utter mortification. Somehow she thought, I suppose, that I had degraded the dignity of the prestigious Johns Hopkins medical institutions. The president, however, sat up and turned sharply toward me. "Do you know anything about chickens?" he asked. He came suddenly alive. I said, "You bet I do! I raised them, had an egg business and was trained in chicken judging at a community college." He responded, "Now we're talking. I raise prize chickens. Let's talk a bit."

Again, my colleague was sitting there both mortified and astounded. Well, the president and I talked chickens for about an hour, high over L.A. At the conclusion, he looked at us and said, "I like you folks, and I shall definitely consider your appeal." Well, the medical school got its money. If I had been concerned with my image and perhaps that of Johns Hopkins—if I had thought that both the university and I were too sophisticated and precious to be associated with the simplicity of raising chickens—this positive result may well have never happened.

Chapter 6

Engage the World, and Good Things Happen

When I was at Johns Hopkins directing the Center for Talented Youth, my writings about talent development attracted the attention of Sir Cyril Taylor, CBE. Sir Cyril lives in London and is founder and chairman of the American International Foreign Study (AIFS). He serves as chancellor and founder of Richmond, the American International University in London. In 1987 he was appointed founder chairman of the City Technology College Trust, subsequently the Specialist Schools and Academies Trust (SSAT). He has served as advisor to 10 successive secretaries of state for education in the UK. Sir Cyril visited me at Hopkins, and we began a sustained conversation about gifted and talented education and its place in a democracy.

In 2001, Sir Cyril asked me to fly to London to deliver a keynote address at the annual conference of City Technology College Trust. Following the presentation, my wife and I were invited to the conference gala, and I was seated at one of the head tables. On my left was the CEO of EMI Music Group, and on my right was Andrew Adonis, then head of Prime Minister Blair's Domestic Policy Unit at 10 Downing Street and now Lord Adonis. My liberal-arts education and exposure to a wide range of subject areas served me well that evening. The head of EMI wanted to talk about his sensational new singing group, the Spice Girls. He asked me, "Have you ever heard of the Spice Girls?" I responded affirmatively. He then took the inquiry to another level: "Well, in that case, can you name them?" Luckily, I had been practicing one of the items in my "Notes to a 21st-Century Student": I do not shun any type of reading based on a preconceived notion of what is intellectually appropriate and what is not. So on my flight to London I read avidly *People* magazine and *Entertainment Weekly* (yes, also *Time, Newsweek* and *The Economist*). Just by chance, *People* had a feature article about the Spice Girls. I absorbed it all. So

I responded to his question without hesitation, naming with great gusto all four "Girls." He was simply astounded. He leaned toward me and addressed Lord Adonis, saying, "You need to talk with this chap. He is up-to-date." Mr. Adonis and I then began a conversation far removed from entertainment and the Spice Girls. We covered the advancement of academic ability in a nation, the definition of the American spirit, the effect of education on an economy and the degree to which government could influence educational advancement linked to economic growth. At the end of the evening we all stood up to leave, and Lord Adonis turned to me and said, "And what might you and your wife be doing tomorrow? If you do not have too busy a schedule, I'd like to invite you to tea at 10 Downing Street." Well, after a socially appropriate pause to consult my schedule that had absolutely nothing on it, I replied, "I think we just might have time."

The next day—in the pre-9/11 world—we simply arrived at the main gate of 10 Downing and said who we were. The guard said merely that we were indeed expected for tea and that all we had to do was enter the compound and knock on the door. I distinctly remember saying, "Which door?" and he responded, "Number 10, of course!"

After knocking on the door, we were met by Lord Adonis and taken to the second-floor landing, where tea was ready for us. We then settled into a rigorous two-hour discussion of the topics we covered the evening before, but in far more depth. At the end of our talk, Lord Adonis looked at me and said, "All right, then. I believe the prime minister would like to talk to you, but not right now. He is currently meeting with the president of France. Simply go back to the United States and we will be in contact." I did not know really what to think. All of this was simply bizarre. I really thought that while the visit to 10 Downing was an honor and our discussion intriguing, I would hear nothing.

Well, a week later, back on the Dickinson College campus, I received an e-mail with the sending address of "10 Downing Street." The message was from Lord Adonis. He said that I was scheduled to meet with Prime Minister Blair in his office the coming Monday. I was to be his "private tutor." I refer at this point to an item in the

"Notes to a 21st-Century Student": engage the world—you have to be out in it—and things happen.

I flew to London the next day. Picking me up at the airport was the prime minister's chauffer, driving an official car. The baby seat of the prime minister and his wife's recent child was still in the back seat. On Monday morning I arrived at 10 Downing and was told again to go to number 10 and knock. Once let in, I was led to the "green room" off of the entrance and told to wait. After a few minutes I heard the rapid, resounding sound of shoes on stairs, and coming in the room to greet me was the prime minister himself—without a jacket and sleeves rolled up for action. He took me to his office, where we were joined by his chief of staff and a prominent British businessman. From that point we were all engaged in one of the most spirited conversations about education and national policy I have ever participated in personally. The prime minister asked insightful and tough questions about talent development and what makes the American entrepreneurial mind what it is—what permits Americans to take risks and act while others deliberate, hesitate and miss opportunity. I really let loose and expressed my thoughts and paths for action for the UK. I remember one exchange that I can hardly believe happened, in retrospect. The prime minister was deliberating over an issue and seeking resolution but could not get there, and his colleagues were only supporting his indecision. At that point I said, "With all due respect, Mr. Prime Minister, I shall now demonstrate the difference between an American and a Brit. Stop talking, make a decision and get it done!"

I left 10 Downing not quite believing what had just happened, but my personal and professional life were just greatly extended and enriched. Simply being out in the world in word and in deed led directly to wider and wider circles of influence and activity. I later found out from Sir Cyril that my remarks led to concrete action in the UK. The prime minister committed tens of millions of pounds to establish a Gifted and Talented Centre at the University of Warwick.

Being out in the world and open to possibility can also lead to being a participant in world events. I share two such incidents.

While I was working for Johns Hopkins, I was called to the President's Office to meet with a prominent trustee. When I arrived for the meeting, I discovered that I was not only to chat with the trustee but also with a Japanese American alumnus of the university. Our conversation was quite general, but my new acquaintance and fellow alumnus spoke compellingly about the many opportunities for Hopkins in Japan. I was not precisely sure about my reason for being involved in this particular conversation, yet I found it intriguing and learned a great deal.

Several months later I was traveling to Tokyo on U.S. State Department business (while working at Hopkins full-time, I was also a senior consultant to the U.S. State Department). When I stepped off of the plane at Narita Airport I was unexpectedly greeted by the Japanese American alumnus whom I had met previously (this also was pre-9/11). I was stunned. He just smiled and said that he was sure I had no comprehension about what was happening, nor did he. He asked me whether I had a dark suit and whether I would be prepared to make a quick turnaround and meet some Japanese for dinner. He reiterated that he also was not quite sure what this was all about but that it involved association with the royal family and the Japanese Foreign Affairs Ministry.

The dinner was held at a special location and was most elegant and elaborate, but it was not particularly revealing. My new acquaintance and I retired to the men's room several times to consult and try to figure out why we were there—to no avail.

Following dinner, he and I went to the American Club of Tokyo to reflect on the whole bizarre experience. When I went to the bar to get a drink, I perceived that alongside me was a member of the Foreign Ministry who was at dinner. Rather urgently, he whispered to me in English, "This is highly serious. Please tell your president that if we do not get this right, we may well be again at war!" I was speechless.

Over the next few days in Tokyo, more was revealed. This is what was relayed to me. I have no way of judging its veracity. I can only relate what I was told and convey how I then proceeded upon this new information.

Evidently, Emperor Hirohito, while quite old at that time, was determined not to pass from this earth without correcting what he saw as a period of very poor relations between Japan and the United

States. Of course, he was emperor of Japan during WWII. He was deeply disturbed that the numerous postwar initiatives to improve Japanese-American relations were, from his perspective, not working.

However, he apparently had heard through the international media of a sport that was played at many of the elite American universities. He had also heard that players could succeed if they were of modest height and fast. He thought Japanese university students could do well if they engaged in this sport. He then apparently watched a match via satellite television between Johns Hopkins and Princeton. The sport was lacrosse, and his ambition was to introduce it to elite universities in Japan and arrange for teams from the United States and Japan to begin playing each other. Through these athletic events, the emperor believed that America's and Japan's future leaders would establish at an early point a respectful relationship on the playing field that would carry over a lifetime and result in improved dialogue between the nations. This was sports diplomacy.

Apparently, I was drawn into this because I was the first senior Hopkins' administrator traveling to Japan. My being out in the world under the auspices of the U.S. Department of State was the catalyst of contact.

Now many events happened quickly. I was appointed a charter member of the first Japanese lacrosse association; I helped bring the Johns Hopkins lacrosse team to Japan to play; I helped facilitate an institutional agreement between Johns Hopkins and Gakushuin University, known as the "royal family university"; through my trustee service at St. Paul's School in Baltimore, a historic lacrosse powerhouse at the scholastic level, I arranged an agreement that includes academic and lacrosse exchange; and my wife and I hosted in our home the first Japanese student of an elite university—Keio—to come to the United States for an extended period to study and learn the sport of lacrosse at Johns Hopkins. Lacrosse became quickly the fastest growing sport in Japan. To my delight and without my intervention, the Keio University lacrosse team visits Dickinson College every few years to scrimmage our outstanding team and dine with them. The emperor, I believe, would be pleased!

Also while I was working for Johns Hopkins and traveling for the U.S. Department of State, I received a telegram while I was in Paris from the U.S. ambassador to the Netherlands. He requested that I see him at his office as soon as I arrived the next day in the Hague. Of course, I did so. He was most engaging and ended the conversation by again whether I had a dark suit with me, just as my Japanese friend had. I was beginning to think that this was some signal for engagement and adventure! I said that I did, and he asked then if I would have dinner that evening with a high-ranking representative of the Dutch Ministry of Education. Well, of course.

I met the minister at a local restaurant and had a delightful dinner. We chatted about all sorts of topics, including the difference between American and Dutch education and our respective approaches toward the advancement of academic talent in children and youth. I thought nothing about the enjoyable encounter until decades later when I was working at Dickinson College. The college and the U.S. Army War College were interested in the erstwhile ambassador—who had gone on to successful diplomatic post after post—to occupy our joint academic chair in leadership. Since I knew him, I volunteered to give him a call. After he shared with me that an unexpected upcoming post from the president would not permit him to accept our offer, he paused and said, "I bet you wonder what that dinner was about years ago in the Hague." I said that I did, and his response was stunning: "I can talk about this after so many years. Thank you for helping the U.S. post missiles in the Hague aimed at the Soviet Union. You were a part of ending the Cold War! That meeting was an obligation of the United States toward the Netherlands in the treaty that was arranged to permit the stationing of those missiles on Dutch soil. A senior U.S. education official was to meet with a representative of the Dutch Ministry of Education. You were it!" In retrospect, I remembered well the controversy in the United States and the Netherlands surrounding those missiles. But I had absolutely no idea at the time that I was involved.

Again, you must be out in the world for things to happen, and sometimes what happens engages you in major historical events, regardless of the modesty of your part. In this case, my professional context expanded greatly. I became far more experienced in Japanese higher education through the new contacts that I developed than I would have otherwise, I was introduced to a sport with which I previously had little contact and I got to know Dutch education much more thoroughly than ever before. These experiences added immense texture to my personal and professional lives and provided me with a lifetime of connection with people and places I never would have encountered in such depth and distinction.

Chapter 7

A Voice on the Diagonal

While president of Dickinson College, I have taken on the challenge of the Dickinson Dimensions to develop a personal voice and speak up about issues that matter. This has been my preoccupation throughout my entire professional career, no matter where I have worked. The appendix contains a selection of previously published work about a variety of topics. Each one provoked both admiration and scorn. Each one therefore fulfilled its civic intention. Each one validated the usefulness of my liberal-arts education. The topics I tackle range, for example, from college rankings to online learning to liberal-arts education to precollegiate education to standardized testing and other such forms of assessment.

Now that I place these commentaries side by side, I search for precisely what in my personal or professional life motivates me to engage with these topics and in the manner that I did. I seem to be always trying to point out an absurdity—better, an outrage—within education from the viewpoint of someone who is both an insider and an outsider. I appear to be trying to disclose with outrage what others might not see from my distinctive perspective. As I noted in the preface, I am an outsider in higher education masquerading as an insider.

But where did this slant originate? Only in writing this piece did it come back to me, and it is quite personal. I am a first-generation college student. Nobody on the direct line of my mother or father's family even went to college, much less graduated. There is no doubt that my mother and father wanted me to be the person to break the cycle. I was going to college, and all their energies were directed toward that goal. I was to live a life of knowledge, culture and wealth that they did not experience. One day when I was about seven, my mother took me to New York City to walk up and down 5th Avenue. My mother missed the city greatly. She had lived and worked there as a secretary right up until I was born, when she was 37. We were now living in a rural area outside Albany, and the adjustment was not easy for her. While walking down the street, she suddenly stopped and asked what was for me an almost unfathomable question: "See all these men and women walking on 5th Avenue? How can you spot the ones who are educated and highly successful?" I was just baffled. She then said, "It's simple. Just look at their shoes. They are always shined. No scuffs. That's the difference. Always shine your shoes!" To this day, I have my shoes shined first thing when I arrive in New York City! I thought she would stop there, but that was not the case. "But remember, even if you shine your shoes, you are not them. You are different. You will never be comfortable in their highfaluting circles. Just remember that and you will be okay. Never lose sight of who you are and where you come from. Be successful—highly successful—but never take on their lifestyle. You don't have time for that luxury. Be your own self. Be independent and self-reliant. Be with them, but not of them."

This disposition of being "with something" and not "of it" was vividly underscored for me on my Commencement Day at Dickinson in 1971. My father was brought up in a poor rural family near Montgomery, Ala. At 15 he faked his way into the military. For the next few decades he served in the army, participated in rodeos in Wyoming and played minor-league baseball. Finally he put together 30 years of military service and retired. I was born shortly after that. My father first worked on a box assembly line and then as a cook/chef in hospitals. As I walked out of the main door of Old West, the event venue for graduation, to receive my diploma, I scanned the audience for my parents. I noticed that my father was nowhere within the limestone walls that defined the audience. I then spotted him standing far beyond them—a wall and a wide street separating him from all others. It became suddenly evident to me that while my father felt proud to see me do what no one in my direct line of ancestors had ever done— graduate college—he could not see himself as part of that audience, comfortably sitting within the limestone walls. He remained "other."

This idea of otherness has had an indelible impact on me—beyond that day in New York City with my mother, beyond Commencement Day in 1971—throughout my life. I am constantly restless at points of achieving success and only comfortable in the quixotic, energetic pursuit of getting things done well. I never pause long enough to exhibit the lifestyle of success. Some friends began to say of me over the years that I live on the "diagonal." What this meant is captured best in a poem written and read at my inauguration as Dickinson's 27th president in 1999 by Kendra Kopelke, a close friend and Baltimore poet:

Striding Across the Diagonal

… as the new president strides across the
diagonal, legs out in front of him
like a drum roll, visions multiplying in his head.
There's no portrait of him in Old West yet,
Only because he can't sit still;
Like [Marianne] Moore's steeple jack, he isn't afraid
    of heights.
What a thrill to live in a place like this,
Where you can see far off
In all directions, where a president promises a noble
    future (no bull!),
Layers of movement foretold in
Something as solid
As the limestone—,
Look at the way it changes when wet, a green
    iridescence
That flows as if it were nothing but pure light.

Another theme that I believe threads my writings is what I would label a typical—yet acute— "first-generation college-student profile." I rage against all types of "phoniness"—assumptions of privilege and distinction without the hard work to earn them, and any form of shirking effort and taking shortcuts to wealth and glory. A case in point is my longstanding diatribe against the *U.S. News & World Report*'s rankings of colleges and universities, which epitomizes phony in that it bestows inappropriate and undeserved privilege and prestige. You simply have to earn it by your own effort.

As a first-gen college student, I grew up drilled in the lifestyle perspective that success is all about your own hard work. Nobody gives you anything for nothing, and if they do, beware! Distrust praise; if possible, avoid it. Praise only distracts you from an accurate and pragmatic assessment of your effort forward. Self-reliance (in the Emersonian sense, although my family knew nothing about him or his ideas while I was growing up) is all important. Self-reliance is gained by honest work that "nobody can ever take from you" and by the prudent, consistent and discrete ("never reveal how much money you have") saving and amassing of wealth (it is not important how much you have, only that you save and have enough to keep you independent and self-reliant). Two childhood incidents that underscore these dispositions carried into my writing come to mind.

Children often receive gifts during the winter holiday season. Sometimes those gifts are money from family or friends—money to buy candy, a toy, something you really want. Well, in my case, I received gifts of money from time to time (my first Christmas gift was some Citi-Service oil stock from a distant entrepreneurial great aunt), but I never bought a thing over the whole span of my early youth! Every gift went immediately into the bank and was then transferred to the stock market—every single gift. When I was old enough, I went with my parents to the bank, filled out the forms and deposited the money into my own account. I then personally transferred the money to a brokerage firm when enough was amassed. Never did I take money out of this account for any expense; reinvestment to gain financial security without excess or display was the objective.

My mother and at least one of her siblings inherited very elaborate jewelry from a distant spinster aunt who took a liking to them. This aunt apparently was a forceful and highly successful business-woman well before this was more common. She owned a major casino and surrounding land on what is now La Guardia Airport in New York City, and she developed a good part of commercial Brooklyn in the late 19th and early 20th century. My mother's sister and her family immediately sold their gift to buy a car and some other ultimately disposable items. But not my mother. She deposited the jewelry in a bank safe-deposit box wherever we lived and kept it there throughout her whole life. She never brought it out; she never wore it. As a child

I remember the "sacred" ritual of visiting the bank a few times a year to behold the jewels and, for my mother, to make sure they were still there. But this viewing served another purpose. During each visit I heard the story of this successful distant relative and was reminded unequivocally that with hard work, I could have such things.

My mother's ritual has actually led me to hide any professional accomplishment and feel complete and content when so doing. Later in life, I received justification for this position when I read the words of an 18th-century German author, Christoph Martin Wieland, who said the definition of outstanding writing, and thus literary production, is when "extreme effort is hidden from the reader by being deposited in a place other than the text."

My early affinity for understatement and a low profile perhaps accounts for why I chose Dickinson College for my undergraduate studies. Although I attended and graduated what is a highly reputable college-preparatory school in Albany, New York—the Albany Academy—I did not receive much college guidance. In those days I think such guidance was principally provided by the families and friends of students and not by the school itself. Since my family did not attend college, I was adrift. On Saturday afternoons in 1965, my father and I would watch college football on TV followed by GE's *College Bowl*, a program devoted to college teams competing to answer factual questions from a spectrum of academic fields. That year there was one undefeated college—Dickinson. My father looked at me and said, "That seems to be a good college." I agreed and applied Early Decision.

It was highly unusual in the '60s for a student from my school to go to a college in Central Pennsylvania. New England and New York were almost exclusively the targets. Of course, I visited a few other colleges in New York and New England with classmates, but there was no emotional connection. When I visited Dickinson with my mother, we drove in on a rather warm spring evening just after a downpour. The campus was carpeted in fog, except for a space at the lower tree-leaf line. At that moment something clicked for me. I felt highly comfortable in that restricted yet internally expansive space, and I could see myself studying, reading and moving within its borders from a first-generation college student to a more informed and engaged citizen of the world. Only upon my return to Dickinson years later did I appreciate what may have attracted me to the college beyond fog. It is what I call a "Mid-Atlantic-state mentality," which stands in stark contrast to a "New England mentality." (This dichotomy is adapted from the 1996 book *Puritan Boston & Quaker Philadelphia*, by E. Digby Bartzell.)

So what is this Mid-Atlantic-state mentality that so attracted me, that spoke to my receptivity to understatement, under-recognition, pragmatism and getting things done—all first-generation college-student virtues? It all starts with the college's founder, Dr. Benjamin Rush.

When Rush founded Dickinson in 1783 he wanted more than just another college. He intended for Dickinson to be the bellwether of a new kind of higher education that would be distinctly American. He rejected the idea of learning solely for learning's sake, which dominated European institutions, and he advanced instead the concept of a useful liberal-arts education. This was a "scrappy" education through which inherited ideas were rigorously challenged and new ideas encroached. Rush instinctively knew that the young democracy would require active, engaged and ambitious citizens if it was to survive. Dickinson graduates, therefore, were not only to ensure the success of the nascent government but also to contribute to the development of a national economy and appropriate social structures.

For Rush, access to higher education for all citizens was so fundamental to the success of American democracy that he intentionally located Dickinson on what was then the western frontier of the nation and in a state, Pennsylvania, that was being established by a unique mix of people and ideologies and was a center of critical activities that formed the new government. As the first American college or university founded west of the Susquehanna River, Dickinson represented a national commitment to extend the sources of formal learning beyond what was already established along the Atlantic Coast.

It was a bold, symbolic move imparting a sense of "frontier pragmatism"—a notion that acknowledged the vast uncertainty and boundless opportunities that accompanied the founding of a new nation and gave citizens the useful skills and knowledge to ensure its success. Rush's choice of location for Dickinson, then, was highly intentional. Born of the Revolution, the college was rooted in America's formative past and, at the same time, welcomed the country's inventive and entrepreneurial future. From its very inception, Dickinson reached outward into the world from a firm yet volatile intellectual base.

What made Rush's vision so workable was the fact that it benefitted in varying degrees from three intellectual traditions that had already converged to leave a lasting mark on Pennsylvania's culture. The first of these was the Scottish Enlightenment, a school of thought that influenced many of our founding fathers, including Rush. This approach to knowledge was driven by a keen sense of utilitarianism and common sense that valued thorough empiricism and practicality. It advanced the optimistic belief in the ability of humans to effect significant changes for the betterment of society and nature. It was a useful, activist, cosmopolitan outlook on life that welcomed diversity of opinion.

The second tradition emanated from the German immigrants who had settled in Pennsylvania. Motivated by a clear sense of purpose and a strong work ethic, these settlers were committed to sharing talents and resources to build cohesive communities in a rugged and untamed environment. Rush's desire for this perspective to influence the college was so strong that when our first president and the Board of Trustees did not move quickly enough to hire a professor of German, Rush assisted in the founding of our collegial institution, Franklin & Marshall College.

The final tradition came from the Pennsylvania Quakers, who reinforced the importance of a sense of community. Pursuing a spirituality that was, in part, outwardly focused led the Quakers to create communities of shared discourse—environments that valued resolving issues through discussion and encouraged social activism and political engagement. This straightforward approach put a premium on simplicity and manifested the virtues of an uncluttered life. Our namesake and the first chair of our Board of Trustees, John Dickinson, however, came from a Quaker tradition, and it is suggested that he refused to sign the Declaration of Independence because of the influence of this tradition. Of course, Dickinson College was never a Quaker institution; in fact, we were chartered in 1783 as a nondenominational college—somewhat of an exception in the early days of American higher education.

This combination of early influences upon the Mid-Atlantic region and arguably Dickinson College stands in contrast, for example, to New England and its colleges. The early years of higher education in New England were set in the prevailing context of Puritanism and an "American transcendentalism" that kept the everyday world at bay by exalting status and distance from a daily, mundane engagement in life. For colleges, these ideas were realized physically by being built "high on a hill"—establishing a physical separation of the college from the rest of humanity, the academy towering symbolically and unreachably over the townspeople below. In contrast, Dickinson College was purposely located in the midst of the town's activity and on an equal plane. Its presence was to be imperceptible and discreet. Personal traits of modesty in achievement and aspiration were defining characteristics of Mid-Atlantic people.

Rush starkly confirmed this disposition for me when he vigorously and unconditionally asserted in one of his letters that he would pay from the grave for a person to wipe out any traces of his name that might be attached to Dickinson because of his financial support for the college's first building—what is now West College or, more familiarly, Old West. He had heard that his fellow trustees were thinking of using his name, and he wanted to put a stop to such actions at once. He didn't desire nor need a naming. In stark contrast to the people of the Mid-Atlantic states, those of New England enjoy pronounced distinction and prestige as well as the elaborate public celebration of accomplishments and the key transitions in life.

By choosing to study at Dickinson, I clearly chose to be influenced in my education by a particular sense of place and the habits of thought and action that accompany it—by the "Mid-Atlantic mentality." Our personalities matched.

Chapter 8

Full Circle

And so I come full circle.

My professional introduction to the world of higher education came when I wrote a Ph.D. dissertation that established the genre of the literary advisory letter, in which an older poet addresses a younger poet to advise on the craft of writing and on living a fulfilling life. As I depart higher education in my early 60s, I return to the genre to write an extended letter—in the form of a short book—to help students maximize their undergraduate education in the 21st century.

In the concluding chapter of my dissertation I wrote the following:

> For the literary advisory letter to exist a number of conditions must be present. There should be a belief that aspiring young men [or women] can be educated by a master to become future poets or be advised to abandon the profession entirely. Correspondingly, there should be a vital master-pupil relationship in which the master is willing to bestow his [or her] experience, wisdom and warning on a youth, and fledglings in turn are receptive to being led and formed.

I leave the college presidency and nonprofit higher education strongly affirming the relationship between mentor and student as the most powerful and influential dynamic in education. Without it, teaching and learning are merely transactional. I leave the field in *medias res*, positing as I go advice to those many young students of future generations. There is no better way to leave the playing field of active undergraduate education than to impart advice and to hope patiently for that advice to help young people find fulfillment in years to come. Education is all about optimism, and these words serve that master.

Selected Op-Eds

The Chronicle of Higher Education
LIBERAL ARTS FOR ALL, NOT JUST THE RICH
Oct. 19, 2001

For years, many of our country's most wealthy and privileged families have ignored shifting educational fashions and continued to send their children to high-quality residential colleges and universities for a liberal-arts education. They are well aware of the many lifelong benefits of such an education. For example, an estimated 40 percent of the Fortune 500 chief executive officers in 2000 graduated from a liberal-arts college or received a degree with a liberal-arts major.

Yet every time poor, minority, immigrant, first-generation, or otherwise disadvantaged college students in the United States stand to benefit from a liberal-arts education, the rules of the game change. Education is suddenly redefined. The liberal arts are devalued, and "modern" educational theories—usually anti-intellectual, practical, student-centered, and vocational—are trumpeted.

The outcome has been clear. The rich have remained rich and powerful. And the poor have remained poor and disenfranchised because they have been diverted, yet again, from obtaining the type of education that has served as one of the primary avenues to leadership and power for generations.

The latest educational fad is distance learning, arriving just as the proportion of black and Hispanic college-aged youths in the general population is predicted to rise substantially, yet their share of the college population will be much less. If we are not careful, many disadvantaged students will, once more, lose access to substantive leadership opportunities.

Why does a traditional liberal education foster leadership? People are "affinity beings" who possess an innate desire to learn among other people in the most comprehensive sense: to see them, hear them, exchange ideas, share food and drink, even to have sufficient stimuli to fantasize about them. The "24/7" nature of a residential liberal-arts institution forces the inevitability of learning through social interaction. Students are addressed by their names and recognized and differentiated by their appearance, distinctive pattern of speech, gestures or written words. They see their thoughts and ideas received and discussed by others, providing external recognition that those thoughts and ideas have value.

At the same time, one can't just strike the "Delete" key or turn off the machine in a residential environment when confronted with a difficult human interaction or an intellectual disagreement. Affinity with others is a "built-in" program, not an option. Through a liberal education, students engage in the study of a wide range of subjects in the arts, humanities, sciences and social sciences, directed by an instructor in ways that ensure that students move beyond what they already know. Such an education aims to free students from preconceptions and encourages them to consider many different, often conflicting, opinions. In an environment that encourages experimentation, students can reconcile their perspectives with the prevailing values of current authorities—represented by instructors and the individuals whom instructors recommend—as well as other students.

Having worked both in a distance-learning company and a residential liberal-arts college, I know firsthand that no existing form of distance learning can similarly affirm students as individuals and also force them to acknowledge the ideas of others. Liberal education is not defined by practicality or the immediacy of occupational goals—which would do little to challenge prejudice, bias or authority. But a liberal education is ultimately useful; it give students the strong sense of self and habits of mind and action to become leaders. And, unfortunately, it is precisely the poor, minority, first-generation, immigrant or otherwise disenfranchised students who most desperately need an educational environment that builds identity and gives them the confidence even to attempt leadership.

The historical pattern of denying disenfranchised youth a liberal education is well documented. In her book *Left Back: A Century of Failed School Reforms* (Simon and Schuster, 2000), Diane Ravitch described how early-20th-century educational reformers created a new curriculum for poor, foreign-born and nonwhite students that excluded them from gaining access to power through a liberal education. "Because the children were 'different,' because many did not come from English-speaking homes, it was argued that they needed a curriculum different from the one available to the children of affluent, native-born families," she noted. "Not for them the 'old limited book-subject curriculum'; the experts in the new schools of pedagogy said these children needed industrial education, vocational education, nature study, sewing, cooking and manual training." Joining the reform movement, colleges built new programs in technical, vocational and professional fields at the expense of liberal education—which was portrayed as irrelevant, inefficient and outmoded.

Ravitch also identified the condescension in the rhetoric on behalf of the poor, detailing how reformers believed that schools and colleges should offer differentiated programs. Providing a similar academic curriculum to all students was "antidemocratic" and "aristocratic." Observed Ravitch, " 'Equality of opportunity' was redefined to mean that only a minority should continue to get an academic education, while the great majority—the children of the masses—would get vocational or industrial training."

Such focused educational marketing did not convince all representatives of the non-elite. As early as the 1890s, W.E.B. Du Bois questioned whether industrial training would best serve African-American students—recognizing that the path to success and power in America traditionally went through a liberal education. He called for the selection of a "talented tenth" of African-American youth, who would receive a college education in the liberal arts in order to prepare for leadership roles.

But, unfortunately, despite the pleas of Du Bois and others, a succession of populist and progressive reforms held sway and were introduced into schools and colleges by faculty members and administrators who embraced such beliefs. Those reforms diverted poor, minority and immigrant students toward industrial, vocational, and technical studies, as well as student-centered learning—and away from access to a substantive education in the liberal arts.

Today, to encourage disadvantaged students to choose distance-learning offerings over a liberal-arts education, people use arguments strikingly similar to those used decades ago to embrace populist reforms. For example, in testimony before Congress's Web-Based Education Commission, Andrew M. Rosenfield, the head of UNext.com, which sells online courses, enthusiastically predicted, "Internet learning has the power fundamentally to transform educational opportunity and democratize access to education"—especially, Rosenfield noted, for "those who because of the happenstance of financial and geographical circumstance never could hope to attend a physical college or university."

Yet, of course, the only area of distance instruction that appears pedagogically effective for great numbers of learners—and adult learners specifically—is vocational knowledge, where a body of technical information is transferred in specific fields like business and information technology. Therefore, the only education that can effectively be delivered en masse to young people is, by necessity, vocational and practical—precisely the type of education advanced in the early 20th century by progressive educators for immigrants, minority groups, and the poor.

While most online-education organizations are not yet offering full undergraduate degree programs for college-aged students, the momentum is growing. The Massachusetts Institute of Technology's decision to place undergraduate course materials online, with basically zero feedback to viewers from professors, is one highly publicized case in point. And in an article in the Bloomberg News Service (February 28, 2000), Christopher Byron, an Internet commentator, urged parents not to send their children to a residential college. He directed them instead to Virtual U., which he equates with the University of Phoenix Online. Why? Simply because it is cheaper. And what type of colleges does the author generally reject? Liberal-arts colleges, of course. According to this perspective, there is little use for an education in the arts, humanities, sciences and social sciences.

What's more, announcements of the triumphant rise of distance learning are linked to predictions of the demise of the physical context for liberal learning: the campus. Several years ago, in an article in *Forbes* magazine on technology and higher education, Peter Drucker pronounced: "Already we are beginning to deliver more lectures and classes off-campus via satellite or two-way video at a fraction of the cost. The colleges won't survive as a residential institution."

Few observers doubt that distance learning will be an important platform for the delivery and sharing of information and practical knowledge in the coming decades. It is already effective at delivering workplace training and adult continuing education. Growing evidence also suggests that it may be a useful supplement to liberal education—providing discrete knowledge or even coursework not readily available in a particular residential setting.

But to predict the death of liberal education and to offer distance education as a viable alternative for college-aged youth is irresponsible. Where's the research that proves the effectiveness of virtual learning for that purpose? The claim is also unfortunate because it comes precisely when more and more disadvantaged youth are ready for college, and when liberal-arts colleges are poised to make it possible for them to attend in unprecedented numbers through financial aid and heightened recruitment efforts.

Disenfranchised students, as much as their affluent and advantaged peers, deserve a chance at a residential, liberal education—not an unproven alternative. Those students deserve the opportunity to break the destructive cycle, finally, and receive, not just placebos, but the education that they need. They deserve a chance to obtain the type of education that will substantially increase their access to power and success.

It is time to let the secret out beyond the privileged: A liberal-arts education equals leadership.

The Chronicle of Higher Education
THE LIBERAL ARTS AS A BULWARK OF BUSINESS EDUCATION
July 18, 2003

The spate of revelations about ethical wrongdoing, greed, financial fabrication and executive arrogance in corporate America these days has shaken confidence in Wall Street and cost millions of investors significant sums of money. Such crises beg for correctives, and many observers are calling upon higher education to serve as an improving, enlightening force. Well, don't count on salvation any time soon—especially from many colleges and universities with liberal arts at their core.

David L. Kirp, a professor of public policy at the University of California at Berkeley, and Jeffrey T. Holman, a graduate student in economics at Berkeley, observed in *The American Prospect* (October 7, 2002) that efforts to apply business practices to traditional colleges and universities elicit cries from faculty members who contend that such measures will move higher education to "the dark side" or are simply "gauche."

In a similar vein, throughout my 25 years in higher education, I have encountered countless alumni with liberal-arts educations—both from small liberal-arts colleges and from universities that offer liberal-arts courses—who are embarrassed that they hold jobs in the business sector. They express dismay that their former professors in the arts, humanities, social sciences and even the sciences tell them in no uncertain terms that they have made a "Faustian bargain" and are living a "tarnished" life. With such outright condemnation from their respected mentors, those graduates tell me that it is difficult to think of themselves and their occupations as other than lacking in virtue.

It wasn't always this way in America. For a brief period, at least, some higher-education leaders appreciated fully the benefit to the nation when liberal education and commerce were equally valued and occupied common intellectual space. Benjamin Rush, a signer of the Declaration of Independence, who, with John Dickinson, founded Dickinson College and helped establish several other colleges and universities, proposed in his writings a distinctively American form of higher education. Rush wanted institutions to produce citizen-leaders who possessed the comprehensive knowledge and virtue needed to build a just, compassionate, economically sustainable democracy. He promoted a liberal-arts education that would be useful and applicable for all graduates, no matter what their occupations or service—including, unequivocally, business.

For Rush, commerce and manufacturing were defining parts of that democracy to which liberal-arts education provided intellectual capital. In a 1769 letter, he stated emphatically, "There is but one expedient left whereby we can save our sinking country, and that is by encouraging American manufacturers. Unless we do this, we shall be done forever."

In proposing this distinct form of liberal-arts education, which placed a premium on "usefulness," Rush exhibited his outright disdain for the higher-education system he experienced in England. There, higher education was purposefully ornamental and elitist— and reserved for those who were already wealthy and privileged. The notion of applying learning to advance society was simply nonexistent.

Rush was harshest, however, in his criticism of those colonial institutions of higher learning that, he judged, had not yet grasped in mission and curriculum the distinctly American education needed by the "new and peculiar state of our country"—in which, as he noted in a 1795 lecture at the University of Pennsylvania, "the business of the principal part of the inhabitants is to obtain the first and most necessary means of subsistence." It was equally regrettable, he said, that "no accommodation has been made in the system of education … to the new form of government and the many … objects of knowledge that have been imposed upon us by the American Revolution."

The "accommodation" that Rush sought for undergraduate students called for a useful education that was grounded firmly and progressively in the liberal arts but that also encouraged students to explore emerging branches of knowledge and communicate across subject areas. He argued strongly, for example, for a radical reduction in the teaching of Latin and Greek, which he thought of as dead languages. Instead, he advocated the introduction of modern languages, like German, French, Spanish, and Italian, which he believed would connect students more immediately to the intellectual, political and commercial activities of the day.

Rush also thought that a redefined liberal-arts education should embrace natural history, geography, divinity, mathematics, logic, moral philosophy (including government and the laws of the nation), grammar and rhetoric, and the natural sciences. He particularly emphasized the importance of studying the then-emerging field of chemistry, which he believed had the capacity to connect seamlessly to other areas of new knowledge and would be of critical importance to the new, fragile nation to "admit of an application to agriculture, manufacturers, commerce, and war."

For American higher education, Rush's legacy—as well as that of several contemporaries, such as his good friend Thomas Jefferson—was to offer to a scrappy nation, born directly out of a revolution, an ultimately practical vision of the liberal arts. That vision gave the new country an education blueprint designed to prepare and commit college graduates to the useful responsibilities of building a democracy—through work in commerce and government as well as in cultural and spiritual institutions.

Regretfully, many colleges that offer a liberal-arts education today deny that legacy vigorously, if unknowingly. Instead, they often pursue a protective "purity" for the liberal arts and ignore, or even belittle, the world of business as too crass for association. Ironically, such institutions promote an elitism more closely aligned with the British tradition—one that America's founders judged inappropriate for the more inclusive and progressive ambitions of our nation.

It is time for the leadership of undergraduate liberal-arts institutions to move beyond arguments for pursuing liberal arts exclusively on the basis of "intrinsic worth" and to embrace instead an imperative derived from the historic compact among the liberal arts, business, and democracy. It is time to educate graduates whose hubris and exaggerated ambition are tempered and balanced by studies that aim to challenge one's understanding of oneself and to prepare one to function intellectually and morally in a complex world.

It is also time for education leaders to affirm publicly that a liberal-arts education is not a mere luxury without practical consequence, but rather encompasses a distinctive preparing of students for positions of corporate leadership. It is time for administrators and faculty members to embrace with pride their graduates who pursue careers in business and finance and to incorporate, both philosophically and structurally, business into the intellectual core of the liberal-arts curriculum.

Rush's emphasis on a broad-based, diverse course of study also rejected any thought of a narrowly focused, vocational education, which has become the model for far too many business majors today. To him, a graduate's success was dependent upon a fundamental study of the liberal arts and the general reasoning and moral skills that they offered. The singular and separate approach that many colleges take to an undergraduate business curriculum represents a fundamental misunderstanding of the distinctively American approach to preparing undergraduate students for business leadership. Pursuit of the liberal arts—which contain those subjects that explore the fullest range of human thought, action, emotion, and character—was expressly intended by Rush and others like him as the most useful preparation for a life of business accomplishment and leadership.

While a liberal-arts education doesn't guarantee integrity or protect the self from its own evils, it does offer students the best chance to grow intellectually and morally. It provides our best opportunity to produce leaders with positive character and intent. A separatist strategy is not the educational corrective to corporate greed. Nor is it the best way for students to form a comprehensive intellectual and moral identity. Rush and Jefferson knew as much centuries ago.

Contemporary leaders of liberal-arts colleges and universities must recommit to that insight in practice. They must advance the agenda of diverse, creative coursework, internships, and field studies—regardless of major—where thoughtful considerations of business theory and application surface, and where questions of intent, equity, leadership, and integrity prevail. And if their institutions offer business or finance courses, those must be complemented with extensive study of the humanities, sciences, social sciences, and the arts. A liberal-arts education in America historically intended such diverse pursuit. Such action is not a sign of academic failure or compromise, but rather the fulfillment of a noble and useful purpose through higher learning.

The Quiet Patriot
May 31, 2005

Of all the college commencements over which I have presided, this year's was bittersweet and exceptional. Following the joy of sending 536 bright, ambitious students into the wider world, I was stopped by a member of the audience who asked me a pointed question, "Why was "The Star-Spangled Banner" not played during the ceremony?" And this was directly after I delivered a presidential address that reminded the audience of our college's American revolutionary origins, praised the democratic tradition and urged our graduates to become the citizen leaders of our nation.

I believe the intent of the question was that because of this omission, (we have never sung the national anthem during Commencement), I and the college are unpatriotic; that we are part of a liberal establishment that disrespects America.

After recovering from my initial shock, I raged inwardly. How dare this person question my patriotism or that of the college? Hadn't he even listened to my remarks during the ceremony or was his judgment of me and my college predetermined? After all, I graduated ROTC from this very college and served in the U.S. Army. Moreover, my college, a traditional liberal-arts college, recently celebrated 50 years of commitment to ROTC in a world where many other colleges and universities have banished such commitment. The day before Commencement, we celebrated with a full auditorium, a commissioning service for our current Army ROTC graduates (where the national anthem was sung). Our institution maintains a long-standing cooperative academic arrangement with the U.S. Army War College in our town—unusual for a liberal-arts college. Through the centuries, many of our graduates have been military leaders and scores of our alumni are currently on active duty with one, a young lieutenant, losing his life for our country in Iraq.

Never, has this question been raised in all our previous graduations. So what is different now?

What I am seeing is that we in America have begun, almost exclusively, to show and accept our patriotism by visible symbols—flags, stickers on cars, etc. We are a country now of "loud" patriotism and failure to be "loud" is judged as unpatriotic. What has been lost is "quiet" patriotism—committed understatement. There is little tolerance or appreciation for that patriotism that is not aggressive, not flying in the face of others, not ready to accuse others of having less on the basis of what is prominently displayed.

Further, what has been lost is the imagination to accept numerous forms of patriotism. The founder of our college, Benjamin Rush, was a revolutionary and undisputed patriot. He signed the Declaration of Independence and he served as surgeon general of the Middle Continental Army. And yet, he cautioned against a standing army (General Washington did not hang him nor did he accuse him of lack of patriotism over this) and he stated unequivocally that an American form of patriotism must also be defined by "quiet service" to one's fellow human being. In that spirit, he argued and "fought" against slavery, the inhumane treatment of the mentally-challenged, and the neglect of education for women. He volunteered to remain in the infested city and to serve the poor of Philadelphia as a physician during raging bouts of yellow fever. Patriotism here got at advancing the "stuff" of democracy.

I think back about how I was raised by a father who was clearly patriotic, but who would never fly a flag on any national holiday, would never talk about the military or his exploits in it after 30 years of service—mostly as an enlisted person before, during and after WWII. A man who would always buy a poppy on Veterans Day (and ask that I buy one too), but not wear it. A man who said to me that patriotism was not so easy as just flying a flag on a certain day, but rather it was a profound, deep commitment that absorbed your whole being and propelled you to service with no visible reward except a quiet readiness to serve and preserve.

It is time for us to regain what was intended by a distinctively American patriotism and exercise tolerance for those of us who enjoy a "quiet," yet steady patriotism. Let us remember that for some, it is through understatement and commitment and not flagrant display where responsibility for our nation resides.

Trusteeship Magazine
COMPLAINTS ABOUT CORPORATIZATION IN ACADEME ARE
OVERSTATED AND POLEMICAL
September/October 2005

The catchword "corporate" has recently gained sufficient traction to
instill fear and trembling in higher education circles. The term is used
by critics to account for a variety of perceived negative developments
within the academy. Supposed ramifications of "corporatization"
are so sweeping that some commentators, such as John Merrow in
a recent PBS documentary and book, *Declining by Degrees: Higher
Education at Risk*, assign all the alleged faults in higher education over
the last quarter-century to institutions that "have become a business
… less [worried] about teaching and learning."

I don't buy it—nor should faculty or trustees. The current pro-
miscuous use of "corporate" is political name-calling at its most mundane. When scrutinized, the charge merely advances the hackneyed
dichotomy of faculty versus administration-with trustees grouped
with administrators. Increasingly, whenever a party objects to a new
policy or development, "corporatization" is evoked as the culprit. The
expectation is that this word is so abhorrent to faculty that most will
immediately empathize and not think about the issue more deeply.
The "true believer" mentality that "all business is bad" is counterproductive in academe.

"Corporate" is, in fact, so misused in academic circles that what is
frequently attributed to the word actually originates in academe itself.
For example, some critics argue that the "corporatization" has led to
the "dumbing down" of content in undergraduate curricula by pushing colleges and universities to "meet consumer satisfaction."

This development—to the extent that it exists—was actually
introduced decades ago by concerned faculty in pursuit of greater rel-
evancy and connection to students' lives. While many in the academy
judge this as positive, critics rail against the "corporate" for breaking up
the traditional coherence of the curriculum—downsizing the "common" course of study. Unsaid is that this breakup occurred decades
earlier during the "culture wars" fought within academe by academics.

Others lament that humanities publications, if not the humanities as a whole, are threatened because the academy so obsessively pursues external support for scientific research- the product-centered business model. But who established such concern for productivity in universities? I suggest that it arose out of academe itself in mid-19th-century attempts to replace the "gentlemanly" (even theological) understanding of higher education in America with the German model that valued the primacy of research, productivity, and the ceaseless creation of new scientific knowledge.

Critics would have us believe there was once a "Golden Age" in American higher education when knowledge for knowledge's sake reigned. Not so. Before the American Revolution, colleges and universities had a vocational purpose—to supply Protestant clergy for colonial society. After the revolution, institutions practiced unabashedly "corporate" techniques that included development, marketing, branding and enrollment management.

Lacking the luxury of benevolent patronage to support higher education as existed in England, early American educators had to be resourceful and self-sufficient. Rush, a physician, signer of the Declaration of Independence, and Dickinson's founder, embraced "corporate" vices with vigor. He joyfully engaged in entrepreneurial strategies to attract students, such as going into debt to procure the most advanced scientific equipment to give Dickinson a competitive edge over its peers.

The basic disposition to advance the reputation and financial status of American colleges and universities has always been present. In fact, it distinguishes us even today from the primarily government-supported universities in other countries.

Finally, campus practices labeled "corporate" in today's rhetorical frenzy are often characteristics of solid leadership. Astute faculty recognize this.

So, what is to be done? I suggest that we all—faculty members, administrators and trustees—avoid stereotype-laden invocation of the term "corporate." Instead, as leaders of higher-education institutions, we should, without rhetorical blinders, develop and evaluate practices that advance our academic excellence and purpose, regardless of their origin and absent potentially misleading or inflammatory labels.

Inside Higher Ed
No God Left Behind—Why Not?
Sept. 21, 2006

The secretary of education's Commission on the Future of Higher Education unequivocally advances the notion that the "business" of colleges and universities—defined primarily in the final report as "preparation for the work force"—is best advanced by the disclosure of data allowing institutions to be compared to one another, particularly in measurements of student learning. Standardized testing of all college students would be required to produce those comparative quantitative data. Such universal application of testing is forwarded as the guarantee of accountability for what this American democracy requires most essentially from its higher-education institutions. In other words, what has already been applied with mixed success to precollegiate education is now to be applied to higher education. In addition to the No Child Left Behind Act, we are to have what might be called No College Left Behind.

In the nation's current zeal to account for all transfer of teaching and insight through quantitative, standardized testing, perhaps we should advance quantitative measurement into other areas of human meaning and definition. Why leave work undone?

I suggest, for example, that a federal commission propose an accountability initiative for those of faith (not such a wild notion as an increasing number of politicians are calling the traditional separation of church and state unhealthy for the nation). This effort should be titled No God Left Behind. The federal government would demand that places of worship, in order to be deemed successful, efficient and worthy of federal, state and local tax-support exemption, provide quantitative evidence of the effectiveness of their "teaching." (Places of worship are not unlike colleges and universities in that they are increasing their fund-raising expectations—their form of "price"—because of increasing costs.) The faithful, in turn, would be required to provide quantitative evidence of the concrete influence of their respective God upon behaviors within a few years of exposure—say four years.

And in keeping with the Commission on the Future of Higher Education's suggestion that one test would be appropriate for all types of higher-education institutions regardless of mission—liberal-arts colleges, private research universities, public research universities, community colleges, for-profit-online universities, vocational schools—a standardized test would be applied to a person of faith, whether Christian, Jew, Muslim, Hindi or other "approved" religions. Additionally, a pre-test would be given to the faithful upon initial engagement with their respective God and place of worship, and would be followed by a post-test after four years to assess "value added."

Of course, I really don't think No God Left Behind is a good idea. The reasons why also are applicable to No College Left Behind and No Child Left Behind. Most people of faith, I believe, would argue that this quality lies beyond mere human quantitative measurement to validate its worth, that it exists in a variety of forms (only the most radical would argue for the exclusion of faiths that fail a test), and that its effects on human beings may not be immediately evident. None of these assertions, of course, makes faith for believers any less real as a source of improving the quality of human life.

My case for faith continuing to flourish for those who wish it, without proof through standardized testing, shares critical affinities with my argument for higher education not being universally subject to quantitative assessment. There are at least four inter-related issues that confound the Commission's absolutism towards quantitative measurement to solve the imagined knowledge deficit and lack of contribution to the nation by American higher education.

First, quantitative testing, to be of application, must have as its subject that which can be empirically assessed. Such limitation leaves out critical areas of human knowledge, meaning and definition that are not readily subject to immediate empirical assessment during the course of instruction but are, nevertheless, very real: the development of character through trial and error in a residential setting, an appreciation of the arts and aesthetics, a literary and poetic sensibility, a recognition of the responsibilities of citizenship, an appreciation of liberty and freedom, a spirit of business entrepreneurialism, and creativity and inventiveness in the sciences (and I am not talking solely about the short-term acquisition of cultural, historical and political "fact" in these areas).

The commission's recommendations—with their focus on workforce preparation—might well reduce the scope of what is taught and discussed in those institutions to only those areas that can be indisputably measured by a test. An abiding respect for learning, which is not so obviously technical and thus not measurable through standardized assessment, is rooted deeply in the intentions for a distinctively American higher education by our country's founders. Indeed, Benjamin Rush, a patriot, signer of the Declaration of Independence and founder of several colleges, to include Dickinson, proclaimed this distinctive American relationship among advanced knowledge, abstract concepts and the future well-being of the nation when he said, "Freedom can exist only in a society of knowledge. Without learning, men are incapable of knowing their rights." The intent of a liberal education is thus defined.

Both propositions are based not on the quantitative assessment of the merely technical, but rather the confidently ambiguous power of existing in a "society of knowledge," one that would influence learners to a much desired and critically important ideal—democracy and the diversity of perspective that it secures. There exists in Rush and his co-conspirators, in founding a distinctively American higher education after the end of the revolution, a mature appreciation of the complexity and variety of the instruction necessary to advance a democracy.

Second, and closely related to the perspective of Rush, is that education in America was not intended solely to provide young people for "the work force" through the empirically demonstrated mastery of a limited set of practical skills. Fundamental literacy, numeracy and scientific knowledge were more properly the task of the grammar schools and the academies (high schools). American higher education historically builds on this "technical" accomplishment and engages students in a democratic way of life through both advanced technical and speculative (creative) learning.

Third, students in the United States at all levels of formal education already are the most "tested" by standardized measurement in the world. Yet, we still seem to be in a position of deficit in improving what students actually know and need to know to function productively in society. Do we truly believe that more testing will lead to improved teaching and learning? Are we so convinced that "to test is to learn" despite so much evidence to the contrary?

Fourth, are we oblivious to the fact that, like the flourishing of spirituality only in societies that are generously supportive, the acquisition of knowledge only advances in political entities for which this activity is esteemed and generally valued? A society and government in which only practical, technical knowledge is lauded and that which is more abstract is derided—such as the long-term, arduous education for the appreciation of democracy, liberty and freedom—have little chance of moving a people to take the enterprise seriously.

I have no doubt that Secretary Spellings, the Commission members and the chairman, Charles Miller, intend an American higher education that offers the nation and the world graduates who can confront, with knowledge, skill, creativity and an entrepreneurial spirit, the challenges and the opportunities that the world demands. My caution—and it is a pointed one—is that in our rush to secure excellence thorough the simplistic and misguided notion of increased quantitative assessment of workforce skills, we will destroy the historic distinctiveness of American higher education.

Derek Bok, in *Our Underachieving Colleges*, cites numerous commentators over the last few decades alarmed at the perversion of American higher education as it progressively leans to practical and technical knowledge at the expense of more generous, less immediately focused ambitions. For example, Diane Ravitch, an education analyst who has frequently criticized the college establishment, states, "American higher education has remade itself into a vast job-training program in which the liberal arts are no longer central." And Eric Gould in 2003 observes negatively that, "What we now mean by knowledge is information effective in action, information focused on results. We tend to promote the need for a *productive* [emphasis added] citizenry rather than a critical, socially responsive, reflective individualism."

We must never forget that a distinctively American higher education, using a wide variety of internal and external assessments already in place, aims to increase competencies and literacies established prior to college (although far greater public transparency is certainly needed). This ambition the United States shares with the rest of the world. American education, however, infuses this globally shared agenda with something extra, something that has secured its distinction for centuries—to extend beyond factual and technical knowledge and to introduce its students to what Derek Bok describes as, "more ethically discerning ... more knowledgeable and active in civic affairs"—and that cannot be captured through standardized testing at the moment of introduction, for it unfolds over time and with experience.

Lose this ambition and American higher education has lost permanently its distinction as a democratic society of knowledge.

Inside Higher Ed
LET US DISARM!
Dec. 8, 2008

It is high time for the federal government to adjust the antitrust laws to allow American undergraduate colleges and universities to "disarm" unilaterally from wasteful expenditures. Current law does not permit us to disarm because we cannot talk to each other about how to control costs without running the risk of being accused of what can only be considered anti-competitive trade collusion.

It is time for all of us in higher education to think about what it would be like to compete only on the quality of our academic programs and not on the excesses of our amenities. Why can't we be bold and courageous enough to come to the common sense conclusion that not competing on amenities would in the long run be good for students and for those who have to pay tuition? Why can't we temper our "capitalistic compulsion" to compete with each other in ways that only serve to drive up tuition costs? Wouldn't we be in a position to render better service to the American public if we arrived at some common conclusions about how to reduce costs?

Colleges and universities are feverishly rushing to cut expenses because of the current and very real economic crisis. Witness all the presidents announcing hiring freezes, postponements of construction projects, furloughs, lay-offs, salary freezes and modest tuition increases. While none of my colleagues want these cuts to affect the quality of the academic program, it may, in fact, be an unavoidable result.

Yet with all this trimming and restraint, the public is not likely to see the price of an undergraduate education decrease any time soon. The traditional higher-education business model does not permit it. At many, if not most, institutions the cost is significantly higher than the sticker price. At Dickinson, for example, it costs us $13,000 above the sticker price of $47,800 to educate a single student. What rational "business" begins with costs always being significantly higher than price and then tries to sustain that model by further increasing costs? The constraints higher education imposes upon itself now might well soften somewhat the threat of the current economic crisis by reducing marginally the gap between cost and price, but will do nothing to alter a business model that does not work because you cannot have your cake and eat it too.

The only way to control cost and moderate price is to perform radical surgery. Since the historic mission for many colleges and universities is to offer a liberal education that prepares students for informed participation in a democracy, the activities that undergraduate education has added over the centuries to this essentially academic intent are the most vulnerable to "the knife"—residential life, student life, athletics. A combination of classroom and out-of-classroom experiences is now defining a distinctively American undergraduate education that is distinguished from classroom-only university programs in other countries. It is this very surgery that for-profit universities have already performed to keep tuition across their sector more affordable. Academic degrees are offered online (excepting short-term residencies on a host college campus or coursework in a modest office building); there are no residence halls; there is no athletic program; and, of course, there is no student life except conversation about coursework online. For-profit universities are already growing rapidly in enrollment and if tuition keeps rising among nonprofits, this opportunity may become increasingly attractive to the American public.

I suggest that nonprofit education will be reluctant to go so far as the for-profits in altering what has evolved over the centuries as the American "model" of undergraduate education. That said, a viable first step to control costs without sacrificing the academic experience is for colleges and universities to pull back as a "sector" from the extravagances that have developed in the out-of-classroom amenities over the last few decades because of a compulsion to outspend the competition in what is most visible to the paying public—sports palaces, fancy hotel-like accommodations, spa-like student unions, gourmet-style dining facilities, etc.

On behalf of the public and our own desire to remain a key contributor to the national ambition, we ought to disarm in at least one aspect of our activity. We should have a positive deflation of our ambitions and our competitive fever (regardless of the numerical ranking gimmicks) in those areas that are not historically related to our role in advancing knowledge.

What would happen, for example, if all of us came to the conclusion that it would make sense only to build residence halls that conform in design and purpose to the academic program of our respective college or university and to the pricing and construction standards of eco-friendly "low-income housing" that offer inhabitants perfectly livable, attractive space without extravagance? The initial cost may still be high (although not higher than luxury-hotel accommodations), but the long-term energy savings would be significant. What if we all agreed that students could, indeed, survive and even thrive in double rooms? What if we all scaled back our competition for student athletes? What if we pledged to reduce conference and meeting costs by relying more heavily on virtual technology? What stands in the way is not only antitrust laws but also our own attitudes and egos.

It is quite obvious that none of this radical change could be accomplished systemically by a single president or a small group of institutions; it would take a sea change across higher education. But even if we have the best of intentions and can overcome our reluctance to change, the antitrust laws stand squarely in our way. Right now, any discussion with the intent of disarmament cannot prudently be attempted.

The federal antitrust laws were applied in the 1990s to challenge financial aid meetings among colleges that had an "overlap" in the students they recruit. The aftermath of that litigation has had the unfortunate consequence of severely limiting discussion among colleges and universities about cost and competition, at great detriment to the public. I assert that if we, as a nation, are serious about reducing the cost while improving the quality of higher education, we in higher education need a "safe" space in which to talk candidly. Congress should revisit the law and permit such conversations for the benefit of the public. We can't disarm if we can't talk. That is Diplomacy 101!

Let me be clear. I am not talking about encouraging discussion among institutions about faculty salaries, annual tuition charges and the like. I do, however, believe we need the will and determination to try to achieve change in those current practices that have escalated our costs. As a first step we need change from the federal government that would give us the legal means to help the public with the cost of higher education. Not to entertain disarmament leaves us with an intolerable alternative—escalating tuition without foreseeable limit.

Leadership is also required and that probably best comes from established associations. It is time for an organization like the American Council on Education to issue that call for us and to work productively with the federal and state governments to revisit the antitrust laws to allow us to work towards affordability.

There will, of course, be those who decry any form of cooperation among those who meet to discuss cost. They distrust us. This caution is understandable were it not for the intractable crisis in higher education. If we do not find ways to reduce the cost of our colleges and universities, students will potentially seek alternatives such as for-profit universities or study at foreign universities, or be shut out of higher education. And many of those who attend our colleges and universities will be saddled with increasing debt that will burden them and/or their families for years—all at the wrong time in our economic cycle. If "self-interest" is not a consoling safeguard for the skeptics, let us request a temporary exemption of two years to allow colleges to address the exorbitant tuition issue to demonstrate that there are benefits to the public in this approach. If there are such benefits, let the exemption be extended. If not, shame on us!

Inside Higher Ed
VERTIGO YEARS
Aug. 17, 2009

> *"All of you to whom furious work is dear, and what-ever is fast, new, and strange—you find it hard to bear yourselves; your industry is to escape and the will to forget yourselves. If you believed more in life you would fling yourselves less to the moment. But you do not have content enough in yourselves for waiting—and not even for idleness."*
> —*Friedrich Nietzsche*

Reducing the price of higher education by offering a three-year undergraduate degree for all students embarrassingly announces to the world that in America finance and clever marketing trump learning. Lopping off one quarter of the current norm for bachelor's degrees seems a compelling way to achieve the big savings we all long for, particularly when coupled with imaginings that college education is inefficient and readily compacted. Higher ed is easy prey to such imaginings because it deals often with what is not immediately per-ceived and readily measured. Its subject is the mind and the maturing young person. Its playing field is the duration of time.

It may be that we can no longer afford the four-year standard for an undergraduate education. If economic realities push against our current model, so be it. But before we fast forward college in the name of affordability, let's at least be honest about what is being lost. Three is usually not more than or equal to four. Not all results—especially in education, where "widgets" are not the product—are available at lower price and the same quality. Perhaps we can "get undergraduates through" in three years. However, what we may have to alter to achieve that end might severely compromise what we hope to accomplish for our students, particularly in areas vital to a thriving 21st-century democracy and economy.

Consider the following areas of concern. Most involve potential dilution of those very educational goals deemed by the marketplace to be critical competencies to a global workforce and by the public to be essential to American democracy.

Global perspective. American higher education has traditionally done a poor job providing students with global perspective, despite the clear importance of globalization for our future. True, more Americans are studying abroad than in the past, but for shorter periods—this despite convincing evidence that stays of up to an academic year yield markedly superior results. A three-year degree program—with the "no frills" philosophy that often supports it—is likely to reduce space for global education across the curriculum; it certainly will constrain study abroad. Not to mention the more specialized but important issue of impact on instruction in critically needed but demanding languages such as Arabic or Chinese.

Interdisciplinarity. The movement in higher education has been steadily toward more interdisciplinary work, and for multiple, good reasons. This is where much of the action is in research and discovery. Think, for example, of such fields as biochemistry, neuroscience, bioinformatics or environmental studies. More generally, most of the problems we currently face are interdisciplinary in nature (think, for instance, of what one needs to know to address the issue of climate change seriously). Both in the workplace and as citizens the ability to "connect the dots" by drawing insights from multiple fields is becoming ever more essential. As a consequence, we now add "synthesis" to traditional demands for "breadth" and "depth" as a key dimension of undergraduate education. A shortened degree can limit our capacity for interdisciplinary programming, whether in majors or general education.

Complexity. As the foregoing indicates, academic fields—and the world at large—are becoming more complex, not less. Look, for example, at what it now requires to be a biologist as compared to 20 (or even 10) years ago. New information, new methods (often borrowed from other fields as in bioinformatics), and new instrumentation have opened doors both to more knowledge and more questions to answer, not fewer. This is not only a matter of mastering an academic discipline but of expanding into contemporary issues from health care to financial markets. We need more thinking and students knowing with some certainty about the complexity of issues, not less.

Choice. Growing complexity has meant that academic majors have become both fuller and more hierarchical (i.e., more courses with more prerequisites). Pushing hierarchical majors back from four years to three will inevitably up the pressure on students to decide on a major immediately, and significantly constrain the possibility of a change in direction. Early specialization is the European model, but should it become ours? Will it maintain America's edge of advancing students and a workforce who are engaged, entrepreneurial and creative in part because they have taken the time to find out who they are and remained open to new possibilities? This question has particularly salience as the new, 21st-century economy demands ever more flexibility.

Creativity. Much of the foregoing focuses on an arena in which Americans, and American students, have been historically distinguished—creativity. Can this quality thrive in a "hurry up," "let's get it done" version of higher education? This goal is certainly more difficult to achieve in a course of study that is predicated upon early specialization and in which combining depth with experience in a variety of fields is minimized?

Democracy. It is true that we as a nation must educate for the skills/abilities that fuel our economy, and at reasonable cost. But we educate for the habits of mind and action that fuel a democracy as well. Educating for democracy as opposed to mere academic coursework is a global differentiator of American higher education. Three-year compacting may very well push out opportunity for the broader tools and vision we need for citizenship to unfold over time in a residential setting—especially among students who are generally the youngest to begin university in the industrialized world. Let us remember that many of the skills of organization and association that since Tocqueville have been identified as guarantors of American civil society are developed in co- and extracurricular activities that characterize current residential education. These, too, are potential victims of degree acceleration.

Meaning. When advocates of a shorter degree call for "no frills" and an end to "waste," likely targets for substantial cutbacks are the humanities and arts. The press for more practical undergraduate degree programs, intensified by global economic competition, has already reduced enrollment in these fields. Is it worthwhile to have a system in which speculation on what it means to be human and exposure to the range of human creativity and expression in the arts are increasingly pushed aside? Our students already do too little of this.

Technology. New online technology is often offered up as the elixir for students of any age that shortens time and improves quality by simultaneously accelerating and enhancing instruction. But this is far from proven. The emerging reality may be that technology works best among younger students when combined with more traditional, faculty-contact based approaches rather than as a substitute. Moreover, mastery of many technological innovations—whether general skills of computing or more specialized skills associated with new instrumentation and techniques, especially in the sciences—itself places time pressures on the undergraduate degree. Not to mention that the substantial costs of developing and applying effective technology in instruction work against promised cost savings through degree acceleration.

It is worth noting that at many institutions the door is already open to a three-year degree. Students can deploy credits earned in high school through Advanced Placement, summer school, and/or a few semesters with a course overload to reduce their time to a bachelor's degree to three or quite easily three and a half years. How many do? Very few. Advocates of degree acceleration would claim, with some reason, that we do not advertise the fast track and have built the system to discourage it.

They might also argue, again with cause, that students who might otherwise finish in three years fear competition from peers who have taken longer to mature, hone their abilities, and develop resumes full of internships, study abroad and senior research experience. But could it also be that many students are in no rush because they sense some of the points made above? Perhaps they have an inkling that four years of study and maturation prepare them better for graduate work, career, and life?

Supporters of the three-year degree often cite the example of Europe as justification for reducing our time in undergraduate study. Indeed, as part of the Bologna Declaration, member countries are required to move by 2010 to a five-year bachelor's-master's degree sequence. Many nations are choosing the 3+2 option. Yet the comparison of the two systems of higher education is highly misleading, most obviously because conditions in Europe are quite different from conditions in America.

Take Germany as an example—a country that has chosen the 3+2 option. There, high school students prepare for the university with a rigorous liberal arts and science course of study until the age of 19. This study is so demanding that numerous colleges and universities in the United States award a full year of college credit for the completion of the Abitur—the German high school degree. In essence, the German secondary school experience de facto makes for a four-year degree. Moreover, German men are required by law to complete a period of either military or civil service and thus will begin undergraduate study generally at 20 and finish at 23 or 24.

Certain fields of study, however, have a limited number of seats for study available in any given year ("Numerus Clausus") and therefore, students have to wait a year or more additionally to begin university. The American three-year proposal would have our students completing college at 20 or 21. The age difference is striking—and not to our advantage. Moreover, at present only 35 percent of German school students proceed to university study versus approximately 65 percent in the United States. Clearly Germany is subjecting a far more uniformly well-prepared and limited number of students to the "three-year" baccalaureate than would be subject to it in the United States. The comparison of the two nations for advocacy of the three-year degree simply breaks down on several fronts.

Importantly, many European professors, students and educational agencies are awakening to negative outcomes of the three-year degree. For example, increasingly German students are forgoing their former practice of study abroad in order to finish on time their tightly prescribed three-year program. The situation has become so alarming that the German Academic Exchange Service (DAAD) is apparently advocating a four-year undergraduate degree program to accommodate a year of study abroad. Students and professors are also discovering that the three-year course of study is so regimented that there is little to no time to engage in studies across disciplines or to reflect upon what has been learned.

Returning to America and looking at our system as a whole, the key numbers may not be four and three. As the Obama administration has clearly discovered, roughly one third of our students are enrolled in community college, and here the issue is improving the quality of two years. Even in regard to four-year institutions, the real challenge may be increasing the number of students who complete on time. Our focus ought to be on the five, six or more years it often takes to complete. For example, more than 60 percent of students with Advanced Placement credit—theoretically prime candidates for an accelerated degree—currently fail to finish in four years. In addition, all of this, as the European example demonstrates, is predicated upon another set of numbers—K through 12.

Underlying the issue of degree non-completion at all levels of our higher education system are the demographics of access. Opening the doors of college to more Americans, including particularly students from groups historically underrepresented in higher ed, creates challenges in regard to cost. But it also raises the issue of quality. Will we expand opportunity and access by diluting the product by introducing a three-year degree at such a critical period of opportunity in their lives?

Of course, the commentary on three-year degrees is typically based on the assumption that it will radically decrease cost. But the new model has yet to be rigorously structured financially. The claims are that three years will save a great deal of money, but are we certain that is so? Implementing an accelerated degree efficiently in regard to scheduling, advising, and facilities will require additional administrative overhead. Offering the necessary courses may well mean additional faculty. And there will be other added instructional costs. These might include extra professors to implement more intensive pedagogy, new monies to support online work, or both. Could it in fact cost the same or at the outside even more to accelerate?

Capturing the spirit of the times, one prominent advocate styled the three-year degree as the "higher ed equivalent of a fuel-efficient car" compared to the "gas guzzling four-year course." A metaphor from the food industry might be more apt. Slow education, as in slow cooking, is enthusiastically replaced by Fast Ed or McEd, with comparable results. Higher education is certainly in need of efficiency. Our current business model, which has yielded steadily increasing costs, needs change and, perhaps, radically so. Let us not be fooled by adapting across the system solutions that appear corrective but may be destructive of the virtue and distinction of American higher education and its ambition—education for the workforce and for participation and leadership in a democracy.

Reducing the undergraduate program to three years from four is a "quick fix." Much is to be lost and much wagered, ironically at a time when the four-year program that has helped so many to success is being made available across American society. We can do better.

Neil B. Weissman, provost and dean of Dickinson College, co-authored this article.

The Philadelphia Inquirer
HELPING STUDENTS GOVERN THEMSELVES
Oct. 31, 2011

Ask national security officials where the greatest threat to the homeland lies, and they're sure to tell you it's in ungoverned territory— those areas around the world where the absence of law and order allows terrorists to operate without fear of reprisal.

In colleges, too, ungoverned student behavior can disrupt order and threaten safety. A small subset of students who ignore the social contract and do what they want, when they want to, can have a disproportionate impact on a campus. They can compromise the quality of life of all students and waste huge amounts of staff time and money.

Colleges have codes of conduct to address this kind of behavior. When it comes to substance abuse and other issues, we support our codes with counseling and, where appropriate, discipline. But if some of a college's students are able to make life frightening, dangerous, or intolerable for others on or off campus, that college has a problem with ungoverned space.

All sorts of military and nonmilitary means are employed to deal with the world's ungoverned territories. Ultimately, though, such places cease to be havens for bad behavior when enough of their people embrace and master effective governance—ideally, self-governance—in all its dimensions. That is, when they see the possibility of a better life through legitimate government.

This idea can inform college leaders dealing with ungoverned behavior. We have our codes of conduct and disciplinary mechanisms, but what ultimately matters is whether our students understand that effective self-governance is the key to their ability to lead productive and meaningful lives on campus and beyond.

We should redouble our efforts to teach students the benefits of surrendering a part of themselves to the social contract. We should instill in them a fuller understanding of what it means to be part of a wider, diverse community. We should encourage them to engage in open dialogue about ethical, moral, and epistemological questions that extend beyond self-interest.

And, most important, we should teach them the simple truth that progress toward the good life depends largely on how well they treat others and subjugate their will to the social contract.

Benjamin Rush, the founder of Dickinson College and a signer of the Declaration of Independence, said it best in a 1773 letter to his countrymen on the virtues of patriotism: "The *social* spirit is the true *selfish* spirit, and men always promote their own interest most, in proportion as they promote that of their neighbors and their country."

If You Think College Is Expensive …
Nov. 16, 2012

Amidst the numerous calls to make higher education more affordable, online learning and classroom technology have emerged as the silver bullets.

While reducing internal costs and providing more variety in coursework at individual colleges, these "fixes" don't address the ascent of tuition, room and board—the ultimate burden to the student and family—that blocks affordability. Cost is not price. Lowered cost has yet to lower tuition.

So why is it that increased use of technology and online learning have not lowered tuition for undergraduate education? The answer is obvious: Faculty and staff would have to be reduced in great numbers and replaced by technologies, and the nation would have to gut residential undergraduate education as we know it. Anything short of that is just rearranging the chairs on the deck.

But is any of this likely to happen? I doubt it. There is little reason to believe that most 18 to 21-year-olds, who are still gaining self-governance and motivation beyond that which provides immediate gratification, would engage online learning successfully without the costly human infrastructure that necessitates higher tuition. Numerous for-profit online universities, in fact, focus primarily on working adult learners because the retention rates among traditional college-age students is abysmal.

Educators—and many parents—agree that the undergraduate experience in America is all about identity. We have historically determined that young people between the years of 18 and 21 attend residential college to learn from mentors and peers about who they are and what they might become. Skills and competencies are critical, but identity formation is primary in our democracy. And America remains, despite the rhetoric to the contrary, a nation committed first and foremost to education for democracy, rather than education for commerce. To accomplish identity development, many residential undergraduate colleges and universities pursue a "high-touch, labor-intensive" course of study with faculty and staff interaction as the defining experience.

Of course, some large universities, where "high-touch" undergraduate education is no longer an expectation, might engage online learning and MOOCs (massive open online courses) enthusiastically to generate extra income. But there is no evidence yet that the funds generated will reduce tuition, room and board. In fact, many public institutions will have to use these extra funds to compensate for monies withheld from the states.

Some small liberal-arts colleges might employ "star" professors to provide a main set of lectures supplemented by tutors. They might even adopt hybrid learning, replacing areas of basic content in existing courses with technologically delivered material.

All of these initiatives might well save a college or university money and reduce its cost, but, again, there is no evidence that reduced cost translates into lower tuition. And the prospect of college-age Americans living at home while taking online courses is probably not broadly appealing.

The future of American education involves choice. Students who can afford it, or those who are qualified and receive a substantial scholarship, would most likely opt for a traditional residential education. It is the American dream. Others, including many first-generation college students, would accept an online education that forgoes identity formation and preparation for democracy. This choice brings up a troubling question of social justice: Why, at the very moment when college is becoming available to students previously alienated from higher education, do those who have benefitted from the traditional model—the decision makers—advance on the basis of affordability that which they would not accept for themselves and their children?

Former Harvard president Derek Bok once said, "If you think education is expensive, try ignorance." In these demanding times, I'd add, if you think education is expensive, try a lack of identity among a democratic populace.

In a recent *Wall Street Journal* interview about college costs and online learning, Stanford University President John Hennessy said, "What I told my colleagues is there's a tsunami coming. I can't tell you exactly how it's going to break, but my goal is to try to surf it, not to just stand there." Stanford and other elite institutions, such as Harvard and Carnegie Mellon Universities, and Massachusetts Institute of Technology are not sitting back and waiting for technology to disrupt higher education—they are out there experimenting with both delivery formats and cost. They are part of the change. This is why they are elite. They boldly anticipate. And they have the wealth, confidence and the unassailable market niche to do so.

But are they looking in the right place for that tsunami? I would argue "no!" Much of their current effort is directed at experimenting with online learning. This is a necessary component of the massive change that potentially will reconfigure higher education in the United States. Princeton and Stanford universities and the universities of Michigan and Pennsylvania have combined to form Coursera, offering free selected courses to the public. Harvard and MIT have announced a new nonprofit partnership, known as edX, to do the same. Carnegie Mellon is offering its Open Learning Initiative (OLI) to the public.

But all of these efforts are not the tsunami. Open online learning is merely a tool that adds variety to how education is delivered. And many 18 to 21-year-olds and their families still believe—despite the rhetoric to the contrary—that a college education is as much about maturing in a residential setting as it is about learning or getting a job.

No, online learning may be part of the current, but the tsunami itself will be something different. The tsunami will come from a notion as old and as distinctive as American education itself. The notion about which I speak is that education takes place not just in the classroom—and now through a computer, iPad or smart phone screen—but literally "everywhere, anywhere, anytime."

Yes, education happens in schools and colleges, but it happens also in the home, on the job, at places of worship and through individual initiative. Education also is never finished. A degree offered decades ago—even a few years ago—is obsolete with respect to up-to-date factual knowledge (critical-thinking skills, leadership skills in a residential setting and historical knowledge stay relevant, however). The "anytime" in a distinctively American education means that there is an imperative to amass knowledge through a lifetime and demonstrate acquisition.

Now, imagine that a highly respected, unassailable institution or set of institutions offers a set of completion exams at the bachelor's level to anyone everywhere, anywhere, anytime. One need only look at the GED, or to some extent the Western Governors University, to say this is possible. Of course, a GED probably doesn't have the "prestige" of a regularly earned degree and the WGU is still a new model. But we are talking here about what is possible over time with experimentation, improved technologies and unrelenting public pressure to offer an undergraduate education at a more reasonable price than currently predicted.

Necessity clearly still drives invention. Imagine that this move is made by those extremely prestigious research universities currently at initial stages of experimentation with online learning, open access and the rewarding of certificates. Imagine that these universities find a way to equal a high level of academic achievement online to that on their residential campuses, are secure in knowing that there will be always sufficient students who wish a traditional residential experience at their respective campus, and convince their alumni and the public that their coursework on campus and online is academically equivalent as far as the transfer of knowledge is concerned. Would they ultimately leave money on the table in times of ever increasing financial constraint and unrelenting demand to fund pioneering research? Would they restrain from total market dominance?

Imagine the moment when these completion exams permit a person to assemble learning from a variety of academic institutions and life experiences to complete a degree. At that moment, the monopoly of institutions over source and cost loosens, and the student gains control of how knowledge is to be gained and at what price. At that moment, the sources of learning are severed from credentialing. At that moment, American higher education is radically changed.

A tsunami is in the making, but it will encounter a wall of resistance in yet another defining characteristic of American higher education—a 24/7 residential learning and living experience that aims not just to transfer knowledge to 18 to 21-year-old students, but also to guide their maturation into citizenship. This pushback will be located squarely in the historically prestigious liberal-arts colleges and in those institutions like the Ivies and the major research universities confident in securing undergraduates regardless of alternative developments because they have the wealth to afford what always was. But this wall of resistance is not very deep when it comes to all students. All the governors and other policy makers embracing WGU and other forms of recognition for prior learning as well as online learning seem to be quite willing to give up that residential experience, at least for other people's children.

This residential learning is often inefficient, costly and repetitive, and that is because many developing young people are emotionally and intellectually unpredictable during undergraduate years. The mission for much of 18 to 21-year-old undergraduate education is to move these students to another level of maturity and corresponding engagement. It is a worthy pursuit. It is education for democracy.

The tsunami is close to shore. The warning siren is sounding. But the outcome is not evident. A barrier—albeit increasingly thin—formed by commitment to undergraduate residential education for democracy confronts a wave of convenience and necessity defined by centralized credentialing, dispersed sourcing of knowledge and learner-controlled pricing. This is the wave to surf and the shoreline to protect.

In my 14-year tenure as president I have often been asked to define and defend the notion of a "useful" liberal-arts education. The general public has difficulty associating the liberal arts with anything useful. That obstacle prompts them to dismiss liberal-arts colleges as repositories of graduates with majors such as philosophy, history, anthropology and American studies who cannot get jobs. The thought that these same colleges also have majors such as biology, chemistry, physics and economics is totally missed.

The public is not to blame. American higher education never really experienced the American Revolution. While we threw away the oppressive dictates of monarchy, we never threw off the privileged notion of an English upper-class liberal education that was literally defined as being only for those with sufficient wealth to do nothing professionally but dabble in learning. We remained enthralled by the notion of learning for learning's sake and despite our emerging pragmatic nature, wanted our education to remain sublime and removed from the business of life.

There were prominent founders of the nation who argued for a new kind of liberal education for a new kind of nation. Thomas Jefferson urged a "practical education" for his University of Virginia. And Benjamin Rush, the founder of Dickinson College, decried the unwillingness of Americans to reform education after the Revolution:

> It is equally a matter of regret, that no accommodation has been made in the system of education in our seminaries [colleges] to the new form of our government and the many national duties, and objects of knowledge, that have been imposed upon us by the American Revolution. Instead of instructing our sons in the Arts most essential to their existence, and in the means of acquiring that kind of knowledge which is connected to the time,

the country, and the government in which they live, they are compelled to spend [time] learning two languages which no longer exist, and are rarely spoken, which have ceased to be the vehicles of science and literature, and which contain no knowledge but what is to be met with in a more improved and perfect state in modern languages. We have rejected hereditary power in the governments of our country. But we continue the willing subjects of a system of education imposed upon us by our ancestors in the fourteenth and fifteenth centuries. Had agriculture, mechanics, astronomy, navigation and medicine been equally stationary, how different from the present would have been the condition of mankind!

But these singular calls for a more pragmatic education in America to match a new form of government went largely unheeded. Rush's founding of Dickinson is particularly illustrative. In his 1785 "Plan of Education" he called for a "useful liberal education." The curriculum was to be absent instruction in the writing and speaking of Greek and Latin, but rich in instruction of German, French, Spanish and even Native American languages as those would be highly useful to Americans striving to establish a native economy that would grow as it interacted linguistically with trading nations throughout the world and in the United States. Democracy was to be established through commerce informed by useful liberal education. Liberal education, commerce and democracy were interdependent. The Dickinson course of study was also to include chemistry as Rush thought this subject held the greatest number of connections to emerging knowledge useful to the nation.

The first president of the college and Rush's fellow trustees ignored his plan. They recommitted to what Rush once called "the monkish" course of study, unchanged for centuries.

Latin and Greek were taught and a chemistry professor was not hired. Additionally, the college refused to hire a German professor. Rush was so angry that he founded nearby what was called Franklin College (today Franklin & Marshall College). It wasn't until 1999 that Rush's notion of a "useful" liberal education was reintroduced and embraced explicitly as part of a revised mission statement some 216 years after it was introduced.

Unfortunately for those in America today who wish to argue the usefulness, and thus the worthiness, of a liberal-arts education, the founding fathers were not explicit. We know that a liberal education was to yield informed citizens who could build and protect the new government. We know that certain courses were to be taken out and others inserted—those that related more to emerging and immediately explicable knowledge, expanded the appreciation of democracy and created new knowledge and wealth that would materially power the nation's development. A useful liberal-arts education was essentially entrepreneurial. But for all the novelty and potent force in this "disruptive technology" in American higher education introduced by the founding fathers, we know little about how a liberal-arts education actually becomes useful—that is, how the study of the liberal arts converts to material effect in the wider world.

Much is at stake to define explicitly and to reassert the usefulness of a distinctively American liberal-arts education. The liberal arts are under assault by those who, under the mantle of affordability and efficiency, would reject it for the immediate, but often temporary benefit of higher education defined as job training. My own experience offers a definition for the 21st century, in fact, for any century, where economic uncertainty prevails. I was a German and philosophy double major. At first glance, what could be more useless? And yet, my professional life has proven such a conclusion wrong.

I have been—sometimes simultaneously—a military officer, a precollegiate teacher, administrator and coach. I founded an athletic team, developed a major center at a prestigious research university, acted as a senior consultant to the U.S. Department of State with diplomatic status, served as a corporate officer at two publicly traded companies and now serve as president of Dickinson College. For none of these careers did I ever study formally or take a class.

I gained competency through independent reading, experience and observation. I appreciated that the breadth of knowledge and the depth of cognitive skill that my undergraduate courses in social science, political science, art and science prepared me for any field of professional pursuit. I was prepared for professional chance. I knew how to ask the right questions, how to gather information, how to make informed decisions, how to see connections among disparate areas of knowledge, how to see what others might miss, how to learn quickly the basics of a profession, how to discern pertinent information from that which is false or misleading, how to judge good, helpful people from those who wish you ill. All of this I gathered in a useful liberal education—in and out of the classroom—and in an intense residential life where experimentation with citizenship and social responsibility were guiding principles.

There were no formal, discrete courses to learn these habits of mind and action—no courses devoted to brain exercises, critical-thinking skills, leadership and citizenship; rather, professors and staff were united in all interactions to impress upon students day after day, year after year, a liberal-arts learning environment that was intellectually rigorous and defining. This was contextual learning at its fullest deployment. We absorbed and gradually displayed ultimately useful knowledge and skill not in a studied manner, but discretely and naturally. Time after time in my various careers, I applied these liberal-arts skills to solve materially wider-world problems. And most important, except for my military service and my college presidency, none of my jobs existed before I assumed them. My useful education has enabled me to maximize opportunity within highly fluid and changing employment rhythms. As I now face another job transition in my life, I go forward with confidence that something appropriate will develop. I have no concrete plans and I like it that way. I know I am prepared on the basis of my liberal arts education to maximize chance. Something will develop. Something that probably doesn't yet exist.

I am not alone in my appreciation of the liberal arts. Those of privilege have appreciated liberal education historically. It has contributed to their access and hold on power and influence. Their sons and daughters, generation after generation, have attended liberal arts institutions without hesitation. There is no job training in their educational landscape. It would be tragic if all the new and previously underserved populations now having access to higher education missed the opportunity for their turn at leadership and influence simply because of the outspoken—arguably purposeful—dismissal of the liberal arts as "useless," often by those who received a liberal-arts education themselves and intend nothing less for their own children.

———————————

The Huffington Post
THE SILENCE IS BROKEN
Jan. 4, 2013

Americans like to forget the unpleasant. It's a new year and the politics of the day and other pressing issues have begun to push from our memories the brutal events that took place at Sandy Hook Elementary. But our waning interest and inability to focus for a sustained period of time will not fix that which has for so long been broken.

College presidents do not speak out on national issues today because the public deems them meddling when they reach beyond their profession. We have listened and remained silent— even about issues that affect our communities. Gun control and mental illness are two such issues.

It wasn't always like this. Decades ago, presidents were regularly called upon to advise public figures and work in government. People listened—even if they did not agree—because they thought that by being involved in educating emerging leaders and engaged citizens, presidents might have something to say. Not today.

But that has just changed. Sadly, it took the loss of very young children and their protectors—teachers and administrators—in Newtown, Conn.—to do it. But it is done.

Presidents have signed on to an open letter initiated by Presidents Lawrence M. Schall of Oglethorpe University and Elizabeth Kiss of Agnes Scott College, calling for better gun safety legislation. I signed this letter, which had more than 165 signatures within 36 hours from presidents across the country. Ultimately 304 signed. This is a national crisis that crosses all boundaries and affiliations. We represent schools large and small, religiously affiliated and non-denominational and presidents who identify as Republicans, Democrats and Independents. As sentinels of our students, we cannot remain silent.

I shall talk to our students and let them know that I support the right to bear arms, but that I interpret the Constitution not to include those assault weapons and high-capacity magazines that are so readily available today.

I will share with them my own story. I shall share that my good friend from Baltimore was indiscriminately gunned down in 2005 because two people just wanted to kill somebody and they had the means to do so readily available.

I shall talk about my father and his attitude toward guns. He grew up in the deep rural South and, coming from a very poor farming family, frequently hunted for meals. He served in the U.S. Army for 30 years and was a veteran of World War II. I grew up in a household with a gun culture. But for my father that meant something definite: It signaled discipline, respect, care and responsibility.

My father sat me down with a rifle at a very young age and described its appropriate use and its irresponsible use. He told me that a rifle was a solemn object that was to be respected. It could be the source of sustenance and protection or, used inappropriately—carelessly, the cause of loss and tragedy. My father impressed upon me that my .22 caliber rifle was just the right power for the purpose intended—to chase away raccoons and rabbits from crops. I needed nothing more powerful. For me, a gun culture had absolutely nothing to do with an indiscriminate amassing of firepower radically out of line with intended purpose.

Yes, I grew up in a gun culture, but it did not carry into adulthood. This is a personal lifestyle choice, not a political statement. The last time I held and fired a weapon was while serving in the U.S. Army. But here again, the weapons were respected, firepower was adjusted to purpose, and discipline was strictly enforced.

I shall also direct our students to study the strong convictions toward mental health of our college founder, Dr. Benjamin Rush. A physician, signer of the Declaration of Independence and surgeon general of the Middle Army in the American Revolution, Rush also is known as "the father of American psychiatry." He advocated vociferously for substantial investment in the humane treatment of the mentally ill to improve their condition and the well-being of the emerging American society. And most remarkably, he both supported militias to win the war and admonished one of his sons for acquiring a gun without his consent and guidance.

I am encouraging our students to talk vigorously about gun control and then to do something. I am asking them to be activists. I am causing trouble on our campus and it's about time. As an Independent politically I shall make sure that all perspectives are represented in this conversation but, from the beginning, our students shall know where I stand. I expect challenges, but neutrality has its limits in life-and-death situations. Gun control shatters silence, political correctness and any concerns of alienation because of your stance on an issue of such magnitude.

So the silence is broken on American campuses. They will be noisy, but that is as it should be. And our energy and sense of purpose will be directed to Washington—to Congress, the Supreme Court, lobbyists, national associations and the partisan politics of parties that increasingly cannot agree even to protect our people. Students will witness democracy by example. It's about time. We can do better.

The Chronicle of Higher Education
A LIBERAL-ARTS HOME FOR THE MILITARY
Feb. 25, 2013

Four decades ago, I participated in ROTC at Dickinson College and was commissioned as a second lieutenant in the U.S. Army. I also had the distinct privilege of going through basic training with one of the first cohorts of women to engage side by side with men in combat simulation.

I didn't think my military service was all that unconventional, and not until I assumed the presidency at Dickinson, in 1999, did it strike me as unusual. I would look around at my peers, and rarely did I see any who had military service in their backgrounds. At first glance, that's not so alarming. There are many ways to serve, and the military is but one—an important one, but not the only one.

While it may be unreasonable to expect the majority of college and university presidents to have served in uniform, the higher-education community itself should be held accountable for ensuring that anyone who leads an institution thought to be part of an indispensable bulwark of democracy understands the vital role of the military in society and finds opportunities to help students gain that knowledge.

This mandate is even more crucial with the announcement last month that women will now be eligible for combat-arms deployment. More than half of American college students are women, and yet only 20 percent of the 20,000 students enrolled in Army ROTC programs are women. Presidents can now inspire and encourage women to consider yet another opportunity for service, leadership, and advancement from which they were previously excluded.

Today's college student knows very little about the military. Both men and women have little understanding of the reality and consequence of combat. With only 1 percent of Americans in the armed forces, most college students will never serve, and they may not have a relative who has served. Those students will come to believe that the nation's military engagements and wars exist as distant tasks for others.

What can we do about this?

Dickinson, with a grant from the Andrew W. Mellon Foundation, has worked to build on opportunities for cooperation between liberal-arts colleges and neighboring military-education institutions. We have seen the benefits of these collaborations in joint classes and cross-institutional visits by students and faculty. Colorado College and the U.S. Air Force Academy, for example, offered a joint course, "The Physics and Meaning of Flight," and Vassar College and the U.S. Military Academy organized a discussion for their students on "Military Academies and the Liberal Arts."

Other colleges might consider adding or re-establishing ROTC programs on their campuses. Having such an organization in proximity permits me to discuss with these young men and women their military commitment and what it means to them in the context of undergraduate studies.

They educate me about commitment, time management, wellness, idealism, and connection, at a young age, to something larger than themselves. And when I visit some of our young graduates at the Walter Reed National Military Medical Center who have served and been severely wounded, I am brought into an emotional dimension of my profession that offers a distinctive connection to the sacrifice of those who are our students.

The Constitution decrees civilian leadership of the military a necessity for a liberal democracy. The founding fathers believed that citizens who know a great deal about the military also understand their responsibility to oversee and control its actions. They also recognized that a nation whose success depends upon an engaged and informed populace demands an education far different from the isolated model that was prevalent throughout 18th-century Europe, and upon which America's colonial, theologically oriented colleges and universities had been modeled.

They advocated instead an education that easily traversed the boundaries between the classroom and the community, where the lessons of the academy could be applied immediately to society. This education was to prepare leaders who would shape the economy, government, and social structures of the young democracy.

That's why the lack of understanding of the military in higher education is so troubling. If we as educators, with access to millions of young people, aren't encouraging these discussions, who will? We are responsible for helping to develop the next generation of citizen leaders who will oversee the military and who, without our support, may have no preparation for this responsibility.

If we are to remain a democratic republic, fulfill the American educational mission and honor what our veterans have fought to preserve, we must reacquaint academic America with the military. We must be certain that those who will become our civilian leaders are educated and equipped to participate equally in the conversation and the relationship with those who serve.

Selected Speeches

Opening Remarks for the 41st-Annual Public Affairs Symposium
Feb. 15, 2004

Ladies and gentlemen, welcome to the 41st-annual Public Affairs Symposium at Dickinson College. The Symposium—better known over the years simply as "PAS"—emerged in the early 1960s as a powerful public forum to connect the liberal-arts curriculum of the college with the "burning point" (the German word "Brennpunkt" comes to mind) events and ideas in the wider world. It was a presumptuous initiative then and remains—with durational intensity—symbolic of what we do at the heart of a "distinctively Dickinson" liberal education today.

We intentionally strive to connect knowledge usefully in and across existing and emerging academic disciplines and place our engagement of ideas—a full and provocative array—in the context of unavoidable global challenges and public policies. Such intentionality is the stuff of liberal education. It is our public morality.

In the early 19th century, Alexis de Tocqueville visited the United States to see our young democracy at work and to take ideas back to France, which at that time was swaying precariously between revolutionary democracy and authoritarian regime. De Tocqueville, of course, wrote *Democracy in America* to record his observations, the first extended commentary about the state of affairs in the United States. He found that one of the abiding strengths of American democracy in the early 19th century was a deep sense of community spirit. Americans displayed a conscious tendency to come together as citizens, to form voluntary organizations for the express purpose of confronting contemporary problems and to advance collectively, a more humane and functional society.

Today, in the early 21st century, commentators from across the political spectrum are worried about an apparent decline in community spirit in America and a weakening of our civic organizations. This retreat, they believe, poses a real threat to those bonds that hold a democracy together and further weaken communal responsibility and action—leaving us, regrettably, with mere individual ego—unconnected, selfish or uninspired and most dangerous, an intellectual unilateralism, a mind moving in the world without productive alliances of other minds.

In this troubling context—a society in which community and service are less important than self—the importance of PAS to the mission of the college is all the more compelling. We know who we are; we know what we are to do. We prepare unabashedly citizen leaders. We are encouraged still by the explicit intentions of our 18th-century founder, Dr. Benjamin Rush, who was also so intimately committed to the founding of this nation that he risked condemnation by England for treason. Inspired by his vision, we commit to building through the thoughts and actions of our students—later graduates—a just, compassionate democratic society. We commit to preparing them for this responsibility by leading them beyond the unilateralism of their prematurely secure egos to positions that take into account the "other"—politically, historically, culturally, environmentally, legally, spiritually and with respect to human rights.

Such a task is not without its challenges. We build citizens by opening minds to contradictory notions. We confront young people daily with other troubling questions, fill them, at least temporarily, with self-doubt and present them with facts and beliefs that, while reasonable to some, are highly objectionable to others. At Dickinson, the mind has no comfortable hiding place. Most in our community thrive. They relish engaging the wide variety and diversity of thought and action; they grow in four years into informed, inquisitive, engaged citizens of the world. However, as in any collective, some seek to flee our confrontation through self-imposed obscurity, numbing silence and avoidance of forums such as PAS.

But we, as a larger community, persist. We persist in introducing those who would flee to new, sometimes unsettling ideas bit by painful bit. As the most recent Morgan lecturer, Michael Ignatieff, stated last week in this very hall, our faculty and administration demand from all students "adversarial justification" for opinions they hold. This process of reasoned dialectic and demand for logical clarity among our students is unsettling and messy. Our institutional devotion to free inquiry and democratic process can, ironically, be as unsettling and outrageously annoying to our general public. Ideas will be heard in our space that some will find highly objectionable. This will surely happen over the next few days during the PAS sessions. Some will ask us not to have a guest speak because the position espoused is objectionable to some group for some reason.

We are, however, clear about our educative role in American democracy. We do not censure thoughts that are merely intellectually threatening and strongly held. We defend this space, this podium, for free intellectual inquiry of all sorts. If not here, then where? We believe ultimately in the redeeming power of reason, spirit and civility guided by education to prevail and to be that which permits our audiences, through reflection and civil questioning, to judge for themselves the ultimate value of what they collectively or individually hear and then believe. At Dickinson, we affirm you as rational, spiritual beings. And just as our founder Dr. Rush and his friends—Jefferson, Adams, Madison, Dickinson and Franklin—hold us all capable of self-government, we hold ourselves and you eminently capable of governing our own ideas. We resist any external party that would shield us and our reason from direct contact with ideas eloquently presented. Judgment of their value remains our collective right and privilege.

LEADERSHIP, LANGUAGE STUDY AND GLOBAL SENSIBILITY
EARCOS 2004 KEYNOTE ADDRESS
Nov. 2, 2004

I am delighted to be again among old friends internationally and to meet new ones. I respect highly and profoundly all of you who engage the world by being out in it daily and preparing through your schools and respective communities a next generation—a new, increasingly hopeful generation—of global citizens.

Most of you know me as a person who has spent decades studying and advancing special-needs students—especially highly able students (and that includes those with learning challenges). About eight years ago, however, I asked myself a fundamental question: "To what use is this high academic talent to be put?" Of course, you might smile at this. My query reveals a distinctively Anglo-American prejudice—that an idea is only as worthy as it can be applied (more on this prejudice later). But to this end, my interests morphed into the study of leadership—leadership for citizenship and societal contribution as a worthy end and application for human talent and high ability. Coincidentally, my pursuit has coincided with a raging preoccupation with leadership in general. The media and popular press are filled with books on leadership and management—not just good leadership, but as of a few months ago, even books dedicated to bad leadership. Anything apparently sells related to this topic.

Last year, about 3,000 books on leadership in business were published in the United States. According to last week's *Economist*, leadership studies is now a distinctive genre of intellectual pursuit. But there is a rub. That enthusiasm exists only in the United States. In fact, most other countries, such as the U.K., find this U.S. obsession bizarre—chiefly because of the U.S. linking of leadership with the personality trait of "charisma," which the Brits think is fleeting and insubstantial. They also distrust anyone who possesses it. Additionally, the Brits find the American advancement of leadership for the world to be highly ironic given its obvious (as perceived by the Brits) challenge to leadership in its own business world and that of politics.

Leadership is big business. I think of Jim Collin's book *Good to Great* and his "hedgehog" concept, or Malcolm Gladwell's *Tipping Point*. Millions and millions of copies of these and other leadership books are being sold. I am convinced that this leadership frenzy explains in large part the overwhelming fascination with the U.S. founding fathers of late and the proliferation of books by McCullough, Ellis, etc. treating them in great detail. I am convinced that this fascination with leadership grows out of the singular question of global and political leadership—or lack thereof—in our contemporary world.

That said, I am also convinced that this focus on leadership—now among the general public, in the world of business and finance, politics and increasingly taught at undergraduate, graduate and professional schools—will soon be a required subject at the precollege level. Leadership is coming your way. You will feel the pressure to teach it. It will be the new buzzword. You will have many speakers in the future seeking to address you here and at other conferences on the topic and they will all link it, I predict, to another current issue—some say "buzzword"—one with a few years head start—accountability. Your charge, of course, is to determine how you will react and ultimately, how you will teach this new area of study. This is a crucial decision. You will either teach it as a separate field in and of itself or you will integrate it into all your existing subjects. You face the same choice you had with, for example, critical thinking and problem solving—standalone subjects merely self-relating or skills set in more comprehensive academic contexts. Those who know me know my strong prejudice. I prefer the latter option.

Today, I wish you to think out loud with me about your new subject and to think in a revolutionary manner—to go where no one has yet gone but where you must go if leadership as a subject of study is going to have any sustained import in education. I am going to ask you to take leadership out of the more common context of business, finance and politics and place it in that of a liberal-arts subjects. I'm asking you to see what you are currently teaching as a surprisingly rich source of leadership skill that is transferable to all areas of vocational and life pursuit. I shall also challenge you to enrich your emerging contribution to leadership study by drawing upon your distinction-precollege education offered within a global context, a global commitment. And finally, I ask you as educators to seize leadership for yourselves and your profession because you now need it. There is a sense of urgency today for concerned educators to produce their own leadership that will provide a powerful challenge to leadership readily taken by others—even within education—who are following a course to reduce you to being mere mechanics and your students to mere widgets.

Let us begin this urgent journey together. I intend as always to be provocative and educationally sacrilegious throughout, for we must jolt out of place prevailing paradigms of educational theory and practice or at least examine them so thoroughly that they are applied with a sense of limitation—and this includes "No Child Left Behind."

There is much at stake here for us as educators. I look forward to your reaction—good, bad or ugly.

The proposition that the study of foreign language/ESL and culture advances leadership skills in a variety of professional settings—military, business, diplomatic, academia, service, for example—appears perhaps to be counterintuitive and confounding, if not disingenuous. Educators today appear to view leadership originating outside the traditional subject area—the liberal arts—and place its source exclusively in business and management. However, I contend that such a claim is valid, and I assert this on the basis of both research in the field of leadership and perhaps as importantly, on decades of personal in multiple adult leadership spheres—as a military officer, the entrepreneurial head of an academic center at a major research university (The Johns Hopkins University), the chair of a U.S. Department of State advisory committee to advance the education of youth throughout the world, the president of a division of a publicly-traded for-profit company and simultaneously, the vice president of yet another publicly-traded, high-tech company, and, currently, the president of a traditional, yet feisty national, "top-tier" liberal-arts college (Dickinson College in Carlisle, Pa.)—with a recognized leadership role in the globalization of American higher education. I assert this association of leadership and foreign language/culture study on the basis of my own long-term study of the German language and culture.

I shall begin with what I consider general leadership skills and then demonstrate how these skills emerge out of the study of language and culture. Most importantly, leadership involves both the telling of a story and the ability to persuade others to engage that story as fully as if it were their own. Leadership at its most sublime is narrative. Like a finely-crafted novel or poem, the story should appear effortless in execution and conceal the exhaustive energy and toil that are expended in maintaining and advancing it. Leadership is exhausting, but it must not appear so.

The concept of leadership as narrative or storytelling is not without precedent. The Harvard educational theorist, Howard Gardner, in his provocative1995 book with the collaboration of Emma Laskin, *Leading Minds: Anatomy Of Leadership*, states unequivocally that "leaders achieve their effectiveness chiefly through the stories they relate." Leadership is thus a matter both of composition and communication. However, for Gardner, it is not enough to draft a story and relate it to others. You must also as a leader embody it; you must live the story yourself—through your own actions—with such integrity, intensity and lucidity that your story becomes the others' story, your vision becomes their vision, your plan of action, their plan of action. In addition, Gardner identifies those stories that are the most effective in persuading followers and to bring about major alterations across a significant population. They are stories that concern issues of "personal and group identity" and "must in some way help their audience members think through who they are." Ultimately, those who follow absorb and use the words and phrases of the leader and his or her story often believing they are their own.

According to Howard Gardner in his most recent book, *Changing Minds*, a leader spends most of his or her time attempting to change minds—that of others and her own, if necessary. But a leadership story is not just a message, a slogan, an image or a vision—especially if it is to change your mind and that of others. It contains the three elements of any good narrative: a protagonist, goals and obstacles to be overcome. Gardner offers the example of Margaret Thatcher as a person forwarding an outstanding leadership story. The protagonist was the British nation, if not British society. The goals were the restoration of stature and the proper international role for the U.K. The obstacles were the misguided consensual governmental policies of recent years, the willingness of the British government to cede leadership to other countries, the power of the unions, the fractiousness of the Commonwealth nations and the absence of a directed national will. For Gardner, in order for a leader to change minds, he must know how to create a story, how to communicate that story effectively and how to alter it if changes are warranted. She must possess interpersonal intelligence; that is, she must have the ability to understand readily other people, be able to motivate them, listen to them carefully and respond to their needs and aspirations. And lastly, a leader requires a considerable measure of existential intelligence. A leader thus must be comfortable with posing and dealing with fundamental questions of human life and resolutely confront "big," existential ideas as part of daily functioning.

I have found in the course of my professional life other elements that contribute significantly to leadership and that are derived, I believe, from my study of language and culture. Some are quite obvious; others are more complex.

For example, I have found throughout my career that it is important for leaders to be able to identify quickly the core challenge in any circumstance and to visualize immediately a way to meet the challenge. There is the need to balance the ability to compose a story that communicates your vision for leadership with a solid knowledge of the more mundane facts of the domain in which you exercise leadership. A leader must temper vision with the practical. A leader is reminded again and again that while a primary focus is upon the strategic, to be totally successful, you must make sure that the details are attended to—often personally. Failure to account for the details, to follow up, often leads to an incomplete, if not unsuccessful, mission.

Before one actually leads, a leader must grasp the "big picture" and deal with big ideas—not just little ones. Big ideas are those that evoke the soul and spirit of people and have a substantive context in the history of ideas as an historic notion. They deal with questions of life, death, aim (purpose) and sensibility. What I am asking is precisely what our Monday keynote speaker, Mike Chinoy, CNN's senior Asia correspondent, demanded of the media—that it/we move beyond an understanding of news/education as mere event to understanding news/education as a process over time with deep, complex, interrelating roots. That said, I am not naïve about those big ideas that are captured in the context of radical idealism and presented in all innocence and good intention. They can be powerfully destructive. I think of a passage from Graham Green's *Quiet American* that took place not far from this very spot. Foster, the seasoned British reporter, says of the young, ambitious American Pyle (working with the nascent CIA involvement in Vietnam) upon first seeing him on the then rue Catinat—today Dong Khoi:

> Why does one want to tease the innocent? Perhaps only 10 days ago he had been walking back across the Common in Boston, his arms full of the books he had been reading in advance on the Far East and

the problems of China. He didn't even hear what I said; he was absorbed already in the dilemmas of Democracy and the responsibilities of the West; he was determined—I learnt that very soon—to do good, not to any individual person but to a country, a continent, a world. Well, he was in his element now with the whole universe to improve.

We know now, decades later, the destructive effect of that idealism, that big idea, on the peoples of both the United States and Vietnam. Additionally, a leader understands what leadership is all about in the domain in which skill is to be exercised and anticipates the likely outcomes of such leadership. There should be no surprises when leadership is exercised. A leader is prepared for the chance moment when leadership is required and is willing to cross all borders in thought and deed to achieve a creative solution to a demanding situation.

A leader envisions the future. A leader, however, must never underestimate nor prematurely dismiss potential sources of insight or inspiration, however unlikely they may seem. For example, there is ample evidence that a number of the world's scientific leaders made their discoveries while experimenting in a totally different context than the one projected for results. They were receptive to change and absorbed readily in the unanticipated context of a source of new knowledge. One only has to think of Roentgen's accidental discovery of the X-ray. Additionally, I personally have profited from never underestimating or dismissing aspects of my own life. A leader must be both constantly active—in motion and engaging the world—exposing herself to a variety of experiences that give a new edge to leadership and yet, simultaneously, be reflective, thoughtful about the implications of experiences gathered and how they are to be applied to move people and organizations forward. A leader must apply "peripheral vision" to a domain of action and thus create a knowledge base that is deeper and more expansive than that of others. A leader "connects the dots" in this frame of reference and thus, leads with distinction. This process of building a large framework of knowledge for leadership is similar to a theory of giftedness proposed by the South African scholar, Ochse.

She states that a gifted person possesses a framework of knowledge deeper and broader than most other people and is constantly scanning that base, seeking the unexpected, the inconsistent, that which others have not yet discovered. It is a combination of the span of the knowledge base, the constant motion through it, and the ability to pick out the remarkable and yet unseen that makes a person gifted.

A leader must have the interpersonal and emotional intelligences to appreciate which approach or voice—which grammar and syntax—are most likely to influence one person rather than another and to know always to whom one is speaking so that person can be reached with the leadership story. The effective leader, no matter how acclaimed on the basis of past successes, never becomes passive in the face of leadership demand, never confuses the authority of reputation—which is short lived—with the authority of voice, which is daily reinvented.

And finally, belonging to any attempt to provide leadership to a group of people are two closely associated elements—urgency and change. A good leader creates and/or maintains a sense of urgency for change. Leadership literature abounds with commentary on the indisputable existence of change as the principal environment in which leaders act. For example, Charles J. Schwahn and William G Spady in *Total Leaders: Applying The Best Future-Focused Change Strategies To Education* state, "The common theme running throughout futurist and leadership literature that has most influenced our work is the inevitability of change everywhere. You can't deny or hide from change. It's constant, accelerating, and here to stay." If change is not confronted, is not advanced through leadership in an organization or society, negative consequences abound. Here lies the urgency: Change or be damaged—perhaps even cease to exist. Again, Schwahn and Spady on the subject: "In this new era of rapid rather than gradual change, organisms and organizations face a certain reality-either adapt, change, and survive, or die." This imperative provides the leader with a sense of urgency to his or her story that can permit people to confront the necessity to deal with change rather than to ignore it. John Kotter of the Harvard Business School is most eloquent on this topic in his book *Leading Change*:

Ask almost anyone over thirty about the difficulty of creating major change in an organization and the answer will probably include the equivalent of 'very, very tough.' Yet most of us still don't get it. We use the right words, but down deep we underestimate the enormity of the task, especially the first step: establishing a sense of urgency ... Establishing a sense of urgency is crucial to gaining needed cooperation. With complacency high, transformations usually go nowhere because few people are even interested in working on the change problem. With urgency low, it's difficult to put together a group with enough power and credibility to guide the effort to convince key individuals to spend the time necessary to create and communicate a change vision.

To summarize then, the general traits required by a leader as I perceive them are:

* Compose a leadership story.

* Communicate persuasively a story to others.

* Create a sense of transparency to leadership that masks the difficulty of the leader's effort to compose the story and execute it.

* Embody a story as leader.

* Identify quickly the core of a challenge requiring leadership.

* Combine effortlessly vision of the "big picture" with a concern for the practical details of context and follow-through.

* Anticipate leadership opportunities.

* Cross borders.

* Remain open to diverse experiences and people that give an edge to leadership.

- Appreciate all sources of knowledge and experience as sources of insight to leadership.

- Appreciate emotional and interpersonal intelligences.

- Accept change as a normal condition.

- Create and sustain a sense of urgency.

- Engage the world and connect experiences rapidly; connect the dots among a wide range of elements; connect where others see no connections.

- And listen well.

Having offered these several components to leadership, let's now relate them more directly to their origins in my foreign language and culture study—and add a few more skills.

Learning well a language other than one's first, and learning it well, is truly a matter of intense, unrelenting composition of the most intimate order. As one acquires a new vocabulary, syntax, grammar and idiom, one rewrites a self-narrative that takes an existing personal story written through one's initial tongue and redrafts it into a new story, albeit with familiar components anchored by who one is fundamentally, and challenged by the expressive, emotive limitations and possibilities of the new language. Language learning then is at its core a basic act of self-story, self-composition. However, it is more. It is also about storytelling and communication to others. With one's additional language one must be able to express to others not only what one desires, but also convey a truthful representation of who one is as a person—definition and character—apart from the new verbal construct. One strive as a learner to inhabit the "second" language so fully that one's fundamental self-definition is transparent regardless of the new vehicle of expression. Thus a person who studies and acquires another language has intense exposure to at least two primary components of leadership—composing a story and communicating that story persuasively to others. And that first story is of the most intimate nature; it is the self-story.

Language learning also involves a constant crossing of borders—linguistic, cultural, aesthetic and geographical—particularly as one literally travels constantly to the countries in which a new language is used. And when first traveling to that new country, one does what all novice language learners do and what even exiles do who return to their home after years at a remove: One attempts to interpret what one now sees and hears in the framework of what one's first language and culture—or in the case of exiles, one's adopted language and culture—have imposed upon one. Unter den Linden in Berlin, for example, is first made accessible through association with Park Avenue, New York; the new cuisine is scanned for aspects that resemble what you eat at home. Andre Aciman describes this inclination well in his book *False Papers: Essays In Exile And Memory*, which examines his return to Alexandria after years in New York City: You do "what all exiles do on impulse, which is to look for their homeland abroad, to bridge the things here to the things there, to rewrite the present so as not to write off the past." However, this act of crossing borders and reinterpreting numerous elements on the other side within the context of who one is or has become, is an act that permits a leader to keep a focus on a well-defined, centered self while extending to engage others of differing persuasions and dispositions. This gesture—practiced early in new language acquisition—is the same movement that builds the character of a leader and permits him or her to welcome and deal with change on the basis of a solid self-definition, and thus lead compellingly.

Language learning also offers a future leader insight into and practice with a field of endeavor that balances simultaneously the big picture (the maturely functioning language and its use in sophisticated conversation and written word) with detail. The detail, of course, is grammar and syntax. Any language learner knows that if attention is not paid to grammatical and syntactical detail, communication is incomplete and meaning is distorted. With regard to this balance, one fuses together two personality traits—those who live in the bone and those who live in the connective tissue. This balance is a most healthy one for leadership, for a leader needs both perspectives to function well. Those who live in the bone require order, routine, the efficient use of time, and structure and predictability from life. Their measure of everything good is that which already exists. Old habits are the only habits. The people bred in the connective tissue, in contrast, thrive on anticipation and ambiguity. They enjoy prolonged reflection without necessary resolution and tend to weave for themselves and others a delicate thread of ideas from a variety of conflicting, often previously unassociated sources.

Language learning further advances leadership skill in that to be a successful learner, one often has to engage in activities that, through daily application of one's native language, one would never approach. However, in the spirit of gaining comprehensive exposure to a second or third language, for example, one indulges in all sorts of different activities—one eats "strange" foods, dines at "odd" hours. For example, to advance my learning of German, I have watched more soccer, sat still in more pubs for longer periods of time, viewed more television (for the pure language exposure), participated in and watched more parades and town festivals and sampled more varieties of sausage than is perhaps healthy for me. This exploration into new territory (what more "serious" people may consider trivial), however, nourishes that leadership trait of openness to engaging all aspects of life, from which emerge the distinctive elements of a persuasive leadership narrative suited to a diverse and rapidly changing world. The key, again, to successful leadership is to be out in the world constantly and to appreciate and make things happen where others are too wary and cautious to go. I think of the renowned literary critic of the 20th century, Hugh Kenner. He related to me once how he engaged the world and thus created a world for himself—indeed, a vocation—when others might have been to reluctant to take the steps he did. As a young, yet impoverished graduate student, he desired to meet a world famous author. He bought a cheap ticket to Paris and found a really inexpensive hotel room. Night after night, he sent a note to the author requesting a meeting. After ten days and no response and with his monies running out, he was about to return to America when there was a knock at his door. The porter brought a note. It said simply, "Dear Mr. Kenner: I am sorry not to have responded sooner. I was away and just returned. By all means come over right now. Simply bring some bread or wine—Samuel Becket." An initial meeting with

Becket in Paris lead to an incredible and life-defining dinner for Kenner the next weekend in London with Beckett, Ezra Pound and T.S. Eliot. Professor Kenner's career was launched in a most distinctive and compelling way. But again, Kenner displayed leadership traits of significance. He took himself out into the world, he persisted and he displayed ambition and confidence that he would be successful in his pursuit—that it was indeed possible to meet Beckett. Persistence, ambition and confidence are increasingly viewed as significant leadership traits. They are related, however, to a distinctively American disposition towards leadership, I posit. For Americans, leadership is almost exclusively an outward, often aggressive entity and is fixated on the achievement of tangible results in limited periods of time. In the process, high intelligence and wisdom are often denigrated. For example, psychologist Rosabeth Moss Kanter, in a recent *New York Times* article, "If at First You Don't Succeed, Believe Harder," states, "Confidence isn't optimism or pessimism, and it's not a character attribute ... It's the expectation of a positive outcome." The *Times* then comments, "As Ms. Kanter sees it, talent, intelligence and knowledge are nice, but confidence is essential" And in a review of Joseph Ellis's new biography, *His Excellency*, of George Washington, the quintessential American leader, it is concluded that "What remains surprising about the narrative of Washington's life is the extremely ordinary nature of his virtues. He was not a military genius ... he possessed neither the wisdom of Benjamin Franklin [nor] the intellectual sophistication of Thomas Jefferson ... What Washington did possess in spades was ambition, stamina and the dogged ability to learn from his mistakes." To be sure, there are distinctive traces of anti-intellectualism in what Americans seem to admire in leadership. Prolonged reflection and changing of mind are not highly rated.

Further, comprehensive language acquisition affords practice in getting quickly and efficiently to the core of a subject or issue, a skill that, I believe, is necessary for effective leadership. For example, when I taught German language for some 15 years at The Johns Hopkins University, I passed on to my students a pedagogical construct that I introduced them to in the first few minutes of instruction. Initially, as a high-school student, I was frustrated by the fact that grammar books never started with an overview of how the language worked comprehensively—how the language "danced." I never received the "whole picture" of the language's basic functioning until the end of four years of high-school study (my fifth year in high school concentrated upon literature). In college I developed a spatial insight and design that permitted me to penetrate to the core grammar of German—that basic "dance"—that got me immediately to the heart of the language's structure and which in the years to come, would merely be slightly adjusted according to differing grammatical and syntactical demands (to include exceptions) and a maturing vocabulary.

In my classes as a teacher, I would begin the first few minutes of instruction by telling my students that I was going to teach them in the next two minutes everything they needed to know about the fundamental structure of German, would then proceed to place the design before them and state that basically they would merely manipulate this construct for the rest of their lives as they acquired more vocabulary, artistic sophistication and grammatical and syntactical exceptions. My students usually appreciated this immediate gesture to the core of the language and could proceed by possessing this overview with confidence from that point forward. Penetrating quickly to the core or challenge—knowing where you are going at the start of any journey, be it linguistic or professional—is, I believe, an essential capacity of a good leader.

Foreign-language/ESL learning also gives one practice in anticipating events, in rehearsing events before they even occur—"visualizing the goal," an essential skill of leadership. Often as a beginning German-language learner, I would have to anticipate both what I was going to say in German to the person with whom I was to speak and, at the same time, I would have to anticipate what they were perhaps going to say then to me. Here, I also had to listen well. Without this dual anticipatory state, I would be both incapable of completing a full sentence in German, much less a complex thought, nor would I be able to comprehend what was said to me in return due to the rapidity with which the language was spoken by a native speaker. Of course, as I gained fluency in German, this practice was no longer necessary.

The primary trait of a leader able to establish readily a sense of urgency is advanced by language and culture study. Foreign-language/ESL learning is by definition an urgent proposition. There is a need as quickly as possible to master the language so that one can communicate one's mature thoughts, dreams and emotions. Failure to do this leaves one severely incomplete in the breech between a high degree of first-language capacity for expressing oneself and a lesser degree of second-language capacity. Secondly, even when one has mastered another language, there is always an urgency to return frequently to the country in which it is regularly spoken so that one maintains a high level of fluency and ensures that the language one uses is inclusive of all contemporary changes in grammar, syntax and semantics that occur naturally in the context of alive, active use.

Successful foreign-language/ESL learning and associated culture studies are fundamentally and unequivocally about inculcating a receptivity to change. A language itself embodies change as a living entity. Acquiring a new language and assimilating the essential habits of mind and action of another people require an ability to become something other while simultaneously anticipating that such exposure will change irrevocably how one inhabits and uses one's primary language and culture. Foreign-language/ESL and culture study also offers to the learner another level of familiarity with change when that language is a vital, "alive" one. Words, phrases, syntax, cultural narratives and norms are constantly changing through natural exposure to, as the literary critic Hugh Kenner calls it, "Elsewhere Communities." As an example of these communities, the German language and culture are daily evolving through the incorporation of English/American words and the pervasiveness of habits of mind and action from rapidly-growing populations settling in Germany to live and work.

In order for a leader to advance powerfully a story that can be communicated well and compellingly to others, she needs to tolerate personally the constant repetition in the telling of the story and those key words and phrases that are defining it. To infuse a leadership story into a community, it is not sufficient to tell it once or even twice. The story simply will not take. Leadership stories must enthusiastically be repeated time and time again over a sustained period of time and without any evidence whatsoever that the leader is bored or tired of the message (the effort must be invisible). The leader must keep repeating the story until he or she hears key words, key phrases coming back from others without extensive or, in fact, any reference to particular authorship. The story must take naturally and exist permanently independent of the leader. Many people cannot tolerate engaging in constant repetition of stories, words and phrases—much less repetition with an always fresh, enthusiastic delivery. However, an accomplished foreign-language/ESL learner knows that repetition—frequent, often painfully tedious repetition of words, grammatical rules and drills—is inherent in the successful acquisition process. A tolerance is developed that can be unobtrusively applied to leadership.

True leadership is tolerant of risk and the accompanying possibility of failure. There is a recognition that as long as one is well-informed and conscientious, to try and fail and try again is not a sign of incompetence but of the progressive, positive spirit that informs good leadership. Leaders persist when others lose concentration and drift. Successful foreign/ESL language study is defined fundamentally by a need to deal comfortably with repeated failure as one steps tentatively into a new area of expression. One does not progress unless one begins to communicate with others who already possess the new language and one is open to the internal and external critique that comes from the first incomplete, frustrating steps of trying to express a conceptual complexity residing in one's head with a few words and the grammatical principles of another language.

Foreign-language/ESL and culture study is ultimately a community pursuit. One develops competencies—linguistic and cultural—according to the degree of and communication with others in the target language population. Exchange and teamwork are inherent in acquiring a new language and culture. And the ability to work in teams is essential to leadership. Indeed, John P. Kotter, again in *Leading Change*, speaks of the need for a "guiding coalition" of key people including the leader or CEO in an organization, as an absolutely "essential part of the early stages of any effort to restructure, reengineer or retool a set of strategies" and, in the current, fast-moving leadership context, "only teams … can be highly effective."

And finally, foreign-language/ESL study permits one to experience a disposition that must be in place for successful leadership. This disposition is best captured by the Nike marketing phrase, "Just do it." A leader is distinguished most often from the follower by stepping up to a challenge and by using all previous experience, knowledge and sensitivities as a guide to move decisively and with unflappable determination against a challenge. The leader can make that tough decision to do something in a timely fashion and, once the decision is made, stick with it despite inevitable criticism and distraction. The acquisition of another language contains explicit practice in developing this disposition. One very tentatively and with great insecurity practices a language—learns vocabulary, studies grammar, repeats drills—and then, based on a hunch that one is ready, one boldly begins to speak, to use the language to communicate, despite the sometime criticism from more fluent speakers. One just decides to "just do it."

In the above commentary, I have tried to isolate those elements of leadership that I have practiced in a variety of settings and that, I believe, have been advanced by my in-depth study over multiple years of German language and culture. I should now briefly like to illustrate how a few of these leadership capacities are applied to my current role as president of Dickinson College. It is beyond the scope of this speech to illustrate concretely the application of all the traits I have cited, but by concentrating on a few interrelated ones, I hope to advance the credibility of my overall thesis that foreign-language/ ESL and culture study advances leadership traits. A more comprehensive treatment of the Dickinson College story (and its success) is contained as a separate chapter, "Benjamin Rush's Brat," in David Kirp's new book, *Shakespeare, Einstein And The Bottom Line.*

One of the first activities when I came to Dickinson College as president in the summer of 1999, was to take a day hike with a group of first-year students during Orientation week. Walking along with me was a senior student who had just returned from a Dickinson study-abroad program in Bologna, Italy. She and I had a good deal of time to converse over the half-day hike, and our dialogue ranged across a host of topics including my perception of Dickinson when I was a student from 1967 to 1971. That evening, I received an e-mail from this student that in retrospect has become a defining moment of my administration. The message started with a few pleasantries, but rapidly moved into a more pressing communication. The student said that she was about to begin her fourth year as a Dickinson student, that she believed she was a successful member of the community, having assumed a variety of leadership positions, and was recognized publicly for her contribution by induction into a prestigious senior women's honorary society, Wheel and Chain. Yet, she had a question of me—despite all her engagement, all her recognition, she was hard-pressed to define to herself and to others what it was to be a Dickinsonian. I was immediately alarmed. If this student who clearly was engaged with the institution was clueless as to the college's identity and comprehensive contribution, what must it be for others? It was then and there that I decided that I had to work with others to give the college a clearly-drawn leadership story, a narrative that would establish unequivocally for its current students—and in turn the alumni and general public—a sense of identity and, through that, a pride. What I needed was a compelling story out of which I could lead the institution to a clear sense of what it was and on that firm basis help it get to where it was going—that is, to take a top-tier national, residential, liberal-arts college (although at the time just barely top-tier) and assist it to achieve its next level of engagement and accomplishment in higher education. This had to be a story so intense that it could stir to action a wide variety of constituents of various ages and relationship to the college as well as attract people to the institution who had no previous allegiance.

A quick survey of my colleagues who had been at the college far longer than I revealed that in its 226-year history, it had never had a comprehensive leadership story—a strategic plan with accompanying vision, mission statement and targeted, concrete objectives to be accomplished within definitive time periods and with assigned staff responsible for execution, and all of this linked with financial realities. Even the founder, Dr. Benjamin Rush—revolutionary, scientist, humanist, and signer of the Declaration of Independence—left unfinished his original plan for the college. Here was an opportunity and a need, and the decision to proceed was made immediately. The college needed this leadership story, and it needed it now. The traditionally recommended timeline and methodology for such an endeavor could not be followed. We didn't have time. The lack of clear identity had in part contributed to some financial challenges that needed attention immediately. A true sense of urgency and intensity had to be created to engage a community in completing this story at a pace and in a manner that challenged orthodoxy.

Working with a small group of key faculty, administrators and students—Kotter's "guiding coalition"—and using the capacity of technology and on-site meetings for extensive, comprehensive and rapid dissemination and exchange among trustees, alumni, parents and additional faculty, staff and students, the Dickinson community accomplished a strategic plan and a Dickinson leadership story in the spring semester of 2000 and has since been using it daily as a guide to our identity as Dickinsonians, common voice, decision making (to include most importantly when not to do something) and future directions.

The story introduces a distinctive language into the community that while appearing to some as new, actually recaptures the original words and intentions—even personality—of our founder and his good friend, John Dickinson, after whom the college is named and who served as the first benefactor of the college and chair of the Board of Trustees. This language and personality are "revolutionary" and require of us a culture and state of mind that balance reflection and decisive action. A sampling of the story follows:

The American Revolution brought into being the world's first modern democracy and launched an ambitious social and political experiment. Our founders, Dr. Benjamin Rush and John Dickinson, were themselves leading figures of the revolution and the new republic. They recognized that the success of the American experiment would depend on the power of liberal education to remake colonial society and to produce a democratic culture.

Dickinson College, therefore, began life as the first college formed under the internationally recognized [chartered five days following the signing of the Treaty of Paris] young republic and, more importantly, as a revolutionary project—dedicated to safeguarding liberty through the creation of an educated body of citizen-leaders. Although the urgency of the American revolutionary period had diminished, the core mission of Dickinson College remains the same and as vital as ever.

Benjamin Rush was a progressive and complex thinker with distinct views about higher education in America and at Dickinson. His guiding principle was to provide a useful education. This emphasis on useful disciplines and practical, interdisciplinary connections was in deliberate contrast to higher education in the Old World, which, he believed, had become rigid, disconnected from the world and overly aristocratic.

Rush valued the wisdom of the past, but he was also an expansive thinker who reached across national, cultural and disciplinary borders. He believed that liberal education should concern itself with those academic subjects that interconnect and reach across to other subjects in a useful manner to create new knowledge. Modern languages should be taught, therefore, because they provide access to far-ranging knowledge in all disciplines. Rush also believed in crossing beyond the borders of the United States and in study abroad—but with a disciplined agenda to return knowledge to advance the republic.

A further aspect of Rush's founding vision for Dickinson is the spirit of institutional innovation and decisiveness. As a revolutionary, Rush defied organizational stasis and recognized that new external circumstances require appropriate internal changes. He wished to engage the world. He pushed to create a college at the edge of the western wilderness, rallying others with the power and persuasiveness of his vision. Throughout its history, the college has continued to display this penchant for enterprise and a willingness to seize opportunities as they arise. Today, the college needs to remain true to its heritage by being receptive to salutary change and by being committed to negotiated change through civil and informed debate.

Thus, according to its leadership story, Dickinson College is an independent, residential, liberal-arts college with *attitude*. "Spunk" defines its institutional personality and is a personal disposition of those associated with it.

The themes and key words that define the leadership story and that are repeated and repeated in all administrative letters, speeches and articles throughout the community are unequivocal: revolutionary; citizen-leaders; a useful, liberal education; a sense of urgency; a clear, compelling voice for change and against stasis; crossing borders; interdisciplinary; connectivity among academic disciplines and the creation of new knowledge; field study (Dickinson was the first college or university in the history of American higher education to take instruction out of the classroom and into the field); engaging the world; innovation and decisiveness; attitude and spunk; and civil and informed debate about things that matter.

This language of change for Dickinson also is accompanied in the story with a clear sense of urgency. The strategic plan contains a candid "environmental analysis" of the college's internal and external challenges and opportunities. Initially there is a provocative question here to the community asking members to consider their disposition toward leadership in general: "For Dickinson to achieve its vision, it must benefit from leadership and it must desire to be led." Again, a fundamental question to any community—does it really want to be led? Internal urgency is further created by a recognition that if the college does not make more timely, sometimes difficult decisions through its administrative and faculty governance systems, considerable momentum and opportunity will be irrevocably forfeited, and those with a talent for leadership will disengage from the institution. This internal evocation of lost opportunity is compounded in urgency by a description of external factors that additionally might limit maximization of opportunity: the declining population of the independent, residential, liberal-arts colleges; the high cost of financial aid; the emerging competition from for-profit education industry; the strong forces to devalue the degree in favor of the certificate; the challenge of distance learning; the escalating costs of health and liability insurance; the rapidly-increasing litigious nature of society and related high costs for legal services; the high costs of technology and scientific equipment; the seeming attractiveness of baby-boomer parents to public education at a lesser price tag for their children (although many of them enjoyed the fruits of a private education); and the increasingly consumer-oriented parents and students who expect business service for all their educational needs. Again, the realities of internal and external pressures upon the college are introduced to advance necessary, inevitable change through a clear sense of urgency and are intended ultimately to position community members to desire to do something, rather than nothing.

This vocabulary, this seemingly new language for Dickinson, now permeates all aspects of our institution and has consequence for its working culture. We must act as we define ourselves. We are absorbing our new leadership story as a new language and culture, and it is the basis upon which the college will articulate its move to its next level of engagement and accomplishment in higher education.

Again, every speech, every article, every press release contains aspects of this vocabulary and this institutionalized story. We make all our institutional decisions with reference to it. However, having been in a foreign-language class year after year—and here I compare a class to an institution—I can appreciate that not all people acquire a new language to the same degree of proficiency or at the same rate and others just don't take to the new language and culture and migrate elsewhere, to another institution that fits their talents and disposition. And I also know because of my foreign language and culture study that possessing a story and repeating it endlessly is not enough for others to embrace it fully. I must, as leader, live it; I and others in leadership positions must embody the Dickinson story and not only mouth the words but realize them through deed. In the terminology of leadership research, I have to be the "lead learner" and model the core organizational values. I have to create a vivid example of what the story looks like when it is transformed into real-life action. I have to animate the words and images. I could not naturally and effortlessly accomplish this movement from word to deed, I could not convince a soul of the validity of the enterprise, I could not establish credence for the story and thus the institution, could not proceed to higher levels of accomplishment, unless this was done. To this end, I and my colleagues engage issues that we believe matter through frequent public speeches, articles and letters/op-eds to such publications as *The New York Times* and *The Wall Street Journal*. When I or my colleagues encounter an issue that violates our story, we do not hesitate, but engage through word and deed. Indeed, the very act of engaging—rather than remaining silent—fulfills our story. Our visible commitment through deed in the last two years has ranged from freeing a colleague, Yongyi Song, from prison in China, where he was being held inappropriately on spy charges and speaking out worldwide against violations of academic freedom and human-rights and affirmative-action violations, to a highly successful counter-celebration with the citizens of Carlisle, Pa., and surrounding communities to protest a KKK rally and any form of hate advancement. Writings have ranged from a *New York Times* letter to the editor protesting against a nationally recognized television news anchor for glorifying academic nonachievement for college students to numerous editorials, articles and speeches criticizing the exclusive use of the SAT in college admissions (with an accompanying change in Dickinson's admission policy to reflect this stance).

Why did I state earlier that now more than at any time in the past, you as administrators (and your teachers) must embrace leadership itself and develop for your school and for your classrooms a strong leadership story and advance it to the public with resolve and tenacity? I say this because your control of what you personally administer and teach is about to be taken away from you—in whole or part. The threat is *accountability*, and it comes at you in all innocence. It offers many good measures—principally seeming security and definiteness about good performance versus poor in educational instruction—but exaggerated and turned into an absolute, it possesses the capacity for much harm in education more generously understood.

The paradigm of innocence as destructive is not without precedent, of course. I refer once again to Graham Greene and *The Quiet American*. When describing meeting Pyle for the first time as he, Pyle, ambled toward the bar of the Continental Hotel in Saigon—the now extinct outside terrace—ironically states, Pyle possesses "an unmistakably young and unused face flung at us like a dart. With his gangly legs and his crew-cut and his wide campus gaze he seemed incapable of harm." Of course, for Vietnam and for a generation of Americans—my generation—Pyle was anything but harmless and innocent. Again, the contemporary equivalent of Pyle for you—a potentially and seemingly beneficial concept gone destructive—is accountability (accountability as interpreted in the No Child Left Behind) legislation.

Permit me to explain this audacious claim—one that will certainly be immediately underappreciated by many in education today as they blithely and unreflectively embrace the latest concept in circulation and favor action at all costs above sustained reflection. I begin by quoting from the Talk of the Town, "Making the Grade" in the Sept. 15, 2003, edition of *The New Yorker*:

> The most striking thing about the sweeping federal
> educational reforms debuting this fall is how much

they resemble, in language and philosophy, the industrial-efficiency movement of the early 20th century. In those years, engineers argued that efficiency and productivity were things that could be measured and managed, and, if you had the right inventory and manufacturing controls in place, no widget would be left behind. Now we have No Child Left Behind, in which Congress has set up a complex apparatus of sanctions and standards designed to compel individual schools toward steady annual improvement, with the goal of making 100 percent of American schoolchildren proficient in math and reading by 2014. It is hard to look at the new legislation and not share in its Fordist vision of the classroom as a brightly lit assembly line, in which curriculum standards sail down from Washington through a chute, and freshly scrubbed, defect-free students come bouncing out the other end. It is an extraordinary vision, particularly at a time when lawmakers seem mostly preoccupied with pointing out all the things that government cannot do. The only problem, of course—and it's not a trivial one—is that children aren't widgets.

And, I might add, learning is not merely a matter of what can be empirically assessed by standardized tests. You see, that is precisely the problem. No Child Left Behind is actually the direct product of a dogmatic Anglo-American sensibility about knowledge—a markedly incomplete vision—and that is that knowledge is only as worthy as it can be measured empirically and then put to some use. Its history emerges most immediately from British empiricism (look to Cambridge University in the early 20th century and its departments of philosophy and mathematics) and the American Metaphysical Club consisting of Charles Pierce, John Dewey, Oliver Wendell Holmes and William James. Yet it was already present in the Scottish Enlightenment and in Benjamin Franklin's singular definition of American character—one that prefers practicality to romanticism and holds that the truth of any proposition, whether it be scientific or a moral or a theological or a social one, is based on how well it correlates with experimental results and produces a practical outcome.

In education—especially that which treats precollegiate education—this turn to pragmatism took place in the early 20th century. We often forget, for example, that it was John Dewey and fellow progressives who framed the intellectual construct for what became the SATs. This empirical turn was motivated in part by insecurity and a feeling of lack of respect by the public toward educators in the early 20th century because education was not scientifically based. In a world that was increasingly valuing science as the measure of all things, education remained undercharged and undervalued. Well, educators remedied that immediately and satisfied their "science envy." Standardized testing became suddenly an integral part of educational practice and was introduced in a comprehensive manner. And since knowledge to be assessed had to be subject to empirical assessment, efficiently and generally delivered, it increasingly became itself factual and technical—focused on short-term impact (note the similarity here with corporate America and its focus almost exclusively on short-term quarter results rather than multiyear production) and partial to little ideas, facts, rather than those big, complex ones involving questions of the meaning of life, aesthetics and moral and ethical judgment that are not readily embraced by standardized assessment. In fact, I would assert that at least since the 1980s, American precollegiate education has been dominated by—and you at conferences such as these have been subjected to—a series of ultimately little ideas, technical strategies, such as cooperative learning, phonics, whole language, classroom-management technique. Education has been short on those big ideas involving the aims of education. This trend is underscored by the now almost total absence of the philosophy of education as a full course of instruction in graduate schools of education. The results are evident. If you ask today's college and university students—as I have—what big ideas influence comprehensively the conduct of their lives, they can come up with none. If you ask them the name of a philosopher or a fictionalist or a poet who influences how they live their lives and define themselves and their actions towards others, they are clueless.

I urge you then today —beseech you—to reclaim for your schools and classrooms big ideas that extend beyond the empirically measurable and thus appear trivial and inefficient. I urge you to reclaim the art of teaching—for today we possess merely the science of teaching and that is inadequate to move forward a total child, much less a people. I urge you to redefine accountability, which is an otherwise worthy pursuit, so that it balances the practical and technical—that which can and should be empirically measured—with that which involves the advancement of spirit, soul, creativity and character of students and which is not so readily subject to general standardization and progressive empirical assessment—much less to short-term results. I urge you to live both "in the bone" (empirical testing) and "in the connective tissue" (the worthiness of intent). I urge you to reject the prevailing mentality of either/or in precollegiate education—that is, that it is either phonics or whole language, individualized instruction or integrated instruction, never a blending of the two based on the needs of the individual child. In fact, I would be so bold today as to urge you to replace accountability as currently understood (after all, facts can readily be manipulated and spun by the accountants, as we all learned painfully with the Enron and Worldcom scandals a few years ago), with another concept for assessment—*transparency*. Transparency is here understood as making available regularly to the public all sorts of data—empirical and subjective—and thus bestowing upon the public the trust to analyze and judge as they will of an education.

I urge you today to assert strongly your own leadership story as administrators for you respective schools and for your sector of education—international schools—and for your teachers to do the same for their classrooms. Already, alarming Orwellian versions of accountability are a reality in the for-profit realm of higher education and I guarantee, having worked in the for-profit education industry, that a version of these methods is eventually headed your way. I am, of course, referring to your total loss of control over what you offer to your students as an institution and what you teach in the classroom in the name of universal empirical accountability to the consumer. The University of Phoenix, the world's largest university, for example, now commissions a panel of third-party subject area specialists to establish a strict curricula for classroom instructors. No deviation from this course of study is permitted by the actual classroom instructors and the tests of this canned knowledge are universal across all campuses. The job then of teachers is merely to deliver and test in a standardized fashion a predetermined course of study. Administrators and teachers are now truly widgets as are the students. All of this is conducted in the name of empirical verification of learning.

As administrators and teachers in international schools, you are in a distinctive position to get accountability (or better, transparency) right—to lead for the sake of others. Firstly, you are essentially free of the accountability as now defined in the United States (pending pressure exerted upon you by the regional accrediting agencies that have taken up accountability in a big way). You are independent institutions and can live up to the full import of that word. Secondly, you possess a really big idea that can be a protagonist in your collective leadership story—global sensibility—an idea that other sectors of education greatly need to (and want to) embrace for future generations. Accompanying global sensibility is an acute appreciation of change since change is an integral part of existing daily on a global basis. What, however, is global sensibility in education? It is the pursuit of all academic and co-curricular activities in a context that takes into account that which is occurring in other nations and among other cultures. It is a fundamental humility that exercises a check upon the imperialism and unilateralism of our own provincial ideas and is based upon the recognition that other nations and cultures possess notions we must gather from afar and integrate into our own pursuit for our own positive advancement.

It is respect for the myriad ways of acquiring knowledge that are gained through the mastering of more than one language—not merely English. It is a recognition that the English language has limitations and does not deliver all areas of knowledge we need for substantive, creative contribution. It is an obligation—through education and experience—to be comfortable and confident in an ever changing world, a diverse set of communities, regardless of place. This is a sensibility that requires a certain type of educational institution— your type of school—defined years ago for America by Ralph Waldo Emerson. Emerson wrote, These schools "have their indispensable office—to teach elements. But they can only highly serve us when they aim not to drill but to create; when they gather from afar every ray of various genius to their hospitable halls, and, by the concentrated fires, set the hearts of their youth on flame."

May you lead by the flame. Best wishes as you achieve your individual and collective leadership stories. Thank you for inviting me to EARCOS and Vietnam.

REMARKS AT THE TOCQUEVILLE AWARD DINNER
Oct. 6, 2005

I am deeply honored to be asked to address the United Way of York County at your annual Tocqueville Dinner. The mission of the Tocqueville Society is "to improve lives by mobilizing the caring power of communities"—a mission that has taken on new meaning in the wake of the recent tragedies on the Gulf Coast. The response of communities across our country reminds us of our compassion as a nation, just as it reminds us of the power of an engaged citizenry. At Dickinson, we immediately reached out to two institutions of higher education with whom we are in partnership through our Crossing Borders program—Xavier and Dillard Universities. Within one week of the hurricane, we were able to bring 14 Dillard students to Carlisle for the fall semester. These students have adjusted phenomenally well to their new situation and are adding a wonderful new dimension to campus life that is benefiting all of our students.

Alexis de Tocqueville, of course, was absolutely on target when he observed in the early 19th century that one of the abiding strengths of American democracy was a deep sense of community spirit. De Tocqueville was most struck by the conscious effort of Americans to come together as citizens for the express purpose of confronting contemporary problems and to advance collectively a more humane and functional society. He found a unique societal infrastructure that existed for the sole purpose of improving quality of life. De Tocqueville was writing approximately 50 years after Dickinson College was chartered in 1783. If we explore the intentions of Dickinson's founder, Dr. Benjamin Rush, we find—perhaps not surprisingly—the seeds of that deep sense of citizen responsibility and commitment that de Tocqueville found so remarkable.

This evening, I would like to take a few minutes to talk about Dr. Rush's views and to think about them in a 21st-century context. Dr. Rush was instrumental in founding several institutions of higher education in the late 18th century, institutions he thought should deliver a type of higher education that was distinctively American. Rush was an ardent revolutionary and a signer of the Declaration of Independence. A close friend and frequent correspondent with many of the founding fathers, such as Thomas Jefferson, John Adams and James Madison, Rush instinctively knew that the success of the young democracy would be dependent upon an active and engaged citizenry. And those citizens would need to receive an education very different from the one traditionally offered across the Atlantic.

Through his first-hand experience as a medical student in Scotland, Rush found English education to be little more than "monkish studies" and virtually "unchanged for 250 years." European education was intended only for the elite, and it was rooted in a study of the past, the esoteric and the unessential. Such an approach was wholly inappropriate for the citizens of the dynamic and entrepreneurial new nation. Instead, Rush advocated a liberal education (in the sense of opening minds through knowledge and experience) that was noted for its academic rigor and excellence, but was also very much a part of the contemporary world. He encouraged, for example, the study of contemporary languages, rather than Latin and Greek, recognizing that a command of French and German would be essential as America established an international presence. He insisted that sciences, particularly chemistry, be included in the curriculum, knowing that they would serve as the foundation for new knowledge, invention and discovery. Recognizing the multiplicity of voices and cultures that already existed within the emerging society, Rush also sought broad access to higher education by advocating for the participation of both women and African Americans just as he argued for the inclusion of the study of Native American languages and culture. Rush was even an early proponent of study abroad, believing that not only every student—but every American—should spend some time in a foreign country.

Active engagement with the community was a particularly important component of Rush's conception of a distinctly American education. For Rush, community service was a measure of one's patriotism and one's commitment to the democracy. In 1773, within a letter to the nation about a distinctively American patriotism, Rush wrote, "The social spirit is the true selfish spirit, and men always promote their own interest most in proportion as they promote that of their neighbors and their country." Rush, therefore, expected students to become actively involved with the community beyond the campus. For that reason, he purposely located Dickinson a mere two blocks from the county courthouse so that students could regularly observe government in action.

Rush also expected students to dedicate themselves to those in need, and he set a stellar example through his own actions. His early and open hostility to slavery, his commitment to the care of the mentally ill and his work as a physician among the poor and the disadvantaged—to the extent that he insisted on remaining in Philadelphia at the height of a deadly yellow-fever epidemic—all underline his commitment to community and to his fellow citizens.

Rush's distinctively American approach to higher education was, then, to be connected to the contemporary world and, above all, useful—useful in building and sustaining the government, the economy and the social institutions of the new nation. Unlike its European counterpart, this new distinctively American education was not intended solely to produce scholars. It was intended to produce citizen-leaders—some of whom would be scholars, and leading scholars at that.

At Dickinson, we consciously strive to fulfill the historic legacy bequeathed to us by Dr. Rush. His vision is woven throughout the strategic plan that guides our short- and long-term actions; his recently installed statue outside my window gives me daily inspiration; and, I am told that Dickinson students regularly count how many times I mention Benjamin Rush in each speech.

I am continually amazed at the timelessness of Dr. Rush's vision and, at the same time, dismayed that the general public and even many colleges and universities themselves have lost sight of the broader purpose of American higher education—to prepare young people for lives of engaged citizenship and leadership so that they might create a more just and compassionate world.

In today's highly competitive and market-driven world, this very fundamental purpose rarely receives attention or thoughtful discussion. Today's students—and their parents—all too frequently select schools on the basis of athletic prowess, the spaciousness of the dormitory room or the size and proximity of the fitness center. Prospective applicants pour over highly subjective national rankings that measure a variety of disparate financial inputs that ultimately reflect the market appeal of a given institution. To be sure, these measures have their place, but shouldn't we more importantly evaluate other institutional aspects more in line with our distinctively American mission for higher education? Shouldn't we be concerned with a college or university's efforts to develop an informed and engaged citizenry? Shouldn't we be asking whether our institutions deliver on their stated missions of producing graduates who are prepared to assume positions of leadership within our communities and our government? Like so many other aspects of our society, the evaluation of the effectiveness of higher education has been reduced to those things we traditionally count and quantify. And in the process, we have forgotten the need to articulate, preserve and value one of the most important purposes for which our colleges and universities were established.

Our institutions of higher learning provide our students with opportunities for developing leadership and citizenship abilities that are hard to find elsewhere in society. It is within our hallowed halls that our students are given endless free rein to learn to think, to challenge and to debate. For many students, college is the first time they will come across individuals whose backgrounds, cultures and ideas are vastly different from their own. It is within these campus communities that students find ways to resolve their differences, to respect—although not necessarily accept—the diverse views of others and to engage in civil, spirited debate. It is—or should be—within our walls that we actively encourage a devotion to free inquiry that is the heart of the democratic process. At times messy and unsettling, it is only through the promotion of the freest exchange of ideas that we will create informed, inquisitive and effective citizens. It is, in short, within our colleges and universities that students learn to accommodate a range of opinions, beliefs and cultures. It is here that they learn how to create and sustain a caring community.

Just today, I received a short note from a student that confirms dramatically young people's appreciation of diversity for academic advancement. "I thought I'd tell you," she wrote, "how I appreciate Dickinson. On Tuesday, I was in my African Diaspora class, and we were discussing double consciousness and nationalism. We have a student from Trinidad, a Native American and a girl from the Ivory Coast in class. Through them, it was absolutely amazing to hear how they associate with the United States and their homelands. How many other schools could you go to and be able to hear those points of view in person and discuss them? I thought it was so neat."

Unfortunately, our society in general gives short shrift to this most fundamental purpose of American higher education and, in so doing, overlooks some of the most positive things that are taking place on our nation's campuses today. As a result, we are presented with a bleak and rather depressing view of the current generation of college students. My summer reading list included several recent books that reinforce this perception.

Set on a fictional campus in Pennsylvania, Tom Wolfe's latest best-selling novel, *I Am Charlotte Simmons*, portrays college life as a "live-for-the-moment" drunken frenzy where students are irresponsible, short on serious study and totally oblivious to the world's challenges. The PBS special entitled, "Declining by Degrees," and the book by the same name came to essentially the same conclusion. "For the vast majority of 18 to 24 year olds," the author stated, "life at college or university may become little more than a four-year frolic through late adolescence with a little learning thrown in along the way." And Thomas L. Friedman in his provocatively titled book, *The World is Flat*, found American students lacking the intellectual requirements and drive necessary to compete with the ambitious young generation emerging in India and China.

Indeed, the prevalent picture by most commentators of the current generation is not pretty. They are thought to be invested with a feeling of extreme entitlement, expecting to live the good life without really having to work to secure it. They are portrayed as disdainful of colleges' rules of conduct, as well as those of society, and incapable of understanding the meaning of the word "no." Most troubling to me, is the perception that this generation lacks true global awareness and a sense of the broader developments shaping our world; they simply expect American prosperity to continue unabated.

I, for one, refuse to be convinced by these sweeping generalizations. Perhaps because I spend my days on a college campus and at an institution that expressly considers the development of citizen-leaders as part of its rigorous academic preparation, I am happily and constantly confronted with countless exceptions to these darker perceptions.

At Dickinson, for example, our students engage in 40,000 hours of community service each year—reaching into our community as tutors to underprivileged youngsters at Hope Station, donating their time and energy to the Project Share food bank, and constructing homes through the Habitat for Humanity program. I receive regular updates from our students who engage in the Alliance for Aquatic Resource Monitoring (ALLARM) initiative as they reach out to the surrounding area to teach communities about ways to improve and preserve water quality. And this year, we are entering the third year of a multiyear study in partnership with the University of Pennsylvania to explore ways to reduce hypertension in the Commonwealth's at-risk populations.

From all indications, our students' commitment to public service extends well beyond graduation. Our latest survey data demonstrated that 39 percent of recent graduates chose professions in the public or nonprofit sector. And, as of January 2005, nearly 200 Dickinson alumni had participated or are currently participating in the Peace Corps. At present, we have, for example, graduates in Guatemala working in applied agricultural science, in Morocco assisting with business development, in Madagascar aiding with public-health efforts and in Thailand teaching English.

I do not, for one minute, think that Dickinson is the only college or university that can provide these examples. I know there are many, many able and committed young people across the country who are prepared to embrace their communities and their nation through public service.

Perhaps we, as a society, are asking the wrong questions—or maybe not enough questions—about the purpose and accomplishments of higher education? Shouldn't we be seeking an accountability from our colleges and universities that is consistent with the intentions of those who created a distinctively American approach to higher education? While there exists a sort of vague and undefined expectation that higher education should have something to do with leadership, citizenship and the furtherance of our democracy, it is certainly not the first thing that springs to mind when one thinks about the mission or excellence of an institution.

In fairness, I was most heartened by the recent release of *The Washington Monthly's* new higher-education rankings. Rather than relying on the traditional financial data, *The Washington Monthly* looked at three different variables: national service, social mobility and the impact of research on the economy and society. In other words, as the publication itself puts it, "While other guides ask what colleges can do for students, we ask what colleges are doing for the country." Not surprisingly, the resulting rankings looked far different from those issued by others, such as *U.S. News and World Report.*

While *The Washington Monthly* methodology, as they themselves admit, needs to be refined, it is a step in the right direction. We do need a better way of understanding how well our colleges and universities are preparing graduates to assume the mantle of democratic leadership—that is, as it has been for nearly 230 years, the essence of our nation's profound success.

As we turn this new lens on higher education, we must remember that, in one important way, American higher education remains true to its distinctive heritage. On most campuses today, there is a significant and very active student-life division—a function that simply does not exist at universities in other countries. Responsible for organizing activities and events beyond the classroom, most student-life organizations focus heavily on developing leadership skills, promoting meaningful public service and establishing a respectful and healthy community on campus.

Most colleges and universities, including Dickinson, are consciously striving to better coordinate in-class and out-of-class student experiences. The emerging pedagogy known as "Service Learning or Integrative Learning"—again, an American creation—is designed precisely to encourage meaningful community involvement through academic coursework, thereby strengthening the connection between students' lives both inside and outside of the classroom. The mission of promoting responsible citizenship, leadership and public service is, therefore, clearly evident, and the commitment to advance these qualities is real.

This commitment derives directly from the intentions of our founding fathers and links the purpose of higher education to the future well-being of our communities and our nation. Shouldn't these aspects of our mission also be criteria by which we are evaluated by the public, the media, our prospective students and their parents? Shouldn't we, as a society, be asking if an institution's approach results in a demonstrable increase in, say, its students'—and to gauge the long-term effect—its alumni's record of voting, running for elective office, serving on nonprofit boards, expressing opinions through op-ed pieces, contributing financially to nonprofit community and educational organizations, and writing letters to the editors? Shouldn't we be consciously exploring connections between higher education, effective citizenship and leadership—particularly as we enter a century that is increasingly complex, challenging and requires not only national but also global leadership? It is time that concerned citizens and higher-education leadership throughout the United States join together to recapture and reassert accountability for a distinctive ambition of America's colleges and universities. Let us hold truly accountable our institutions for the reasons for which they were founded in the first place.

The American Revolution gave birth not only to a new democracy, but also to a new approach to higher education that was distinctly suited to a society dependent upon the active involvement of its citizens. It was this willingness to become engaged, to confront together contemporary challenges that de Tocqueville found so remarkable as he traveled across America in the 1830s.

Today, many commentators worry about an apparent decline in community spirit and a weakening of our civic organizations. It is, in my judgment, an observation that merits both concern and attention. As we face the realities and opportunities the global society of the 21st-century present, many of the mechanisms that traditionally bound us together are either strained or evolving. It is time for Americans—as they have done repeatedly in the past—to rethink and perhaps redefine active and engaged citizenry for the 21st century.

Our nation's colleges and universities have already begun, albeit in an uncoordinated manner, this renewed dialogue. As we proceed, it is, I believe, imperative that we revisit the vision and intentions of individuals such as Benjamin Rush. The qualities he valued still resonate today—an academically rigorous education that is ultimately useful and clearly grounded in the contemporary world; broad educational opportunity for all segments of society; expectation of active engagement with community; and, above all, preparation of the citizen-leaders of future generations.

These are the qualities that distinguished American higher education—and therefore, American society—from our earliest inception as a nation. These qualities still exist within our colleges and universities, but they deserve greater focus and visibility as well as the explicit acknowledgement that they are, in fact, important. By so doing, we will reinforce those expectations of active citizenship and the deep sense of commitment to community well-being that de Tocqueville found so remarkable and so distinctively American nearly two hundred years ago, and which you, as Tocqueville-level donors—as leadership donors—to the United Way value highly. My call tonight, if heeded, will inspire generations of citizens to display the same leadership and generosity you display to secure our nation and our communities.

REMARKS AT THE RECTOR SCIENCE COMPLEX GROUNDBREAKING
May 5, 2006

This is an extraordinary day for Dickinson College. Today, we break ground for the most ambitious and potentially "useful" building project in our history—the Keystone Phase of our newly conceived science campus. The Keystone Phase will be constructed adjacent to Tome Hall, the first phase of the overall project, and will consist of two additional halls. This phase will be followed at a later date by the construction of the Capstone Phase, a fourth hall. This integrated facility, together with Althouse Hall and potentially Dana Hall, will support our visionary, nationally recognized science program and serve as a defining model of undergraduate science study and research for the 21st century.

With this action today, we are taking a major step toward realizing the historic vision for a distinctively American liberal-arts education initiated by our founder, Dr. Benjamin Rush. As a physician, Rush instinctively understood the importance of science in a liberal-arts curriculum. For Rush, science was to play a central organizing role in Dickinson's course of study. The sciences along with the study of modern languages, Rush believed, would help students make connections between existing and emerging disciplines, global connections that would lead ultimately to the creation of new knowledge and new frontiers of intellectual inquiry.

Rush knew that scientific discovery would become a central and highly useful force in the development of the new nation, driving economic expansion, improving public health and fueling America's innate passion for innovation. As the future citizen-leaders of the new democracy, Dickinson students would gain the best preparation through a liberal-arts curriculum that not only included but also integrated the sciences. As we stand at the threshold of a new century that will be dominated by advances in scientific discovery, Rush's vision has never seemed more prescient.

Our faculty has created a progressive science curriculum appropriate for the challenges and opportunities of the 21st century. This building will provide them with a facility that will allow their energy, creativity and intellectual curiosity—and that of their students—to grow and thrive. The Keystone Phase of the science campus will assert—through architectural design and academic content—the centrality of science in a distinctively American liberal-arts education and, specifically, the centrality of science to the mission of Dickinson College .

At Dickinson, our approach to a liberal-arts education has been made more distinctive by the unique and meaningful way we have integrated science into our overall course of study. Our emphasis on active pedagogy, our quick willingness to embrace cross-disciplinary explorations and our insistence on including our science faculty and students in our global mission set us apart from our peers. Science at Dickinson mirrors our total academic experience.

Creating the vision for a three-phased science campus—not to mention defining and refining the endless details that will make it a reality—has required the talent, tenacity and energy of many, many individuals. I must thank, as Provost Weissman will, the science faculty and the students who gave countless hours of service on the science-building steering committee. They are to be commended for their passion, their patience and, most of all, their perseverance in participating in this process. And they are to be applauded for their flexibility and ultimate trust, for contributing their knowledge and expertise, and for their willingness to continue monitoring this project until completion.

Vice President Nick Stamos must be heartily commended for his leadership as he has steadily marshaled this project from conception to design to groundbreaking. Nick, of course, has been ably assisted by Associate Vice President Ken Shultes and many others in the facilities division.

We also must extend our deep appreciation to Fred Bean, the Carlisle borough manager; Michael Kaiser, Carlisle director of public works; and Alicia Reiter, Carlisle planning, zoning and codes manager, as well as Carlisle Borough Council President Don Grell. These individuals have shared in our dream and have worked quietly and cooperatively to secure the zoning requirements and permits to make it a reality.

And finally, I must extend my most sincere gratitude to trustees Byron Koste, Sylvia Smith and the other members of the Committee on Facilities for their extraordinary contribution in both time and expertise. They have been with us every step of the way, providing wise counsel, enthusiasm, encouragement and, when appropriate, a healthy dose of caution. We would not be here today without their strong guidance. I must also extend personal thanks to General David Meade for his enthusiastic conversations with me about the project and its execution, conversations that I know will continue and to which I look forward.

ASSOCIATION OF AMERICAN SCHOOLS IN SOUTH AMERICA (AASSA) 2006 KEYNOTE ADDRESS
Oct. 19, 2006
Portions of this speech are taken from "Leadership, Language Study and Global Sensibility" (Page 105).

I am delighted to be again among old friends—especially AASSA Executive Director Jim Morris—and to meet new ones. I respect highly and profoundly all of you who engage the world by being out in it daily and preparing through your schools and respective communities a next generation—a new, increasingly hopeful generation of young citizens prepared for a life of global awareness and engagement.

Most of you know me as a person who has spent decades studying and advancing special-needs students often in this region of the world—especially highly able students (and that includes those with learning challenges). Indeed, AASSA took the lead years ago in this area with its embrace of the Optimal Match and its sponsoring of the first Optimal Match institutes in the world. About eight years ago, however, I asked myself a fundamental question: "To what use is this high-academic talent to be put?" Of course, you might smile at this.

My query reveals a distinctively Anglo-American prejudice—that an idea is only as worthy as it can be applied. But to this end, my interests morphed into the study of leadership—leadership for citizenship and societal contribution as a worthy end and application for human talent and high ability. Coincidentally, my pursuit parallels a raging preoccupation with leadership in general. The media and popular press are filled with books on leadership and management—not just good leadership, but as of two years ago, even a genre of books dedicated to bad leadership. Anything apparently sells.

Last year, about 3,500 books on leadership in business were published in the United States alone. According to the *Economist*, leadership studies are now a distinctive genre of intellectual pursuit. But there is a rub. This enthusiasm appears to exist only in the United States. In fact, most other countries, such as the U.K., find this U. S. obsession bizarre—chiefly because of the U. S. linking of leadership with the personality trait of charisma, which the Brits think is fleeting and insubstantial not to speak of as typically America. The Brits also distrust anyone who possesses it—this charisma. Additionally, they find the American advancement of leadership for the world to be highly ironic given its obvious (at least to the majority of the British public) challenge to good leadership in its own business world and that of politics. The British people cite Enron, WorldCom, Tyco and Iraq as examples of glorious messes in leadership.

Leadership is big business. I think of Jim Collin's record-selling book, *Good to Great*, and his follow-up booklet dedicated to the nonprofits or Malcolm Gladwell's *Tipping Point*. That said, I am also convinced that this focus on leadership among the general public—in the world of business, finance and politics and increasingly taught at undergraduate, graduate and professional schools—will soon be a recommended, if not required, subject at the precollegiate level. Leadership is coming your way in international schools. You will feel the pressure to teach it just as you may have felt the pressure to teach whole language, self-esteem, critical thinking, cooperative learning—even gifted-and-talented education. Leadership will be the new buzzword. You will have many speakers in the future seeking to address you here and at other conferences on the topic, and they will all link it, I predict, to another current issue—some say buzzword—one with a few years head start—accountability. Your charge, of course, is to determine how you will react and ultimately if you will even teach leadership. If you do, however, how will you teach this new area of study? This is a crucial decision. You will either teach it as a separate field in and of itself or you will integrate it into all your existing subjects. You face the same choice you had with, for example, critical thinking and problem solving—standalone subjects merely self-relating or skills set in more comprehensive academic contexts. Those who know me know my strong prejudice. I prefer the latter option.

This evening, I ask you to think out loud with me about your new subject and to think in a revolutionary manner—to apply it personally, each and every one of you—in altering the course of your current instruction, pursuing change in three key areas: self-esteem, accountability and either-or thinking. For me, these three areas properly handled would go a long way to restoring professionalism to teaching and setting the basis for leadership among both teachers and administrators. I am going to ask you to take leadership out of the more common context of business, finance and politics and place it in the classroom. I shall challenge you to refine your emerging contribution to leadership study by drawing upon your distinction—precollege education offered within an independent, global context, a global commitment. And finally, I ask you as educators to seize leadership for yourselves and your profession because you now need it more than ever before. There is a sense of urgency today for concerned educators to produce and exercise their own leadership, which will provide a powerful challenge to leadership readily taken by others—even within education—who are following, I believe, a disastrous course. These pseudo-leaders and experts not only wish to reduce you to being mere mechanics and your students, mere widgets, but also they would reduce your professionalism and critical judgment to the simplicity of the reductionist choices of partisan politics. Those who know me and have heard me speak, also know that I shall not tonight leave you with seven easy steps to take for application in the classroom tomorrow. I find that approach naïve, simplistic and disrespectful to your professionalism and limiting of your opportunity at such a conference to have space away from the classroom to engage the big picture. I will ask you, however, to engage tonight some complex ideas and challenges in education, to take the discussion into your social and professional settings (at the bar or restaurant following this session, for example), to engage in spirited argument and, at some point in the future, determine if there are indeed practical steps you yourself devise and you can apply in the classroom.

Several years ago in a speech before an international-schools audience in Vietnam I also pursued the topic of leadership. At that time, I urged the audience to seek lessons for leadership in places where it is not usually sought but which is under your direct control as classroom teachers—in the acquisition of academic content itself—in my case, in the study of foreign languages and culture. I urge you to refer to this speech, which evidently caused quite a debate in the United States. Tonight I take you in yet another direction.

Let us then begin this urgent exploration. I intend as always to be provocative and educationally sacrilegious throughout, for we must challenge prevailing paradigms of educational theory and practice or at least examine them so thoroughly that they are then applied with a sense of limitation—and this includes selected applications of the current U.S. educational policy towards precollegiate education—No Child Left Behind. There is much at stake here for us as educators. I look forward to your reaction—good, bad or ugly.

Throughout my relatively long career, I have been fortunate to have exercised leadership in several domains—often simultaneously, and frequently, in sectors that the pundits believe to be in essence contradictory and mutually exclusive. I have worked in the military, the government, the nonprofit college and university world, and corporate America . The one unifying insight that I have taken from this service is that leadership at its most sublime is narrative. It involves both the telling of a story and the ability to persuade others to engage that story as fully as if it were their own. Like a finely crafted novel or poem, the story should appear effortless in telling and conceal the exhaustive energy and toil that are expended in maintaining and advancing it. Leadership is exhausting, but it must not appear so.

The concept of leadership as narrative or storytelling is not without precedent. The Harvard educational theorist, Howard Gardner, in his provocative 1995 book in the collaboration with Emma Laskin, *Leading Minds: Anatomy of Leadership*, states unequivocally that "leaders achieve their effectiveness chiefly through the stories they relate." Leadership is thus a matter both of composition and communication. However, for Gardner, it is not enough to draft a story and relate it to others—you must also embody it; you must live the story yourself—through your own actions, with such integrity, passion and lucidity that your story becomes the others' story, your vision becomes their vision, your plan of action, their plan of action. A good leader most subtly and agreeably changes another person's story to become her story. Additionally, for Gardner, any good leadership narrative involves three components—a protagonist, a set of clear goals and a foil. I have found in the course of my professional life that several other elements contribute significantly to leadership. Some are quite obvious; others are more complex.

For example, I have found that it is important for leaders to be able to identify quickly the core challenge in any circumstance and to visualize immediately a way to meet the challenge. There is the need to balance the ability to compose a story that communicates your vision for leadership with a solid knowledge of the more mundane facts of the domain in which you exercise leadership. A leader must temper vision with the practical. A leader is reminded again and again that while a primary focus is upon the strategic, to be totally successful, you must make sure that the details are attended to—often personally. Failure to account for the details, to follow up, often leads to an incomplete, if not unsuccessful, mission.

Before one actually leads, a leader must grasp the big picture and deal with big ideas—not just little ones. I would provocatively assert, by the way, that in education today, you are usually presented with little ideas—procedures and applications such as cooperative learning, ability grouping, phonics, whole language and classroom management—not big ideas—those that approach the very meaning of what it is to be an educated, reflective, ethically receptive person. Big ideas are those that evoke the soul and spirit of people and have a substantive context in the history of ideas. They deal with questions of life, death, aim (purpose) and sensibility in historical context and, thus, over the course of time. What I am asking for education is precisely what Mike Chinoy, CNN's former senior Asia correspondent, demands in public statements of the media—that it move beyond an understanding of news as mere event to news as a process over time with deep, complex, interrelating roots. That said, I am not naive about those big ideas that are captured in the context of radical idealism and presented in all innocence and good intention. They can be powerfully destructive. I think of a passage from Graham Green's *Quiet American*. (It is quite appropriate to refer to Greene here in Asuncion as he traversed this country and found it eminently qualified for the subject of literature. I refer you in particular to *Travels With My Aunt*). Foster, the seasoned British reporter says of the young, ambitious American Pyle (working with the nascent CIA involvement in Vietnam) upon first seeing him—"Why does one want to tease the innocent? Perhaps only ten days ago he had been walking back across the Common in Boston, his arms full of the books he had been reading in advance on the Far East and the problems of China. He didn't even hear what I said; he was absorbed already in the dilemmas of Democracy and the responsibilities of the West; he was determined—I learned that very soon—to do good, not to any individual person but to a country, a continent, a world. Well, he was in his element now with the whole universe to improve." We know now, decades later, the devastating effect of that idealism, that big idea, on the peoples of both the United States and Vietnam.

A leader understands what leadership is all about in the domain in which skill is to be exercised and anticipates the likely outcomes of such leadership. There should be no surprises when leadership is exercised. A leader is prepared for the chance moment when leadership is required, and she is willing to cross all borders in thought and deed to achieve a creative solution to a demanding situation. A leader envisions the future. A leader, however, must never underestimate, nor prematurely dismiss, potential sources of insight or inspiration, however unlikely they may seem. For example, there is ample evidence that a number of the world's scientific leaders made their discoveries while experimenting in a totally different context than the one projected for results. They were receptive to change and absorbed readily in the unanticipated context a source of new knowledge. One only has to think of Roentgen's accidental discovery of the X-ray. Additionally, I personally have profited from never underestimating or dismissing aspects of my own life.

A leader must be both constantly active—in motion and engaging the world—exposing herself to a variety of experiences that give a new edge to leadership and yet, simultaneously, be thoughtful about the implications of experiences gathered and how they are to be applied to move people and organizations forward. A leader must apply peripheral vision to a domain of action and thus create a knowledge base that is deeper and more expansive than that of others. A leader connects the dots, sees what others overlook in this frame of reference and, thus, leads with distinction. This process of building a large framework of knowledge for leadership is similar to a theory of giftedness proposed by the South African scholar, Ochse. She states that a gifted person possesses a framework of knowledge deeper and broader than most other people and is constantly scanning that base, seeking the unexpected, the inconsistent, that which others have not yet discovered. It is a combination of the span of the knowledge base, the constant motion through it and the ability to pick out the remarkable and yet unseen that makes a person gifted.

A leader must have the interpersonal and emotional intelligences to appreciate which approach or voice—which grammar and syntax—are most likely to influence one person rather than another and to know always to whom one is speaking so that that person can be reached with the leadership story. The effective leader, no matter how acclaimed on the basis of past successes, never becomes passive in the face of leadership demand, never confuses the authority of reputation—which is short-lived—with the authority of voice—which is daily reinvented. And finally, belonging to any attempt to provide leadership to a group of people are two closely associated elements—urgency and change. A good leader creates a sense of urgency for change. Leadership literature abounds with commentary on the indisputable existence of change as the principal environment in which leaders act. John Kotter of the Harvard Business School is most eloquent on this topic in his book *Leading Change*: "Ask almost anyone over 30 about the difficulty of creating major change in an organization and the answer will probably include the equivalent of 'very, very tough.' Yet most of us still don't get it. We use the right words, but down deep we underestimate the enormity of the task, especially the first step: establishing a sense of urgency ... Establishing a sense of urgency is crucial to gaining needed cooperation. With complacency in organizations high, transformations usually go nowhere because few people are even interested in working on the change problem."

With this background in leadership, it is now appropriate to turn attention to those three challenges I mentioned above and get you involved personally. If we accept Gardner's definition of a leadership story, I suggest that you—the teachers and administrators in this room—are the protagonists in this educational story. It is you who must apply all the manifestations of leadership that I described above. It is you who must embody the story, create the vocabulary of change and communicate it to diverse audiences and people. The goals of the leadership story I offer you tonight are clear. You are to expose three popular educational practices that, when embraced in an absolutist manner, represent severe danger to learning. You are to replace them with much more rational, effective and commonsensical strategies in your classroom, in the faculty lounge and in conversation with parents and the general public. The foils—those people or ideas whom you must oppose—are also obvious. They are these three practices and those absolutists who advance them. It is against these entities that you must rail daily in a professional, well-informed, yet pointed way.

Beginning in the 1980s, there was a massive, worldwide effort to increase children's and young peoples' self-esteem. According to Professor Jean M. Twenge in her 2006 book, *Generation Me* (to which I shall refer extensively in this section), "the number of psychology and education-journal articles devoted to self-esteem doubled between the 1970s and the 1980s. Journal articles increased another 52 percent during the 1990s, and the number of books on self-esteem doubled over the same time. Magazines, television talk shows and books all emphasize the importance of self-esteem for children, usually promoting feelings that are a lot closer to narcissism (a more negative trait usually defined as excessive self-importance)." Twenge thus already introduces a considerable negative that grows out of an exclusionary focus among young people on their self-esteem. This obsession will have extreme consequences for what I say this evening.

Of course, once society in general seized upon the self-esteem mantra, the schools were not far behind. They bought into it completely. A veritable "self-esteem curriculum" was introduced in the years following 1980, and it remains pervasive and strong today despite overwhelming evidence that such targeted focus on self-esteem clearly does not yield results that help individuals nor society at large. Again, Twenge on the subject: "Many school districts across the country [the U.S.] have specific programs designed to increase children's self-esteem, most of which actually build self-importance and narcissism. One program is called 'Self-Science: The Subject Is Me.' [poor grammar, of course] (Why bother with biology? I'm so much more interesting!) Another program, called 'Pumsey in Pursuit of Excellence,' uses a dragon character to encourage children to escape the 'Mud Mind' they experience when feeling bad about themselves. Instead, they should strive to be in the 'Sparkle Mind' and feel good about themselves. The Magic Circle exercise designates one child a day to receive a badge saying 'I'm great.' The other children then say good things about the chosen child, who later receives a written list of all of the praise. At the end of the exercise, the child must then say something good about him- or herself. As John Hewitt points out in *The Myth of Self-Esteem*, the implicit message is that self-esteem can be taught and should be taught. When self-esteem programs are used, Hewitt notes, children are 'encouraged to believe that it is acceptable and desirable to be preoccupied with oneself [and] praise oneself.' In many cases, he says, it's not just encouraged but required. These exercises make self-importance mandatory, demanding of children that they love themselves. 'The child must be taught to like himself or herself. The child MUST take the teacher's attitude himself or herself—'I am somebody!' 'I am capable and loving'—regardless of what the child thinks.' Most of these programs encourage children to feel good about themselves for no particular reason. In one program, teachers are told to discourage children from saying things like 'I'm a good soccer player' or 'I'm a good singer.' This makes self-esteem contingent on performance, the program authors chide. Instead, 'we want to anchor self-esteem firmly to the child so that no matter what the performance might be, the self-esteem remains high.' In other words, feeling good about yourself is more important than good performance. Children, the guide says, should be taught 'that it is who they are, not what they do, that is important.'"

Teacher-training courses are, of course, affected by this demand to advance at all costs self-esteem through instruction regardless of the actual quality of a student's academic performance. And classroom teachers are often instructed by their administrators not to correct students mistakes in class or on homework; if they do so, to use a pleasant colored pen (not red; it has a negative connotation built up over the centuries and thus does not build self-confidence—I kid you not here!). According to Twenge, in 2005 a British teacher even "proposed eliminating the word 'fail' from education; instead of hearing that they have failed, students should hear that they have 'deferred success.' "

Now one would think that this decades-long demand for self-esteem instruction in schools would yield positive results—that we would graduate young people who were realistically confident, who truly felt good about themselves, who achieved well in school and out of school, who could handle any challenge, who possessed the highest integrity. Well, actually, the very opposite is the case, but that does not at all stop the absolutists, the true believers, in demanding self-esteem instruction in the schools. Today's students in general are emerging from secondary school unable to deal with personal criticism or defeat. They become rude and unfriendly when challenged by anyone about anything. They are unaccepting of anyone asserting more knowledge than they about a subject other than the self—a teacher, a professor, a boss in the workplace—since they have been instructed for years that they get to determine what is true and what is important. They exist absent deep and sustaining commitments to society and other people and, in fact, are more depressed and unhappy with life than any previous generation—including those that experienced in the U.S. such massive events as WWI, WWII and the Great Depression. It seems that their exalted sense of self-worth, which they now take for granted because of years of instruction, does not hold up to the harsher realities of the wider world and its indifference to their sense of inevitable achievement and reward just for existing as an individual with self-esteem. According to Twenge and citing the most extensive research on the subject (Martin Seligman and Roy Baumeister), self-esteem instruction unquestionably does not lead "to better grades, improved work performance, decreased violence or less cheating. In fact, people with high self-esteem are often more violent and more likely to cheat. 'It is very questionable whether [the few benefits] justify the effort and expense that schools, parents and therapists have put into raising self-esteem,' Baumeister writes, 'After all these years, I'm sorry to say, my recommendation is this: forget about self-esteem and concentrate more on self-control and self-discipline.' " Twenge hits it right on the mark when she says, "Self-esteem is an outcome, not a cause. In other words, it doesn't do much good to encourage a child to feel good about himself just to feel good; this doesn't mean anything. Children develop true self-esteem from behaving well and accomplishing things."

My message to you tonight is exactly that of Twenge and Baumeister. It is time to move away from the folly of self-esteem, feel-good instruction and advocacy and reclaim a teaching that advances children both through a sustained, supportive and progressive engagement with their variety of abilities—alone and in interaction with others—and by repeated exposure to substantive content and skill well beyond the subject of the self and its value. Indeed, there is no doubt that a child's ego is most thoroughly prepared for interaction with a world beyond the precious confines of school by early and sustained interaction with a variety of challenges they have to figure out how to overcome for survival and high performance. This opportunity, indeed, resides on the streets in some pretty tough neighborhoods, and it often—and sadly—attracts more interest in young people than the friendly, overly nurturing, hugging and perpetually smiling environment of contemporary schools—an environment where how an individual child *feels* about something or someone in the learning landscape trumps what is truly known and knowable.

This issue of self-esteem is one that I have taken on personally. Just this past summer I presented a paper along with former first lady Roselyn Carter and the director of the Princeton University Health System on the state of academic and resident (student) life on America's college and university campuses. In my presentation, I noted that today's undergraduates appear publicly as "confident, assertive and entitled," and yet, they are also the most personally miserable and depressed generation in American history. I then proceeded to develop my argument taking direct aim at the results of the self-esteem movement and its related manifestations.

This is what I said: "I suggest that this alleged 'depression' among the seemingly 'confident' is in part a result of decoupling the academic and student-life divisions within colleges and universities. It is unconscionable of us as professors and administrators to blame students and their parents solely for these problems. We have become enablers. We have provided students with a huge, all-absorbing extra-academic world in which they can create a comfortable, but insular niche that at once feeds their inflated sense of self and its need for constant praise and fulfillment. We have removed academic knowledge from the place where they spend the majority of their time among us—residential life. We have left them bereft of substantive encounters beyond this personal, self-indulgent realm. And thus we leave them adrift at a very fundamental human level.

This disturbing development at the undergraduate level has been handily anticipated by several decades of the self-esteem movement in precollegiate education during which all students are endlessly praised as excellent and unique without grounding these claims in actual individual performance. This movement has created a most unhealthy state for a student's honest definition of self by confusing the noble pursuit of equality of opportunity with equality of achievement—disregarding in the process any actual differentiation of performance among students. They truly are unprepared for a discriminating, highly competitive world that does not yield to their unrealistically high and inaccurate estimations of their own abilities and expectations; they are, in essence, bereft of both authentic self-understanding and a grip on that which lies beyond themselves—a most depressing state of mind. Indeed, a recent Hart Focus Group initiative sponsored by AAC&U reveals that public high-school seniors who plan to go to college to pursue a baccalaureate degree went "so far as to suggest that activities like service learning might distract from the more important work of their own *individual* self-development—the primary reason they gave for attending college."

We have not fulfilled our educative responsibility to open students' minds, to encourage serious inquiry and to develop an understanding of what it means to be a part of a wider, diverse community that is not always cast ultimately in a student's own image and opinion. By simply enabling our students' selfish desires, we have denied them the defining human instinct of genuine sociability and connectivity necessary for continuous learning. Instead, we have fallen prey to the students' own definition of success as we assist them in their quest for personal advancement at the expense of communal progress. The whole notion of a useful education, in other words, has become focused on a personal usefulness as each student asks him or herself, "How can I get ahead?" The only reasonable remedy for this situation is to aggressively pursue a mutually beneficial alliance of academic and residential student life on American campuses.

Again, I invite you to join with me in your educational domain—precollegiate education—to bring commonsense, reason and good practice back into teaching and learning. I invite you to work with me to regain professionalism for teachers and professors.

Why did I state in my introduction that now more than at any time in the past you as teachers and administrators must embrace leadership itself and develop for your school and for your classrooms a strong leadership story and advance it to the public with resolve and tenacity? I say this because your control of what you personally administer and teach is about to be taken away from you—in whole or part. The threat is *accountability* taken to extremes, and it comes at you in all innocence. It offers many good measures—principally seeming security and definiteness about good performance versus poor in educational instruction—but exaggerated and turned into an absolute, it possesses the capacity for much harm in education more generously understood.

The paradigm of innocence as destructive is not without precedent, of course. I refer once again to Graham Greene and *The Quiet American*. When describing meeting Pyle (a freshly-minted, naive CIA agent) for the first time as he, Pyle, ambled toward the bar of the Continental Hotel in Saigon, Foster ironically states, [Pyle] possesses "an unmistakably young and unused face flung at us like a dart. With his gangly legs and his crew cut and his wide campus gaze, he seemed incapable of harm." Again, for Vietnam and for a generation of Americans, Pyle was anything but harmless and innocent. The contemporary equivalent of Pyle for you, a potentially and seemingly beneficial concept gone awry, is accountability—accountability as translated in the No Child Left Behind legislation. Permit me to explain this audacious claim—one that will certainly immediately evoke protest from certain quarters. I begin by quoting from "Making the Grade" in the Sept. 15, 2003, edition of the *The New Yorker*:

> The most striking thing about the sweeping federal educational reforms debuting this fall is how much they resemble, in language and philosophy, the industrial-efficiency movement of the early 20th century. In those years, engineers argued that efficiency and productivity were things that could be measured and managed, and, if you had the right inventory and manufacturing controls in place, no widget would be left behind. Now we have No Child Left Behind, in which Congress has set up a complex apparatus of sanctions and standards designed to compel individual schools toward steady annual improvement, with the goal of making 100 percent of American schoolchildren proficient in math and reading by 2014. It is hard to look at the new legislation and not share in its Fordist vision of the classroom as a brightly lit assembly line, in which curriculum standards sail down from Washington through a chute, and freshly scrubbed, defect-free students come bouncing out the other end. It is an extraordinary vision, particularly at a time when lawmakers seem mostly preoccupied with pointing out all the things that government cannot do. The only problem, of course—and it's not a trivial one—is that children aren't widgets.

I might add that learning is not merely a matter of what can be quantitatively assessed by standardized tests and thus directed by an extreme rationality. Such a disposition reflects the radical conviction that inputs must yield anticipated outputs in a predictable and highly efficient manner, with cost thereby controlled and penalties exacted for inefficiencies. This disposition, of course, represents a rather crude, macho distortion of a business mentality that defined the

19th- and early 20th-century industrial age, not that of a 21st-century entrepreneurialism where informed, yet highly risky and inefficient investment (risk capital) is engaged with the expectation—but not certainty—of yielding groundbreaking discoveries, technologies and products. You see, this is precisely the problem with No Child Left Behind and its current successor at the collegiate level, the U.S. Secretary of Education's Report of the Commission on the Future of Higher Education, dubbed recently in a *New York Times* op-ed piece by the former federal education official who directly oversaw the implementation of No Child Left Behind as "No Undergraduate Left Behind." What we have here is a naïve science, indeed, the naïve notion that we can find a purely technical solution to a perceived social or educational problem. These reports and similar documents are actually the direct product of a dogmatic Anglo-American sensibility and rationality about knowledge—a markedly incomplete vision resolved that knowledge is only as worthy as it can be measured quantitatively and put to some targeted use and, further, that all instruction to be defensible and publicly supportable must adhere to this paradigm. Its origin is a humanism crafted by the scientific revolution of the 17th century—in essence, a position that the more we measure, the more accurately we see what things are actually like—quantitative assessment reveals the truth. Its contemporary history emerges most immediately from British empiricism and the American Metaphysical Club, consisting of Charles Pierce, John Dewey, Oliver Wendell Holmes and William James. Yet it was already present in the Scottish Enlightenment and in Benjamin Franklin's singular definition of American character—one that prefers practicality to romanticism and holds that the truth of any proposition, whether it be scientific, moral, theological or social, is based on how well it correlates with experimental results and produces a practical outcome.

In education—especially precollegiate education—this turn to pragmatism took place in all earnestness in the early 20th century. It was John Dewey and fellow progressives who framed the intellectual construct for what became the SATs. This empirical turn was motivated in part by insecurity and a feeling of lack of respect by the public towards educators because learning was not scientifically based. In a world that was increasingly valuing science as the measure of all things, education remained underpowered and undervalued. Well, educators remedied that immediately and satisfied their "science envy." Standardized testing became suddenly an integral part of educational practice and was introduced in a comprehensive manner. And since knowledge to be assessed had to be subject to quantitative scrutiny and efficiency, it increasingly became itself technical, focused on short-term impact (note the similarity here with traditional corporate America and its focus almost exclusively on short-term quarter rather than multiyear results) and partial to little ideas, facts and procedures, rather than those big, complex ones involving questions of the meaning of life, aesthetics, and moral and ethical judgment that are not readily embraced by standardized assessment. Education has been short on those big ideas involving the aims of education. This trend is underscored by the now almost total absence of the philosophy of education as a full course of instruction in graduate schools of education. The results are evident. If you ask today's college and university students—as I have—what big ideas influence comprehensively the conduct of their lives, they can come up with none. If you ask them the name of a philosopher or a fictionalist or a poet who influences how they live their lives and define themselves and their actions towards others, they are often clueless.

I urge you then today—I beseech you—to reclaim for your schools and classrooms big ideas that extend beyond the quantitatively measurable and thus appear to the misguided as merely trivial, inefficient and without power and effect. I urge you to proudly and defiantly speak up for that which cannot be quantified but which securely belongs to learning and the ultimate definition of an educated person in a complex world. I urge you to reclaim the art of teaching—for today we possess merely the science of teaching, and that is inadequate to move forward a total child, much less a people. I urge you to redefine accountability, which is an otherwise worthy pursuit, so that it balances the practical and technical—that which can and should be empirically measured with that which involves the advancement of spirit, soul, creativity, entrepreneurialism and character of students, which is not so readily subject to general standardization and progressive quantitative assessment, much less to short-term results. I urge you to live both in the bone (quantitative testing) and in the connective tissue (the worthiness of seemingly ambiguous intent). In fact, I would be so bold today as to urge you to replace accountability as currently understood (after all, facts can readily be manipulated and spun as we all learned painfully with the Enron and Worldcom scandals in the United States, and teaching can be radically circumscribed to correspond merely to that knowledge required by the tests) with another concept for assessment—*transparency*.

Transparency is here understood as making available regularly to the public all sorts of data—empirical and subjective—and thus bestowing upon the public the trust to analyze and judge an education. I urge you to consider that students in the United States are already the most tested by standardized measurement in the world, and yet we still seem to be in a position of deficit in the actual improvement of what students know and need to know to function productively in society. Is there truly the belief that more standardized testing will lead to improved teaching and learning—that is, are we so convinced that "to test is to learn"? Are we so convinced still, historical evidence to the contrary, that more testing will fundamentally change the learning and instructional culture and practice of schools—right into the classrooms where teacher and student meet an idea, a skill, so that these institutions can finally complete their mission for all students? Are we so blind to the fact that, despite the massive testing that is already occurring in the United States, the results are seldom if ever used in a diagnostic-prescriptive manner in the classroom to improve the fundamental literacies (verbal, mathematical and scientific) and learning deficits of an individual student? Despite our ideological statements of practicality on all things—to include testing—we are in fact hypocrites as we regularly negate the usefulness of standardized testing to advance the core mission of education—helping a child academically in the classroom on a daily basis. You see, I am not against application of standardized diagnostic testing at the precollegiate level to identify verbal, mathematical and scientific competency skills and then guide individual compensatory or advanced instruction so as to deliver remedial-free university education.

Are we so blind to the machinations of individual schools and state school systems throughout the nation that find clever ways to ensure that standardized testing results are manipulated to appear more substantive than they really are and, in so doing, make a mockery of accountability for improved learning? Are we so blind to the fact that substantive, sustained learning is actually advanced by a shared cultural disposition, a common belief that a substantive, rigorous education advances individual and national accomplishment, and absent this most fundamental community disposition and its application in the classroom and throughout society, no technical measures (such as standardized testing) will advance learning or a sustained society of knowledge?

I urge you today to assert strongly your own leadership story as teachers and administrators—yes, as classroom teachers—for your respective schools and for your sector, international education. Already alarming Orwellian versions of accountability are a reality in the for-profit realm of higher education, and I guarantee, having worked in the for-profit education industry, that a version of these methods is eventually headed your way. In fact, it is already being applied in some proprietary international schools. I am, of course, referring to your total loss of control over what you offer to your students as an institution and what you teach in the classroom in the name of universal empirical accountability to the "consumer." The University of Phoenix, the world's largest university, for example, now commissions a panel of third-party subject-area specialists to establish strict curricula for classroom instructors. No deviation from this course of study is permitted by the actual classroom instructors, and the tests of this canned knowledge are universal across all campuses. The job then of teachers is merely to deliver and test in a standardized fashion a predetermined course of study. Administrators and teachers are now truly widgets as are the students. All of this is conducted in the name of empirical verification of learning.

Dualistic, mutually exclusive thinking permeates precollegiate education both in the United States and often internationally. It has done so historically, and we can't seem to escape this well-imprinted cycle. A mutually exclusive set of educational either-ors—ability grouping versus cooperative learning, phonics versus whole language, exclusion versus inclusion, homogeneous grouping versus heterogeneous grouping. Even quantitative testing versus qualitative assessment is involved, and the potential harm both to educators and students is immense.

Teachers today are asked repeatedly by theoreticians and their supporters in professional associations and corporate America (education is, after all, big business and the acceptance of a particular program can mean millions of dollars to certain parties) to make choices between polar opposites. In so doing, you are deprived of a reflective professionalism. Each pole of your choice is championed as a solution for an astonishing and dissimilar array of education problems. Moreover, your decision must be made between dualities in which both of the poles are politicized and ideologically framed and where often there appears to be only one politically correct choice.

In essence, choice for you is illusory, and the basis of selecting instructional strategies becomes more of a matter of advocacy than of scholarship. The distinction is not without consequence. You are in this way being asked to be intellectually acquiescent in the face of political and emotional deck-stacking.

Cooperative learning versus ability grouping is a case in point. Two scholars held in considerable regard by the education-research community have nevertheless characterized ability grouping in their writings as "running against our democratic ideals," in one case and, in the other, "against our national ideology that all are created equal and our desire to be one nation. The questioning of another's patriotism in this educational context is clearly emotionally charged power politics and is the moral equivalent of a politician or a politician's assistants claiming that a citizen's honest disagreement with a particular administration's practice and policies is un-American. It is simply a cheap shot for partisan political reasons. Equally alarming is when advocates of, in this case, non-ability grouping call for the suspension of rational study. For example, a Texas school principal stated in an educational journal that "the ability grouping of educational opportunity in a democratic society is ethically unacceptable. ... We need not justify this with research, for it is a statement of principles, not of science." In a display of the most egregious application of post-modernism to education, it is clear that here facts don't matter and that you should give up your rational, scientifically based professionalism for blind trust. This is simply insulting to you and your profession.

When these kinds of educational dualities are examined philosophically, the poles in each case are organized consistently around differing conceptions of where meaning originates in education and what criteria are brought to bear in judging appropriate instructional format—either upon the most discrete, most differentiated unit or upon the most comprehensive entity, where the demands of the whole prevail.

For example, in the phonics-versus-whole-language dichotomy, which is really about how one best learns how to read, phonics advances the most discrete, most differentiated unit as the source of all meaning—sound units or phonemes. In whole language, meaning derives from a collection of sounds, that is, the story.

The same conceptual dichotomy holds for ability group versus cooperative learning. Although the term "ability grouping" has an array of definitions, in general, it refers to the pairing of students for instruction by differentiated academic status, ability or achievement. Cooperative learning, in the most general sense, simply means that students work together on a school-related task regardless of educational differentiation. Ability grouping, then, represents more than does cooperative learning, a breaking down of a larger group of students into smaller, more discrete units for instructional purpose based on individual difference. Again, such distinction holds for exclusion versus inclusion and homogeneous grouping versus heterogeneous grouping.

What ardent advocates of any of these polarities demand from you as teachers is nothing less than an unequivocal decision about the origin of the meaning of education. But there is more to it than that—something that never achieves attention or commentary. Your decision, when so starkly drawn by these specific, mutually exclusive concepts, also forces you—perhaps unwittingly—to accept a partisan political stance of far-reaching consequence. Selection of the practice that is organized upon the most individualistic unit places you squarely in the politically conservative camp (at least in the United States). Individualism and its preservation run deeply in conservative (right) Republican ideology. Choice of the collective or the group as the basis of orienting instructional approach, places you squarely on the left or liberal Democratic side of the political perspective, where

shared community values—the greatest good for the most people—
dominates. Implicitly, you as teachers and administrators now are
confronted not just with pedagogical decisions, but also politically
divisive ones.

For precollegiate education to regain its intellectual integrity in
this politically charged atmosphere will not be easy. It will take substantive, forceful leadership from precisely you. A possible alternative
leadership story, however, lies before you, and it is found, I believe,
in an article by Peter Schrag appearing decades ago in the progressive
public-policy journal *The American Prospect*. In "The New School
Wars," Schrag comments:

> It's striking how quickly our struggles about curric-
> ulum ideas escalate into quasi-religion controversies
> over social or moral absolutes. The right [political
> right] sees a conspiracy by the federal government
> and its secular humanist legions [this was before
> the Bush administration and alleged receptivity to
> religious fundamentalism in government and argu-
> ments over creationism versus evolution] to strip
> parents of control over their children and incul-
> cate them with relativistic values, witchcraft and
> Satanism. The left looks at every parent who walks
> into a principal's office complaining about a book
> or school assignment as a tool of religious fanatics.
> A generation ago people who challenged the abso-
> lute primacy of phonics were attacked in school-
> board fights as socialists; now Fair Test [which no
> longer exists today] regards anyone too devoted to
> the SATs as, at the very least, an unconscious racist
> or sexist. In the face of such heat, and in the absence
> of vigorous *centrist forces* [emphasis added] speaking
> for parents, it's not surprising that politicians and
> school bureaucrats tend to capitulate easily.

Mr. Schrag pinpoints in the words "absence of vigorous centrist
forces" the plight of educators trying to help children without falling

victim to diametrically opposite ideologies—either-ors—masked as innocent instructional strategies. Demanding allegiance through blind faith (science and research are not necessary!) to a particular ideology leads to the loss of honest professional perspective on what the actual instructional needs of particular children are. Often, a school becomes entrapped by the zealotry of a superintendent, principal or school-board member who attends a spirited conference like this and obsessively seizes upon a one-sided and perhaps unsubstantiated (although charismatically presented) educational technique to such a degree that instructional hegemony emerges back at the school. Of course, this happens every year when the administrator hears yet another wizard idea for instruction at the next conference. The school declares itself *all* cooperative learning, *all* phonics, *all* individualized learning, *all* inclusion, regardless of the variety of strategies necessary to educate most fully the wide diversity of students requiring instruction. The entire educational community is unreflectively forced to teach or learn according to ever-changing and arbitrarily imposed ideologies and practices. A one-size-fits-all position prevails, and teacher dissention is penalized.

Precollegiate educators need to re-establish with confidence the leadership story that no one instructional strategy fits all students, but rather that, after an enlightened assessment of each child's strengths and weaknesses, an instructional method is applied from among a wide arsenal of possibilities. Indeed, numerous methods will be applied over the course of a single child's education. I urge you here tonight to assert the value of individual difference in a school setting and reclaim for your profession a commonplace that people learn (and achieve) at different rates, in different styles and at different levels. And the system must embrace this leadership story organizationally and attitudinally. In essence, the proper role of the administrator and teacher is to take the centrist position and assert that kind of high-level professionalism that restores professional judgment and individual choice to the classroom teacher—that respects your dignity and professionalism—and, thus, helps a child receive an appropriate match between educational need and educational service.

The forces in opposition to your move to centrism are formidable. Despite the need for this centrist approach in the classroom and the numerous laments about its absence, it will not so readily be established. The problem lies with centrism as a force (much less a "vigorous force") and its being accepted as such by educators and the general public. The simplicity of strongly drawn dualities (the either-ors), the uncomplicated adherence to one pole rather than the other and the comfort brought by the deceptive promise of one seemingly magical instructional solution for all children are welcome in educational settings that are often characterized, regrettably, by chaos, lack of time, deprivation of resources and underperformance. Either-ors are equally welcome as simplistic political solutions and battle cries—left/right, capitalist/socialist—in a politically, culturally and economically complex world.

Centrism, however, is often viewed in the contemporary United States as a position of indecision and weakness, an amorphous no-man's land possessing no force whatsoever. I ask you tonight to move beyond this inherited, limiting and unimaginative notion and begin the exploration and practice of framing centrism in a quite different way—an approach first recommended as distinctive to the United States by Ralph Waldo Emerson in his essay "Self Reliance"—a position that suggests that human cognitive force is actually achieved by an individual entertaining simultaneously a set of multiple, seemingly contradictory positions and applying each one selectively depending upon the situation at hand—not by staying the course with an educationally conservative or liberal set of practices, regardless of changing circumstance. Another way of putting this is that I ask you to entertain a sustained situational decisiveness that matches instructional imperatives with a vigorous array of well-defined strategies otherwise held mutually exclusive ideologically and thus devoid of the expansive power a full arsenal of instructional strategies might lend to help an individual student achieve (note the more forceful language of this reframed centrism). I am asking you to join with me and destroy the enduring cycle of mutually exclusive duality in educational practice from which there appears until now to be no escape.

As teachers and administrators in international schools, you are in a distinctive position to get not only accountability (or better, transparency) right for the sake of your current and future students, but also the two other challenges I presented tonight—self-esteem and either-ors. First, you are essentially free of the extremism of accountability as now offered in the United States (pending pressure exerted upon you by various external agencies that have taken up accountability in a big way without being absolutely clear what it is and what they are actually demanding of you! Luckily for you, your regional accrediting agency, SACS, is most reasonable and creative about accountability). Most of you here represent *independent* institutions and can live up to the full force of that word. You have choices that you can make free of encumbrance. You can stay free of the endless stream of buzzwords and ungrounded instructional strategies that bombard educators in your home countries every new academic year. Second, you possess a really big idea that can give you as protagonist substantive definition in your collective leadership story—global sensibility—a disposition that other sectors of education greatly need to (and want to) embrace—they are just not sure what it is because they have never fully engaged it. You have. You are living and teaching globally every day. Accompanying global sensibility is an acute appreciation of change since change amidst unpredictability is an integral part of existing daily on a global basis.

What, however, is global sensibility in education? It is the pursuit of all academic and co-curricular activities in a context that takes into account that which is occurring in other nations and among other cultures. It is a fundamental humility that exercises a check upon the imperialism and unilateralism of our own provincial ideas and is based upon the recognition that other nations and cultures possess notions we must gather from afar and integrate into our own pursuit for our own positive advancement. It is respect for the myriad ways of acquiring knowledge that are gained through the mastering of more than one language—not merely English. It is recognition that the English language has limitations and does not deliver all areas of knowledge we need for substantive, creative contribution. It is an obligation—through education and experience—to be comfortable and confident in an ever-changing world, a diverse set of communities, regardless of place. This is a sensibility that requires a certain type of educational institution—your type of school—actually defined years ago in general intent by Ralph Waldo Emerson. Emerson wrote, "[These schools] have their indispensable office—to teach elements.

But they can only highly serve us when they aim not to drill but to create, when they gather from afar every ray of various genius to their hospitable halls, and, by the concentrated fires, set the hearts of their youth on flame."

May you lead, made passionate by the "flame." Best wishes as you achieve your individual and collective leadership stories. Thank you for inviting me to AASAA and Asuncion, Paraguay, a country named, some believe, for a generosity and diversity of color—Paraguay—"a river of feathers" so called from the variety and brilliancy of its birds—Paraguay—"a variety of colors" evoked from not only its many birds, but its innumerable flowers—Paraguay— "spotted, speckled and multifaceted in display." My best wishes as you lean into the diversity and rich color that is also teaching at its most accomplished and useful.

Opening Remarks for Charting the Path for a Sustainable Dickinson
April 16, 2010

Welcome to Dickinson College's first sustainability summit. I thank all of you for making the effort to travel to Carlisle to participate in what I know will be an engaging and exciting conversation that is central to Dickinson's future.

My remarks this morning will be brief as you will have ample opportunity during the next day and a half to hear directly from faculty, students and others about the college's comprehensive environmental and sustainability initiatives—initiatives that cut across all aspects of college life, from the classroom to residential life to campus operations.

Although we have just recently created the Center for Environmental and Sustainability Education with the help of a $1.4 million grant from the Mellon Foundation, Dickinson's focus on these critical issues began several decades ago. We come by this focus naturally. We were, in fact, one of the first liberal-arts colleges to establish an interdisciplinary program in environmental studies in the 1970s. Our Alliance for Aquatic Resource Monitoring, or ALLARM program, which involves students in useful research with community groups, dates to 1986 when it was founded by Professor Candie Wilderman. And we have steadily been incorporating sustainable practices in our campus operations so that today, for example, 100 percent of the College's electricity consumption is offset through the use of wind power, and all of our construction projects are designed to gain LEED certification.

Our efforts have not gone unnoticed. In the past year alone, Dickinson was given an A- on the 2010 Sustainable Endowments Institute Report Card, the highest overall grade given by the organization. We are also listed as a "cool school" by the Sierra Club and as one of the 20 greenest colleges in America. And we earned a place on The Princeton Review's Green Honor Roll. Dickinson, moreover, was one of only five institutions to be listed on all three. The others were the University of New Hampshire, the University of Washington, Middlebury College and Harvard. Not bad company! And most recently—yesterday, in fact—we were notified of two additional awards garnered by the college. The U.S. Environmental Protection Agency (EPA) will announce on Monday, April 19, that Dickinson is the Centennial Conference's EPA College and University Green Power Champion. This award is in recognition of our efforts in green power use, leadership and distinction as a Green Power Conference Champion. And ALLARM has been chosen for the Pennsylvania Association of Environmental Professionals (PAEP) Karl Mason Award, given to the organization, project or program that has made a significant contribution toward maintenance or restoration of Pennsylvania's environmental quality.

Given the level of achievement and recognition we have already reached, you may wonder why we feel it is so important and necessary to convene this summit this weekend. While we have clearly emerged as a leader in this area, it is imperative that we continue to press forward to solidify our permanence and to ensure that sustainability becomes a unique and defining characteristic of a Dickinson education. Please remember that everything we do is directed to one purpose and one purpose only—preparing undergraduates for lives of professional high achievement and public service and commitment. Ambitious and successful institutions don't take time to rest on their laurels but always push for higher accomplishment. Other colleges and universities are already emulating our practices. Our challenge is to find ways to continue to set the standard in environmental and sustainability undergraduate education in the United States (and potentially globally, now with the Bologna accord introducing some uniformity to the degree process) as these issues are destined to play a central role in the 21st century.

There is, in fact, great urgency and a historic responsibility for us to do so. Our founder, Dr. Benjamin Rush, understood the importance of establishing a curriculum for Dickinson College and for the emerging United States of America immediately following the American Revolution that not only prepared students through a useful, intentional and pragmatic liberal-arts education to address contemporary societal needs, but he also anticipated future challenges and opportunities. It was for this reason that Rush insisted that chemistry—then a relatively new discipline typically not included in traditional Euro-centered curricula—be a cornerstone of Dickinson's academic program. Rush believed that chemistry would serve as the center of multiple points of connectivity from which new knowledge, new discoveries and new paradigms would emerge. If Dickinson graduates were to be the leaders of the new democracy and the new economy as Rush intended, they needed preparation in this key new discipline. They needed to be educated so as to be at the center of knowledge production and contribution.

Dickinson replicated this pattern of anticipating fundamental forces of change and connectivity to emerging educational trends several decades ago when we consciously chose to focus our efforts and resources on global education. Our experience with our Bologna program, which dates to the early 1960s, demonstrated how critical it was for students not only to be given the opportunity to study abroad, but also to integrate a global perspective throughout the curriculum. We anticipated that the world would become a smaller place in which travel and technology would blur national and cultural boundaries on many levels while, at the same time, exacerbating them in other ways. This world of heightened connectivity would demand the skills and understanding of those educated with a broad-based, interdisciplinary global perspective. Today, global education continues to be one of the central defining characteristics of a Dickinson education as we offer our students the opportunity to study in 40 programs in 24 countries on six continents and consciously provide a global context in all curricular and co-curricular activities.

And now, just one decade into the 21st century, we once again are anticipating the emergence of a major force that will both shape and challenge our future. Environmental and sustainability concerns now permeate virtually every issue, problem and opportunity at every conceivable level—local, state, national and global. Just as chemistry served as the central point of connectivity during Rush's time, we believe that sustainability occupies that place today and will continue to do so for this generation and those to follow.

Our graduates will be called upon to make some of the most difficult decisions about the future of our planet, which will require fundamental changes in individual behavior, global resource allocation and national and international policy. Breakthroughs in environmental technology will reconfigure our economy and workforce, just as they will pose threats to national security.

At Dickinson, we have a responsibility to prepare our students to meet these challenges. Environmental and sustainability education at Dickinson is not just a single class—or even just a concentration of major study. As with global education, we expect sustainability to pervade our curriculum and become an integral component of discussion in all subjects both in and out of the classroom. We expect it to become a way of life that asks us to reflect on our individual and collective behavior as members of an environmentally conscious community. And we expect our graduates to become recognized in the 21st century as those who are prepared to envision points of connection that will lead to creative and constructive solutions to tomorrow's environmental challenges.

This weekend's meetings will help shape the future of this important all-campus initiative. We want to use this time to tap your expertise and interest to help us identify the key elements of the undergraduate programs we are planning for the future. We hope an informal advisory network will emerge, with those of you here today serving as the core, to help us tackle these fundamental national and global issues that intersect so many areas of knowledge and activity. Your own networks will help us to develop wider-world opportunities like internships and service-learning projects that will shape the preparation of our students as global citizens ready to engage the important decisions, challenges and opportunities that will affect our planet now and in the future.

2012 CONVOCATION SPEECH:
FROM THE UNCERTAIN TO THE CONCRETE
Aug. 26, 2012

Welcome to Convocation, the official opening of the 2012-13 academic year of Dickinson College, the 240th year in our official history. Although we had hoped to be conducting this ceremony in front of Old West as usual, the weather had different intentions. But this provides us a moment to reflect upon rain, Carlisle, Pa., and Dickinson College. One hears frequently—certainly even in my days here as a student some five decades ago—that "it only rains in Carlisle" or "it rains all the time in Carlisle" as if no other place on earth has rain and a front sits right over our borough and comes from nowhere and goes nowhere. Well, one of the Dickinson Dimensions is to separate fact from inaccuracy, myth and rumor. So let's do so here. Quick referral to data maintained by the Weather Channel focusing on New York, New England, the Mid-Atlantic states and the South reveals, for example, that New York City averages annually 8.2 more inches of rain, Boston 2.1 more inches of rain, Baltimore 0.2 more inches, Wilmington, Del., 7.6 inches more, Atlanta, Ga., 8.1 inches more rain and sunny, beautiful Miami Beach, Fla., 10.0 inches, not to speak of sunny Naples, Fla., with 13.9 inches more rain. Thus, the beloved, treasured thought that it only rains in Carlisle is no more than urban myth. It is simply that you are here when it rains. So now that that issue is cleared up (although I have no confidence that the myth will cease; it is too delightful!), let us proceed.

I extend special greetings to the members of the class of 2016 and transfer students who are about to become lifelong Dickinsonians. I also welcome back our seniors for what will be their last year as undergraduates.

Convocation is intended not only to permit students, faculty and staff to assemble ceremoniously and commit as a community to the new academic year, but also—and rather mischievously—to provide an opportunity for a president to suggest to incoming students those big ideas that might concern you and engage your intellectual and emotional energies on and off campus during your undergraduate years. Given that, it is not uncommon for my comments to be provocative, not merely for the sake of the cognitive disruption they might cause, but also to indicate that this college is a noisy place and does not shy away from candor and reasoned, yet passionate engagement with issues that matter.

But first, let me offer a bit more about this ceremony.

At the conclusion of today's Convocation, weather permitting, you will walk to Old West—led by college marshals—to participate in one of Dickinson's most treasured traditions when you ascend the old stone steps into Memorial Hall to sign in to the college. Several years from now, you will reverse this symbolic action when you descend these same steps to receive your diploma and move beyond these limestone walls to engage the world as Dickinsonians. For the seniors who have joined us today, this rite of passage will occur in just nine short months.

When you ascend the old stone steps, be sure to glance to the right at the statue of our founder, Dr. Benjamin Rush. You will hear much about Dr. Rush over the next four years. Dr. Rush, a signer of the Declaration of Independence, serves as a constant reminder that Dickinson College is linked inextricably to the founding of our nation with all its triumphs and blemishes. By extension, you also are connected. Benjamin Rush was one of the most passionate and eloquent advocates of a distinctive American education—a useful liberal-arts education. His fundamental precepts offer us important directives as we explore ways to define the relevance and value of liberal education in our own rapidly changing, revolutionary era.

I begin by congratulating you on your decision to matriculate at Dickinson College for your undergraduate education. By so doing, you proclaim to the world that you desire the real thing—the "object itself"—in higher education and not a substitute. Let me explain what I mean. Two summers ago I read in the *International Herald Tribune* about the "exploding" audience for original works of art. The head of the venerable London auction house, Christie's, Steven P. Murphy, explained the increased appeal in the following words:

"I think that the virtual world, the ease of access to images in high definition, the total availability of art online—all those things have increased the value of the object itself." The role of an institution like Christie's, he says, is that of "honoring the object."

Well, in a strange way, Dickinson College is like Christie's—our primary mission is to "honor the object itself." You are the initiated who realize just how precious and ultimately useful the pursuit of the object itself is as opposed to its mere image—a facsimile—even if it costs more. Of course, it has to cost more! It is the "object itself!" It is created by high labor intensity and unfolds in intricate, complex precision. Undergraduate research universities, and increasingly colleges, are overwhelmingly filled with exceedingly large classes, radically diminished in- and out-of-class resources, graduate-student and adjunct instructors, professors obsessed with their own research agendas rather than your learning, online virtual courses, degree programs that often extend over six or more years because of the unavailability of required courses and an outcome-based accountability that neglects you and your complex development in its drive to be quantitatively precise.

Instead, you have chosen to experience a premier undergraduate education. This encompasses direct interaction with a small group of similarly motivated learners in a physically and emotionally safe 24/7 residential setting. It also includes interactions with dedicated professors—committed solely to you and your intellectual development, with sustained focus on original texts and objects, and engagement in those skills and experiences in and out of the classroom that mature your mind and emotion. And all of this is concentrated in an efficient four years of study. This object—as all such precious objects—costs a considerable amount to honor. And like the "object itself"—like the original work of art—it only continues to increase in value as its scarcity becomes apparent in a broader world where a mere reflection of the original undergraduate education seemingly and deceptively suffices.

Over the years I have also used these Convocation addresses to mentor students in a non-curricular way—to give advice that might prove helpful as you mature intellectually and emotionally. In reviewing my advice from the past 13 years, I realized that much of what I offered—even years ago—is still relevant for today's students. But rather than keep you in your seats here until nightfall, I decided to make the more provocative passages available to you on the college's Web site when this speech is posted tomorrow. I encourage you to take a few moments to read through these snippets at your convenience.

In terms of today's address, rather than looking backwards, I would instead like to look forward with the introduction of a new tradition at Dickinson College. While the tradition is new, it is composed of pieces of the college that have always existed, and that is comforting. I have merely assembled them in a new way.

Every summer my wife and I travel the world to challenge our preconceived notions, to unsettle the tyranny of familiar place—no matter how appealing and comfortable that place may be—and to remain receptive to seeing what always has been in ways that cause it perhaps to no longer be. I attribute this lifelong habit of purposeful, disruptive travel to my Dickinson junior year abroad in Freiburg many decades ago, when I was about your age and in this community as a student.

Two summers ago was no exception.

Among the cities we wanted to visit was Dresden, Germany. Our primary motivation was to experience its historically high level of cultural offerings in the arts. Additionally, we were curious about reports of its reconstruction after near total leveling in WWII and abject neglect during the Cold War Communist era. Dresden historically has attracted people as its citizens who defy authority and any limitation they perceive upon their personal freedom. It was, for example, an early location for the rise of the Reformation. A large statue of Martin Luther stands today in one of the city's main squares.

During the Revolution of 1848-49, they dramatically rose up against the dominant and oppressive nobility. In June 1953, citizens of Dresden rose in protest of East German communist rule and demanded freedom and the right to vote. They were violently suppressed by the ruling authorities. However, the Dresdeners have also partaken—as knowing silent witness or participant—in some of the most brutal events in human history, to include the elimination of Jews in WWII and the destruction of the historic synagogue in Dresden that served for centuries as the focal point of a vibrant community. On Nov. 9, 1933, the synagogue burned to the ground—excepting astonishingly the Star of David. Of the 20,000 Jews who resided in Dresden in 1933, fewer than 200 survived the war. The synagogue has since been rebuilt on the exact same historic site and rededicated in 2001. The Jewish community is thriving again in Dresden.

Dresden was also the scene of a massive, horrific firebombing in 1945—at the end of WWII—with the resultant destruction of just about all of the city's buildings and an overwhelming loss of life. Debates rage today as to whether this firebombing by the British and Americans was really necessary, as the war was essentially over. Priceless historical treasures were lost in the act. A friend of the college through our long-standing partnership with the University of East Anglia, the late W.G. Sebald, published an extremely controversial book on the bombing titled *On the Natural History of Destruction.* Among the historic buildings totally razed—fried actually—was the architecturally exquisite Frauenskirche. This building was, however, also recently rebuilt and reopened in 2010 and is located only meters from the synagogue.

While my wife and I were walking past the brilliantly reconstructed Frauenskirche on the old marketplace square, I noticed fragments of a surviving old stonewall on display and a pile of little stones scattered at its base. There was also a message in German accompanying the stones. It read as follows:

> [In 2011] the 'Church Day' began with a procession from the Old Marketplace to the synagogue

for the express purpose of being reminded of the destruction of Jewish life in Dresden, of the guilt and complicity of the church and of the courage of some unspoken heroes. Those who marched [from the Frauenskirche to the Synagogue] carried these stones that you see before you on the ground. History is concrete. Whoever returns and communicates this message to his or her community may take one of the stones and present it to his community.

Well, I have indeed returned, and I give to this community one of those small stones that is so filled with meaning. I commit it to our archives.

I ask you as a community to look long and hard at this stone from Dresden and what it means. I ask you—especially those just joining the Dickinson community as undergraduates—to pause and reflect on how you want to live your life here and beyond. What kind of community do you want for yourself and those around you? What is the quality of life you want to establish and protect? How will you protect that life? For the new students, you have begun to articulate those aspirations in the life-path letter that you will deposit as you ascend the old stone steps. This is a letter that you will review periodically throughout your time at Dickinson and beyond to assess your progress in advancing quality of life and commitment to community.

Most profoundly, this stone from Dresden in particular, reminds us all of the extreme danger and harm of unmitigated hate, intolerance, misinformation, greed, ungrounded idealism, ignorance and racism—dispositions that can all too readily be exercised even in this college community. This stone likewise asks us to secure a world of understanding, tolerance and forgiveness. We also must pursue actively these attributes in our college community. But it also asks that we never forget—never—the destruction that people can inflict so readily upon others through action (violence) or words (rumor).

And, lastly, this stone has everything to do with identity—who one is and how one will act. An American undergraduate education for young people of your age is first and foremost about identity—identity formation. Academic skills, competencies and knowledge gained over the next few years and your engagement in out-of-class activities are essential to identity formation. They inform your subsequent ability to evaluate and absorb new knowledge and to live a life of fulfilling quality and commitment to citizenship. The undergraduate years are both an exhilarating and fearful period. (And it is OK to be apprehensive—everybody is, or at least they should be if they are honest with themselves!) You are inheriting the responsibility of defining who you are and how you will think, feel and act for a lifetime. The process you confront is, I think, best described in D.H. Lawrence's novel *The Rainbow*. With reference to his character Ursula at about the age of 17:

> As Ursula passed from girlhood towards womanhood, gradually the cloud of self-responsibility gathered upon her. She became aware of herself, that she was a separate entity in the midst of an unseparated obscurity, that she must go somewhere, she must be something. And she was afraid, troubled. Why, oh why must one grow up, why must one inherit this heavy, numbing responsibility of living an undiscovered life? Out of the nothingness and the undifferentiated mass, to make something of herself! But what? In the obscurity and the pathlessness to take a direction! But whither? How take even one step? And yet, how stand still? This was torment indeed, to inherit the responsibility of one's life.

Let us remember: History is concrete; this stone I hold is concrete, and your identity is ultimately concrete. It is who you are when you cease becoming. (Of course, there are arguments that one never ceases becoming; but the ages 18-21 are especially intense, formative years in human development.) And your identity is of your making. It lies in formation before you at this college and to be formed among the people with you today and those with whom you will connect through this community over the next few years. But please remember that even for Ursula in *The Rainbow* identity is a formative, constructive process out of vagueness, uncertainty and lack of concreteness—"How to become oneself, how to know the question and the answer of oneself, when one was merely an unfixed something—nothing, blowing about like the winds of heaven, undefined, unstated." Identity formation involves trials and errors, risk and restraint, responsibility and obligation and most of all attention—"attention must be paid" by you and this community as you progress the next few years from somebody arguably "unfixed" and only vaguely stated to a concrete personality ready to engage the world.

As you begin your tenure at the college, it is important to be reminded that the actions you take and the decisions you make—the wise ones and, unfortunately, those not so wise—are indeed ultimately concrete and will set the pattern for who you are as a person both at college and beyond.

To remind you of the concreteness of your college experience, of our community of opportunity and obligation, and of the self-responsibility of identity, I begin a new tradition at the college. It is based on the stone I just presented to the college and the recognition of the role that stones—limestone—have played in the history of our college. It was the architect of the U.S. Capitol, Benjamin Latrobe, who designed West College, or Old West, and decided that our campus should be a limestone one. We also have our own quarry not located far from here.

As you, the new students, ascend the old stone steps to sign into the college formally, you can pick up your very own piece of limestone—a piece from the quarry—the very same quarry that supplied the stones for Old West. You shall take the stone, and you shall give us your life-plan letter. You may keep the stone for your years as an undergraduate. It is your concrete link to your aspirations for yourself and our community. It is a symbol of your identity in formation. At your Commencement, I ask each of you to bring your stone with you. As you descend the steps to receive your diploma, you will face a choice between two equally valid actions. You may retain the stone and refer to it for a lifetime—a reminder of your opportunities and obligations to yourself and others—or you may return your stone as you receive your diploma. This stone will then be "recycled" and given to the next generation of students. These simple gray pieces of limestone unify us as Dickinsonians and signal to the wider world that we build community stone by stone, thought by thought, action by action. We carry the limestone!

New students, as Dickinsonians, you will carry a unique historic legacy into the future as the engaged citizens and leaders of your generation. Again, you carry the limestone. This stone concretely represents our obligation and our opportunity. We are together Dickinsonians for life.

CONVOCATION ADVICE THROUGH THE YEARS

Over the years I have used my Convocation addresses to mentor students in a non-curricular way—to give advice that might prove helpful as students mature intellectually and emotionally. Here are some of the more provocative passages that will continue to resonate with today's students.

2000

To the newest Dickinsonians—welcome to Dickinson. Lean into it intensely as all those before you have. Engage it with intellect, good humor and passion. Engage yourself, engage Dickinson, engage America, engage the world. And above all, preserve and always advance Dickinson College's reputation and visibility as one of America's most distinguished independent, residential, liberal-arts colleges.

2001

Avoid those social and ideological cliques that, while seemingly offering friendship, consensus and comfort, inappropriately circumscribe your experience and connection to people and events—those groups that seek sameness and control, not diversity and exploration. Do not betray your individuality at the very moment it is prepared to grow and serve you well for a lifetime.

Serve the spirit and intention of our founder—be a revolutionary in thought and action. Challenge your own future and that of your generation with a vengeance. A life defined by feigned boredom, adolescent cynicism, preoccupation with the mundane and the trivial is not an option for a Dickinsonian. Our only path is that of an energetically engaged, useful life in issues that matter.

2002

Seize as many opportunities as you can—but also select them carefully. Merely being busy is not a virtue. Remember Benjamin Rush—education must, above all, be ultimately useful. It must serve a noble purpose. To achieve this requires discipline and focus.

2003

Liberal education favors a life of rational argument and integrity with accompanying civility based on "what is" rather than a life skillfully crafted on rumor, pretension, invention, preconceived bias and what is clearly not. The latter—like the ubiquitous talk shows—may, indeed, be momentarily entertaining. Rumor and unexamined claims are always easy and invigorating, but they are ultimately dishonest, unfulfilling and unworthy of pursuit.

2004
THE DICKINSON DIMENSIONS

High Accomplishment Pursued Modestly: Be solid enough in personal identity to think for yourselves and be guided in your choices at college by the strength that comes from such self-knowledge. I urge you now to get a grip as soon as possible on the absurdity of status anxiety and peer pressure. Discuss them and their potential effect with your new classmates here at Dickinson. Make them a subject of extended late-night conversation. Embrace rather a Dickinson dimension of self-knowledge and independent thought guided by community values. At Dickinson, liberal education does not intend you to abdicate judgment in favor of others' opinions and to be at the mercy of those who intend you to be actors on their own foolish stage. Be extraordinary rather than merely ordinary by being yourself. Be rather than seem. "To be rather than to seem" was actually the family motto of our college namesake, John Dickinson. We come by this dimension naturally.

Speaking out Passionately for What You Know to be True and Believe Important: A second Dickinson habit of mind is to speak out passionately for what you know to be true and believe important and to do so in an informed manner. Again, at Dickinson we seek what is indeed the case, what is fact, not merely what seems to be. This habit of mind demands self-discipline. A Dickinson liberal-arts education asks of you a life of rational argument and integrity. Our community asks that you argue on the basis of what is in fact the case rather than what might be fueled by rumor, invention or your preconceived biases and ideologies and those of others. This requires restraint and hard intellectual work—we must learn to listen carefully, to investigate thoroughly before conclusion (to include the human decency of going first to the source of an issue of reputed controversy to get another perspective than that in common circulation), to make sure that we speak from a single point of reference (this is simply good scholarship) and to argue ultimately with civility—that is, to question the issue, not attack the person.

Global Sensibility: Embracing global sensibility is for you a priceless advantage and privilege for a life of high accomplishment in the globally complex world that is the 21st century. Dickinson College gives you that world.

2005

Defying Your Generation's Stereotypes—Dickinson-Style

Note: This year, alumni were asked to provide advice to the incoming class, and the quotes below are from them.

"Read the books on the reading list," wrote one alum. "You will never have as much time to read them again."

"I know I missed a huge portion of the Dickinson experience by not immersing myself fully in the academic life of the college," wrote another alum. "If I could do it again, I would not let the excitement of campus life, new friends or living on my own overshadow the true gift of a college education—the opportunity to think about and explore new ideas in a leisurely and self-directed manner. Never again will I have the luxurious amounts of time to dig deeper to learn about whatever captures my interest ... Never again will I be surrounded by such ... fascinating educators and peers who were so willing to teach me so much!"

"Don't worry too much about class selection," advised another, "and I (as someone hiring you) won't either. Take the courses necessary for your major—but also take those that capture your interest. Dickinson provides wonderful opportunities for learning in lots of areas—by all means take advantage of them."

"Take risks," urged yet another alum. "Try courses out of your chosen field ... There is plenty of time and room to explore and learn for the sake of learning."

"Don't be afraid to address huge global issues with your fellow students," advised another. "Dickinson is all about the discourse of ideas and options."

As one alum put it, "What has affected my life the most is the ability to think across disciplines, to see connections between conflicting ideas, to perceive overriding themes and patterns in complex contexts. You can't learn to stretch your brain unless you approach and wrestle with new ideas."

"Learn how to write." "Learn a second language." And most importantly, "Learn how to learn. Life should be an ongoing learning process. It doesn't stop when you get your degree. Dickinson is a superb place to try out different learning styles. Determine what works best for you and make it an intrinsic part of your life."

"Study abroad, study abroad, study abroad," wrote not one, but many alums. The time spent abroad was clearly a turning point for those who had the opportunity to do so. "Dickinson prepared me to be a 'citizen of the world,'" reported one alum. Another wanted me to remind current students that "America needs ambassadors to the world who display prowess and sensitivity. You cannot know the whole world well; you cannot affect all places; but you can know one place well and be an ambassador there for our nation—one who will belie the stereotype of the well-entertained and aloof American."

Other alums spoke of the attitudes and outlooks they thought befitted a true Dickinsonian. "Lack cynicism," urged an alum. "I know it's hard these days to show idealism, but it's the only attitude that makes anything truly important happen."

"Persevere," wrote another. "Significant, worthwhile achievements generally take a long time. If you are embarking on a slightly new or different path, you will encounter many obstacles and receive little positive reinforcement. You will need perseverance."

"Dickinson is a place where you can learn not only from classes and books, but also from your relationships and experiences outside the classroom," wrote one alum. "The way you spend your time when you are not in academic pursuits will also define the way you grow and mature into the person you are meant to be."

I encourage you, therefore, to stretch your social circles. Aim to connect with those you might not normally approach. Remember, as another alum put it, "Each person at Dickinson is unique, each has his or her own story and we have so much to learn from each other. Tell the class of 2009 to not only engage the world, but to engage each other."

Allow me to close with yet one final quote from an alumna, class of 2001: "You will be successful—if you want to be. If you take advantage of all Dickinson has to offer, there is no doubt you will be prepared for the world. ... It will be amazing to you how far ahead of the game you will be when you leave. ... It didn't take me long to realize that I was unique, that no one else had the opportunities I did and that no one else around me was as prepared and mature as I was. I didn't have a college experience; I had a Dickinson College experience. There is a difference."

2006

It is counterproductive to apply the statement, "you are not listening to me," when attempting to get what you want from someone such as a faculty member or administrator. What you really mean by "you are not listening to me" is "you are not agreeing with me!" Expect people on occasion not to agree with you at this college. There are often conflicting positions toward issues, and they are equally valid.

You also will probably initially be stunned that your immediate opinions about people or events—even incidents you hear about on campus—do not receive serious consideration unless they are informed by facts (and in some disciplinary issues the facts cannot, by federal law, be revealed). Rumors need substantiation; they are not a form of entertainment. They hurt other people needlessly, and they ultimately turn the source of rumors into unlikable people. The mere rush to statement and the expression of what you *feel* about someone or something are of a far lesser order in this college community (and ultimately in the wider world) than substantive, responsible communication. Such rashness is particularly inflamed by the instantaneous nature of e-mail or tweets.

2007
The Defining Dimensions of a Dickinson Education

I urge you while at Dickinson to study and explore the Bible, the Koran, the Upanishads, the myths and cultures of ancient Egypt, Greece and Rome, Confucian teachings, the Renaissance, the Reformation, the Enlightenment, modernism, postmodernism, the scientific and technological revolutions, capitalism, communism and socialism. You should also seek those counter texts and theories of marginalized groups that have been largely ignored or forgotten entirely in the above litany. I challenge you to be demanding of yourself, your fellow students and our faculty and to engage fully in this dynamic community of inquiry. Do not forgo this rare opportunity—these very few years to absorb unimpeded those intellectual fundamentals that will guide you for a lifetime.

I also challenge you to use the knowledge and critical-thinking skills you acquire through your academic pursuits to engage the world beyond the classroom. Engage experience. Strive to apply your intellectual acumen to your own life and your community.

You will "engage the world" in the ultimate meaning of that phrase only when you confront and absorb conflicting intellectual material and points of view—those that extend well beyond what you already know and that often confound positions you already believe are securely yours.

2008
Global Environmental Sustainability: An Unprecedented Challenge for Your Generation

Indeed, I hope that you experience many moments of instructive discomfort during your years at Dickinson. Your Dickinson liberal education—fully embraced—will ask you to directly confront and come to grips with the very notion of fundamental change and ask you to re-evaluate what you know or believe you know, even though you might end up reconfirming a good deal of your existing knowledge and beliefs after thorough examination.

We have before us a remarkable opportunity to embrace change as a community of inquiry. To accept change, you must be willing to explore your level of discomfort and not be afraid to voice well-reasoned opinions and concerns. We encourage you to engage in spirited conversation about environmental and sustainability issues with your peers, your professors and campus administrators. Don't hesitate to responsibly question new campus policies and seek evidence of their effectiveness. Think broadly about the state of the global environment. Talk with those who have studied abroad about environmental concerns and policies in other countries. Quite simply, engage the world.

I urge you to take advantage of this opportunity for engagement with the issues of your generation both in and out of the classroom. I know that the majority of you will do so. But I am a realist and I, too, learn from experience. I know that some of you will be inclined to enter your college career luxuriating in uninformed cynicism, lethargy and indifference. But let me suggest that what was fashionable behavior in high school is no longer so. Passivity and the cultivation of indifference will not prepare you for a life of engagement and fulfillment. Nor will those behaviors that compromise the quality of our community of inquiry. Disruption and inattention to speakers and others who enrich our campus life are demonstrations of pure self-indulgence and immature ways of being that are totally inconsistent with the vibrant and engaging environment we offer. Passivity, the cultivation of indifference, insincere cynicism and disruptive inattention are but immature self-indulgence, a glorious waste of your and our time and unworthy of all the reasons for which you have chosen Dickinson as your undergraduate institution and we have chosen you to be among us.

2009

FRONTIER PRAGMATISM: THE IMPORTANCE OF PLACE IN AN UNDERGRADUATE EDUCATION

We must, however, acknowledge that with noise comes responsibility. Civility cannot be assumed or simply inherited. Every cohort of students, faculty and staff has to reinvent and recommit to civil discourse not only in words, but also in deeds. Listening in a sustained and focused way is an indispensable part of speaking out responsibly. It is foolhardy merely to prepare in your mind your response to a person while he is speaking to you and in so doing, disregard understanding his position while you blithely assert yours. It is foolhardy to bring to a conversation a predetermined ideology that you attempt to force—loudly and disruptively—upon another person simply to remain the last person talking—never growing in perception or understanding. It is foolhardy to assert that a person is not listening to you—not valuing you as a person—when what you really mean is that she is not agreeing with you. It is foolhardy to perpetuate rumors before proactively investigating their origin and accuracy or their particular context—a most common malady on college campuses that is both destructive and dangerous to you as an individual and the community of which you are a member.

You will be able to stand firm in your convictions and find the courage to be tenacious in the face of adversity if you have taken the time to validate the foundations of your views. If you have not made sure of the distinction between what is true and what is not, if you lash out rashly with accusation against or about others, if you like to be cynical and incorrect for the sake of merely being so, you will at the very least discredit yourself and most likely advance needless alarm in the community, as well as potentially malign another person or group.

2010

IN DEFENSE OF OUR COMMITMENT

Academically we urge you to see relationships from one course to another and to take risks by enrolling for elective courses well beyond your comfort zone. Only then do you expand your preconceived notion of yourself and your talents. Out of class, we urge you to engage people who are dissimilar to you and to be surprised that your preconceived notions of the world and its people just might at this early stage be premature. What I often hear from some alumni is regret that while they were students their preconceptions about people actually thwarted them in growing as a person. They often ask why in the world they did not talk to someone who later turned out to be quite interesting only because in their youthful preconceptions they thought the person was not "cool." We also encourage you to think outside your current portfolio of personal interests and consider joining or trying out entirely new groups or activities. This is the perfect place to go in new directions.

2011
Changing More Than Just the Size and Color of the Room

You assume the personal responsibility and exercise the restraint that permits the existence of a civil and tolerant community. By your words and actions, you create a community that is safe and accommodating to all responsible identities.

On a related note, your experiences both in and out of the classroom will determine your advancement as an informed, increasingly mature and tolerant person nurtured by a liberal-arts course of study and an undergraduate residential life. You will have to think more intentionally about why you are in college—at Dickinson—and who you are and wish to be as a result of your time in this community. Beliefs and behaviors will undergo intensive examination and perhaps need to change.

JUST DO SCIENCE: A LIBERAL-ARTS COLLEGE PERSPECTIVE ON TEACHING THE SCIENCES TO UNDERGRADUATES, KEYNOTE ADDRESS AT JOHNS HOPKINS UNIVERSITY'S GATEWAY SCIENCES INITIATIVE SYMPOSIUM
Jan. 17, 2013

I am delighted to participate in this engaging meeting at my graduate alma mater focused on the continuing improvement of gateway science education at Johns Hopkins. Thank you for the invitation.

I intend to offer concluding remarks to the day's activities that introduce you to some best practices in teaching the sciences at a representative liberal-arts college—my undergraduate alma mater and the college of which I am currently president, Dickinson—a college that arguably has been a leader in undergraduate science pedagogy in the United States. I believe that it is especially important for you to be familiar with what we do because of the results we in the liberal-arts sector achieve through science education. Victor Ferrall Jr., a former colleague at Beloit College, cites key data points in his book, provocatively titled *Liberal Arts at the Brink*, that may be of interest: "Twenty-eight of the 50 baccalaureate-granting institutions that, proportionate to their size, graduated the most science and engineering doctorate recipients from 1997-2006 were liberal-arts colleges."

Of course, I am keenly aware that we in the liberal-arts college sector do not possess a magic potion and that, in turn, we could learn a great deal about science advancement from a major research university such as Hopkins. I share then to grasp the best of both worlds for a shared purpose and to challenge you to determine whether what I describe can be adapted to science teaching at Hopkins. The obvious issues to reconcile are mission, class size, pedagogy, classroom design and disciplinary ownership.

I assert four points of differentiation between Dickinson and Hopkins in the teaching of science (of course, I do so dangerously, not knowing in detail what you do currently!): history and mission, pedagogy, student-faculty research and interdisciplinarity. I am dismissing one point of distinction I hear often among my colleagues at liberal-arts colleges because I believe it is bogus. Some claim that liberal-arts undergraduate colleges have better results with science education because they do *not* have graduate programs. Faculty do not have to direct time and energy, as well as intellectual capital, to graduate students who are attending the university to accomplish research toward a Ph.D., and, in turn, they do not have to spend an inordinate amount of time seeking grants to support an elaborate graduate-school-oriented agenda. I reject this notion because I believe that good undergraduate science teaching can benefit from a graduate research university environment in many ways (resources, scope of study, contact with bright, striving graduate students and shared research projects), if—but only if—the university makes an effort to diminish any unnecessary divide in terms of instructional support and the personalization of teaching and learning. Unfortunately that does not happen at all research universities—undergraduates are not always given the attention they need to be prepared for both science literacy and advanced study in the sciences. Additionally, if I were to defend this claim of my liberal-arts colleagues, I would give an exceedingly short presentation, as Hopkins, I trust, is not about to forgo its distinguished graduate programs—its DNA from its founding and the base, I believe, of its most creative possibilities for enhanced undergraduate teaching in its future.

Dickinson comes by its scientific disposition quite naturally. Its founder, Dr. Benjamin Rush, was not only a signer of the Declaration of Independence but a physician and scientist. He argued for Dickinson College in 1783 to reject the "monkish" higher education inherited from the elite British and to adopt a new form of education—a *useful* liberal education—suited to the new and emerging democratic form of government that was the United States of America.

Dr. Rush centered the new American higher education on the sciences—particularly chemistry (he was, of course, America's first professor of chemistry at what is now the University of Pennsylvania). It was this subject, he believed, that would have the most connectivity to emerging fields—fields that, in turn, would help the nation grow in political substance and financial stability. In a 1787 letter to Jonathan Smith, he wrote, "Chemistry is not only a science of importance in itself, but serves as a key to a thousand other sources of knowledge." Already we perceive that, for Dr. Rush, science in America's undergraduate liberal-arts curriculum was of central importance. Its influence extended well beyond the confines of the subject area itself. Dr. Rush understood that the study of science in America had to be about something larger than the subject itself to capture the energy and creativity of the population. For him, that something larger was informed participation in an emerging democracy. The teaching of science brought students directly into the progress of humanity and democracy.

It is precisely at this early point in my presentation that a difference of founding missions between liberal-arts colleges and particularly Johns Hopkins—albeit representative of all major research universities—must be mentioned, as it could well confound Hopkins adopting anything I say today about science instruction among liberal-arts colleges. Hopkins was, of course, founded "to realize the scholarly ideal of an institution devoted to the *creation* of knowledge" (from Richard A. DeMillo, in *Abelard to Apple*). As Daniel Coit Gilman so explicitly stated, at Hopkins, "No love of ease, no dread of labor, no fear of consequences, no desire for wealth will avert a band of well-chosen professors from uniting their forces in the persecution of study. … By their labors, knowledge has been accumulated, intellectual capital has been acquired." Clearly the primacy of university activity and distinction is located in outstanding faculty who are singularly devoted to the creation of knowledge. However, this focus on professors is problematic historically, as noted by Richard A. DeMillo: "But it was always a delicate, and sometimes confusing balance—even for Johns Hopkins—between research and teaching the thousands of students who were pouring into colleges and universities and whose interests did not necessarily lie in the laboratory."

An early graduate of Dickinson and later professor, Spencer Fullerton Baird—of course, the second secretary of the Smithsonian Institution—introduced field study into the American curriculum for the express purpose of teaching science. For the first time in American educational history, students went out of the classroom and into—in this case—the surrounding Central Pennsylvania mountains to gather specimens that were later classified and studied in a college laboratory. The formal acquisition of science in our institutions lost its fixedness to confined space and extended out into the world. Students and their professor were involved directly in the collection and the analysis of scientific data.

Let us now fast-forward a few centuries. In the 1980s, before many of our peer institutions, Dickinson embarked on a comprehensive, long-term science initiative that has included an infusion of new faculty, innovative pedagogy and curriculum, and upgraded instrumentation and facilities. Critical components of this initiative have been the application of active, discovery-oriented approaches to science education and the integration of student research throughout the curriculum. Numerous liberal-arts colleges and some universities have adapted their science instruction to this model. Progress began with the development of an award-winning program of Workshop Physics in the 1980s funded extensively by the National Science Foundation—throwing away the textbook and permitting students to discover scientific principles by personal experimentation. This was followed by curricular reforms in mathematics, geology, chemistry and biology in the 1990s. More recently, the college has instituted new programs in biochemistry & molecular biology (BMB) and neuroscience and explored the role of bioinformatics, genomics and nanoscience in the undergraduate curriculum.

Science education at Dickinson focuses on the following goals:

* participatory, discovery-oriented pedagogy for both majors and non-majors

* opportunities for students and faculty to engage in intensive research, often leading to publication in peer-reviewed scientific journals and presentations at professional conferences

* and encouragement of faculty and students to engage in interdisciplinary science and to write frequently about their progress and discovery.

The combination of pedagogical innovation, a research-intensive curriculum, an emphasis on interdisciplinarity and—as importantly—writing has produced, I believe, an exceptionally dynamic undergraduate science program at Dickinson with very positive commitments of our graduates to continued engagement in science as researchers, practitioners and informed citizens.

First and foremost, most introductory science courses at Dickinson—and increasing numbers of intermediate and advanced courses—focus on active learning using discovery-based approaches, enhanced fieldwork, and/or laboratory-based investigation of issues and themes. Implementation of this pedagogy across all disciplines has placed Dickinson on the vanguard of national science-education reform. Retired faculty members Priscilla Laws in physics and Nancy Baxter Hastings in mathematics pioneered the workshop method of science teaching. Their work centers on the principle that students learn most effectively through direct and active experimentation. Similarly, our faculty introduced a discovery-based approach to biology and geology by building introductory courses around themes such as cancer or global warming.

Discovery-based teaching and learning also has influenced the design and equipment of many science classrooms and laboratories. For example, spaces in our Tome Scientific Building were specially configured and equipped with computers and other technology to support the Workshop Physics and Workshop Mathematics curricula. Cooperative-learning design was complemented by the immediacy of experimentation space. In biology, a grant from Merck in 1996 enabled us to equip laboratories and classrooms for physiological and pharmacological research. Very early, therefore, our faculty and students were engaged in our construction process and guaranteed that what was built met completely their emerging needs for teaching informed by research. Form met function head on, and faculty were engaged architects of their instructional space.

In addition, the college's recent and successful $150 million campaign provided funds for the construction of the first two wings of the new Rector Science Complex, which opened for classes in fall 2008. Featuring 90,000 square feet of laboratories, classrooms and research facilities, Rector houses the entire department of chemistry, as well as portions of biology and psychology relating to our interdisciplinary program in neuroscience. It includes areas of inquiry in place of the traditional department structure—meaning that groups of offices, laboratories, classrooms and equipment are largely grouped by function, rather than by department. Offices and laboratories of biologists are situated next to those of psychologists in neuroscience, and the chemists' offices are spread through both wings. Rector has a vivarium on its lower level shared by biology and psychology. Since the opening of this new building we have seen a steady increase in student enrollment in introductory biology, chemistry, neuroscience and BMB courses—especially among women. A further expansion is currently underway to enhance our science facilities and unify all members of the biology department in the Rector facility.

The college itself also actively encourages curricular development. Many of the external grants noted above—and there are many more—were secured by faculty who first received planning grants for their ideas from the college's own Research and Development Committee.

Discovery-oriented teaching at Dickinson mirrors a strong focus on research by faculty and students. We strive for a student-centered experience in which faculty self-interest is balanced by student needs and interest. Dickinson requires senior science majors to conduct capstone research. We also encourage interested students to work one-on-one with faculty for intensive research collaboration either in the summer or during the academic year.

Beyond the undergraduate-assistant roles that many faculty have incorporated into their own research proposals, Dickinson has won multiple institutional grants specifically for collaborative student-faculty research. Over a decade ago, external grants helped us establish a regular summer program of student-faculty research projects.

Thanks to a challenge grant and the generosity of alumni and friends, considerable internal funds are now available for summer projects through the college's own Student-Faculty Research Endowment.

Dickinson faculty members also have worked to ensure that students understand and experience the increasing interconnectedness and interdisciplinarity of modern science—that they appreciate collaboration—a principle already suggested in the 18th century by our founder. The college has made many strides in recent years to break down disciplinary silos and to build a curriculum that encourages problem posing and solving from multiple perspectives. For example, our BMB major, created in 1997, combines the teaching and research expertise of faculty in biology, chemistry, physics and mathematics. BMB joined Dickinson's existing interdisciplinary environmental-studies major, which integrates work in biology, chemistry, earth science, environmental science and policy studies. Most recently, Dickinson's commitment to interdisciplinary science prompted the creation of a new major in neuroscience, composed of coursework at the intersection of biology, chemistry and bio-psychology.

Dickinson has also worked to develop interdisciplinary bridges among the sciences, humanities, arts and social sciences. External grants funded the construction of new laboratories in archaeology and biological anthropology. In addition to providing arenas for the further application of discovery-based pedagogy, these new labs extend the reach of the sciences. Archaeology now actively integrates geology with the classics, art history and history. Anthropology and its collaborating major in sociology now have a strong grounding in biology.

Dickinson has made great progress in interdisciplinary science with the help of a grant from the Andrew W. Mellon Foundation in 2008. We established a Center for Sustainability Education (CSE) to serve as a point of connection for all academic activities and resources at Dickinson related to the study of sustainability. CSE is working across the curriculum to link classroom learning with co-curricular programs, greening of campus operations (facilities), and both global and local civic engagement.

We have also been assisting other institutions in increasing their interdisciplinary approaches to learning. With a grant from NASA's Global Climate Change Education Program, Dickinson is leading a consortium involved in the teaching of global climate change in the liberal-arts curriculum at four-year and two-year colleges. Members are jointly implementing a multifaceted campaign to build faculty competency for interdisciplinary teaching about climate change and developing and implementing a core curriculum of climate change-focused courses.

Dickinson's ambition to have its science students and faculty profit intellectually from interdisciplinarity and collaboration appears to challenge longstanding practice in the academy. Richard A. DeMillo describes the challenge: "Academic biographies—especially in the sciences—are filled with stories of stars who are not only distrustful of methods and techniques they did not create themselves, but also are actually disdainful of lessons that could be drawn from related fields. Many prefer instead to invent everything that needs to be invented to solve the problem at hand. Fearful of committing themselves to courses of action, they are often suspicious of strategy. They have been rewarded for solving problems in isolation from distracting contexts." In contrast, Dickinson intends by its discovery-based instruction to prepare a different kind of mind for a different kind of graduate—one that can recognize problems, create, make connections among seemingly disparate elements and thread meaning and application from the juxtaposition of past, present and future.

When I was preparing this presentation, I asked our science professors to tell me what they thought was distinctive about how they taught science—especially in contrast to what they were familiar with as TAs at the excellent graduate institutions they attended to receive Ph.D.s. The response was unequivocal. To a person they declared, "*we do science!*" Being a humanist I asked for clarity. The response was clear, "We personally take students through the scientific method. We are in this jointly. The students are partners with us at the undergraduate level and our research is intended solely to improve their introduction into the complexities and mysteries to which science permits access and solution."

Another faculty member attributes the apparent success of the science program to the college's substantial investment in sophisticated equipment in the 1980s, continuing through today—equipment normally only available to graduate students. Such equipment directly in the undergraduate classroom and used daily by undergraduate students facilitates an immediacy of problem posing, research methodology, data collection and analysis, thus eliminating the delay associated with sending classroom data to an external third party for tabulation. All students respond positively to this immediacy of result—but especially those who are nonscience majors.

Another professor stresses that, while the physical arrangement of a classroom is often thought to be the most important ingredient in the success of workshop science, this is not the case. The most important ingredient is the curriculum and its adaptation to workshop pedagogy and discovery learning. The curriculum must be conceived such that the student discovers for herself, at the data collection and analysis points, the logical link between what has been engaged and observed and an understanding of the associated general principles.

Yet another example comes from a senior English professor—of all things!—who participated in a Mosaic program this fall. At Dickinson a Mosaic is an intensive, interdisciplinary, semesterlong research program designed around ethnographic fieldwork and immersion in domestic and global communities. In this particular Mosaic, titled "Natural History Sustainability Mosaic," students spent the entire semester with three professors engaged in natural-history field work informed by both an array of sciences and a commitment to intensive writing. Considerable emphasis was directed to writing about scientific matters as a 19th-century English essayist or science journalist and how to engage in citizen-science that can be communicated to fellow citizens and national and international leaders. This mosaic is a prime example of utilizing small class size, interdisciplinarity and beneficial balance of core classes with focused topic work so that our students see science as part of the wider world and as part of their lives beyond graduation. The professor with whom I spoke admitted that the size of the class does matter and that such results would be extremely difficult to achieve in a large research-university setting—particularly at the introductory levels. (But might the creative use of MOOCs and other digital technologies in a blended instructional context overcome this apparent obstacle? More on this later.)

The comprehensive pedagogical principle behind "just doing science" extends today to most areas of the Dickinson curriculum. It complements work initiated in disciplines other than science at the college. It involves our students in an activist, useful liberal-arts education wherein their direct confrontation with, and manipulation of, existing knowledge causes them to connect the dots among reflection, engagement, understanding and application. Such a compelling dynamic is essential, we believe, to accomplish the ambition of a 21st-century undergraduate education and to set the stage for the more focused creation of new knowledge in graduate students and professions. There are several examples at Dickinson including the engagement of our students directly in excavation at the ancient Greek city of Mycenae, as we possess the exclusive rights for such activity; also, an environmental outreach project throughout Pennsylvania, known as ALLARM, which engages our students in helping citizens evaluate regularly the quality of water in local streams and rivers. Another project has our students combing historical records to establish and maintain one of the most thorough online repositories of families involved in the American Civil War. This much acclaimed effort is called A House Divided. And then, there is the senior art-history majors' project that requires students to prepare an exhibition from beginning to end—in all aspects—and that has been cited for its contribution to Dickinson joining Williams College in graduating the most museum professionals among liberal-arts colleges.

But "doing science" and discovery-based teaching/learning extends well beyond academics and into some surprising places at Dickinson—for example, into student life. Connectivity is reaching new levels of complexity and applicability. Dickinson presents its students with a series of axioms to guide their thoughts and actions while at college and to serve as reasonable mentorship for what lies beyond in the wider world. We call these the Dickinson Dimensions. And for the past few years, the Dimensions have been guiding the evolution of our residential-life/student-development effort. More and more opportunities are being created for and with students to exercise these dimensions in residential activities that increasingly cross with academic life. Here are a few of the Dimensions:

- Associate confidently in unfamiliar environments.

- Move beyond that which is comfortable to embrace intellectual risk and gain self-knowledge.

- Use the energy created by these connections to generate meaningful action.

- Exert intellectual flexibility and innovation.

- Discover new knowledge to shape the future.

- Search out facts to support opinion.

- Think independently but objectively, and act responsibly.

Each of these Dimensions, applicable to all meaningful aspects of human activity, can be advanced through application of the scientific method, and we are assisting our students to appreciate just that. Scientific pursuit involves moving confidently into unfamiliar settings that involve considerable risk-taking as a student asks what the problem is and poses a hypothesis to determine a solution. Intellectual flexibility is required, and the method itself assists a student in sorting out ultimately fact from fiction. The hypothesis is either proven or refuted. You know where you stand at the end of the process. You have, as a student, gained an objective, pragmatic take on the world, and you have done it by your own independent engagement.

We are now about the business of linking even more compellingly our students' academic track at college and their non-curricular activities. In so doing science is about to help us overcome a gnawing deficiency in American residential higher education—the almost insurmountable divide between academics and student life where distrust and suspicion reside in both parties.

What I have talked to you about today is not just workshop science or discovery-based pedagogy. It is all about *change-directed pedagogy*—a way of teaching that pervades life in and out of the classroom and that is a powerful preparation for substantive contribution and leadership in the rapidly evolving world our students face ahead. For Dickinson discovery-based learning is now a powerful and essential part of our total *brand*. We have harnessed our disparate pedagogical innovations in all disciplines over the last few decades and now set them moving in the same direction as one college.

I wish you well in your future endeavors as you perhaps take what appears to define successful undergraduate science teaching at the liberal-arts college into a different institutional environment. Again, five key areas, I believe, must be examined and adjusted to the research-university setting for successful adaptation: mission, classroom size, classroom design, pedagogy and disciplinary ownership.

Hopkins may well be especially successful precisely as an entrepreneurial research university experimenting with and adapting into the traditional course-setting digital technologies and thus achieve some of the advantages of science instruction at a liberal-arts college— albeit on its own terms. "Successful" is defined here as appealing to all modes of identity recognition needed by a human being to learn—to include among contemporary students, digital recognition. Digital technologies' capacity for customization and one-on-one instruction could well achieve intimacy of learning and identity affirmation comparable to a liberal-arts college without compromising your research imperative. Ironically, your historical practice should not cause you to resist experimentation. Whereas at small liberal-arts colleges there is often a tendency to defend vigorously what you at Hopkins currently do not possess, a brand critically dependent on small classes, close student-faculty in-person contact and—by definitional necessity—little to no direct instructor-replacement instruction via technology. Many of your current and prospective students and faculty will not expect of you an exclusively high-touch, in-person instructional platform as might be expected of liberal-arts colleges. In fact, the types of students you attract may very well have already fused their physical identity with their digital identity, thus making it easier for you to introduce digital learning and have it accepted at your tuition price point. Additionally, you possess reputational leverage and proven scalability that will attract necessary third-party financial support for the complex ambition of approximating that human "intimacy" necessary for total learning through digital technologies. You may well at once embrace your original mandate to "create new knowledge" and posit a new pedagogy for science teaching. In so doing, you will distinguish yourself by the quality of the experience you offer your undergraduate students that deftly matches the emerging realities of acquiring knowledge with institutional capacities and distinction.

Thank you for permitting me to be part of your dialogue.

I wish to thank the following Dickinson professors for their insights about our science program:

Tom Arnold, *associate professor of biology*

Marcus Key, *professor of earth sciences and Joseph Priestley Professor of Natural Philosophy*

Priscilla Laws, *research professor of physics and astronomy*

B. Ashton Nichols, *professor of English language and literature, Walter E. Beach Distinguished Chair in Sustainability Studies*

Jeff Niemitz, *professor of earth science*

Neil Weissman, *professor of history, provost and dean of the college*

Selected

Dickinson Magazine Columns

Greetings from Old West. We have just started another academic year here in Carlisle and welcomed the class of 2003. Elke and I have now completed our move to campus and look forward to welcoming you to the President's House during events in the coming months and years. It is a fabulous residence. We are deeply honored to make our home there, and our thanks go out to the entire college community for this privilege.

A recent big event on campus was opening ceremonies on the afternoon of Aug. 31. We welcomed the class of 2003 and formally accepted its entrance to the college. It was a superb ceremony steeped in Dickinson tradition—some old and some recently invented.

This is the last edition of *Dickinson Magazine* that will come to you precisely in this format. Over the next few issues, you will see some changes to the format and content of *Dickinson Magazine*. You should also notice a change in the contents of the magazine. For one thing, I intend to write a regular column in this space. You shall also hear more in depth about the various accomplishments of alumni faculty in their research, teaching, travel, professions and service. We also have hired a new editor. Sherri Kimmel brings to the magazine an exciting set of experiences and skills, and we are going to craft a magazine that will make us all proud to be Dickinsonians.

One of my goals is to make Dickinson relevant for its alumni of all ages—to add value to your Dickinson education well after you leave these old limestone walls. We have made some progress in this direction. For example, recognizing that most of you will be pursuing education for a lifetime, I recently concluded agreements with two providers of postgraduate and continuing education—the University of Texas at Austin and the Caliber Learning Network Inc.

These agreements will allow Dickinson alumni to take courses on distance-learning networks at a discount. The University of Texas at Austin is a leading provider of graduate and professional education with extensive offerings in business and management courses as well as in other traditional academic subjects. Dickinson is the first liberal-arts college in the country to accomplish this type of arrangement with a nationally renowned research university. And Caliber, the distance-learning affiliate of Sylvan Learning Systems, offers a wide range of professional-development courses from such outstanding institutions as Wharton, Teachers College (of Columbia University), Johns Hopkins School of Medicine and the business school at the University of Southern California. Dickinson has always excelled at teaching students how to learn. Now we are using our associations in the academic and business communities to make it easier for you to continue your formal education as a graduate. You can learn more about how to take advantage of these opportunities in this issue of *Dickinson Magazine.*

For those of you who live or do business in New York City, Dickinson is now affiliated with the Williams Club (of Williams College, that is) on 39th Street in midtown Manhattan. This new agreement allows alumni to join the club and have access to its facilities, which include lodging and dining as well as excellent social and academic programs. I have been a member for years (through Columbia University) and often use the club while in New York. I also have taken advantage of the club's reciprocal agreements with other clubs across the United States and abroad. Most recently, for example, I stayed very reasonably and comfortably at the Sloane Club in the heart of central London. There will be an open house on Sept. 16 at the club for alumni in the New York City area. However, if you live outside the metropolitan area and are interested in membership, please call the club directly at 212-697-5300 or see the Web site at www.williamsclub.org.

Plans are being developed for a program that will allow alumni to lodge at the college's apartments in Bologna, Italy, when they are not in use by our students. If you missed out on going to Bologna, or if you want to revisit the site of your junior year abroad, the apartments there will be available to you starting during the summer of 2000. Don't feel like traveling on your own to Bologna? Then set aside June 2000 in your calendar and sign up for the Dickinson alumni tour to Bologna and enjoy the beautiful and historical city, which has been declared one of the European cultural capitals for 2000. (Watch future editions of the magazine for details.) We also will be celebrating the naming of the Dickinson Center as the K. Robert Nilsson Center for European Studies in Bologna in honor of the late

Professor Nilsson. He was instrumental in establishing the center 35 years ago.

If you were here for Alumni Weekend, thank you for the very kind and warm welcome you extended to Elke and me. We felt gratified by our reception into the community.

I look forward to communicating regularly with you throughout the coming year. Feel free to drop me a line by e-mail. I can be reached at billd@dickinson.edu.

Spring 2000

Thank you very much for all the recent feedback on a wide range of topics. As I reported in the last issue, we are engaging in a comprehensive strategic planning process at the college, and your ideas are a very important source of input for the plan. Changes to the draft plan have already been made as a direct result of your comments. By the time you receive this issue of *Dickinson Magazine*, the draft will be posted on the college Web site (www.dickinson.edu/plan). Please check it out and e-mail your comments to the Strategic Planning Committee at plan@dickinson.edu.

This is an important moment in the history of the college, and I invite you to be an active part of it. As part of the strategic-planning process, I have convened a Greek Life Action Group composed predominantly of alumni whose role is to make recommendations about how to preserve and strengthen Greek life at Dickinson. Their challenge is to envision a system that is safe, sustainable and appropriate to contemporary realities. As you may know, I was a member of a fraternity at Dickinson as a student, and I am committed to resisting the national trend toward abolition. According to recent surveys, our faculty also favor retaining Greek life as long as the Greek system returns its focus to the founding ideals of fellowship and service and commits to the mission of the college. At the same time, be aware that we also wish to promote a vibrant, diverse student life with considerable room for those who choose to remain independent and who pursue alternative arrangements. Engaging the issue of Greek life is one of my top priorities.

Another key project is energizing the extensive network of Dickinson alumni for the benefit of one another and for our current students. To this end, I have been meeting with groups of alumni in various cities, introducing them to one another and encouraging them to think of ways to build a Dickinson network in their regions. These meetings (which I think of as Rolodex meetings) have been enthusiastically attended. The college Web site soon will launch a new alumni section with new services and tools to further encourage networking among Dickinsonians. Now some plain, hard facts. We are a college very rich in talented faculty, students, alumni and staff. However, when we compare ourselves financially with our peers, it becomes clear that relatively speaking Dickinson is not a rich college. This hinders our ability to maintain our status as a top-tier, national liberal-arts college, committed to protecting and adding to the value of our degrees.

There are several ways to analyze the financial position of the college. The one that captures the most variables and is the simplest to present is the endowment. The endowment of the college is like a savings account, and we use the annual interest to supplement tuition. (Tuition and fees only cover about two-thirds of the cost of a Dickinson education.) The size of the endowment, as you can appreciate, has enormous impact on the quality of our programs and, ultimately, on the prestige of the college.

Our endowment has grown very nicely during the last 10 years, mostly due to wise management by the trustees and the strength of the stock market—not through substantial new gifts to the endowment or for capital projects. While we were pleased last year when an estate provided $5 million, we are reminded regularly of the success of our peers and competitors. Bowdoin College, for example, recently received $21 million from a living alumnus to endow its information-technology infrastructure. (This follows a $35 million gift received in 1997–98.) Williams College just received $20 million from an alumnus to build a new performing-arts center. And closer to home, a Juniata College trustee recently gave $18 million for a new science center. Such major infusions of resources either to the endowment or for a building project clearly have an impact upon a college's academic quality and reputation.

Where does Dickinson's endowment actually stand? At the moment, Dickinson has about $166 million in the endowment, which sounds like a great deal of money. And, in absolute terms, it is. But when we look at our competition, especially at schools that are ahead of us in the rankings, our endowment is conspicuously small. Here are endowment figures (as of June 30, 1998) for a few schools that are ahead of us in the *U.S. News and World Report* rankings.

Report ranking:

Swarthmore	$873 million
Washington and Lee	$818 million
Williams	$778 million
Middlebury	$616 million
Lafayette	$477 million
Bowdoin	$388 million
Bucknell	$355 million
Franklin & Marshall	$284 million

As the adage goes, the rich get richer, and, in our case, they continue to press their advantage and pull away. Even more troubling, other schools seem to be gaining on us. Gettysburg, Ursinus, Susquehanna and Muhlenberg have advanced in recent years and have begun closing the gap. Although their endowments lag behind ours, other measures of financial health such as alumni-giving rate, alumni giving per student and endowment per student are improving. We must and we will create energy, excitement and a culture of commitment and philanthropy at Dickinson to rectify this situation. Positioned near the bottom of the first tier, we are a mere nuance away from relegation to the second tier. This is not an option for Dickinson, and we need to do everything to maintain the college's reputation. Rest assured that we are working hard to identify and cultivate donors with the needed potential, and we will engage them to help propel this grand institution into the future. We look forward to seizing every opportunity to secure Dickinson's place as one of America's most distinguished liberal-arts colleges.

FALL 2000

Thanks for all of the supportive letters and e-mails that have arrived recently, especially regarding the new format of the magazine and the direction of the Strategic Plan. This feedback has been very welcome and helpful. One of my top priorities this year has been to start establishing what I like to call the "Dickinson story." This is a narrative about a liberal-arts college "with attitude"——respectful of its traditions but also enterprising, innovative and confident about the future. The new magazine and the Strategic Plan are both elements of this story, and your feedback will continue to be instrumental in shaping their messages.

Thanks also for making the last fiscal year (which ended on June 30) a success. Giving by alumni increased substantially—both in terms of the amount raised and in the participation rate—and five reunion classes broke standing records. With your help again this year, we can keep this momentum going and achieve our goal to be considered permanently one of America's leading independent, residential liberal-arts colleges.

I spent a few hours each week this summer visiting the college archives, and I have found some interesting things to weave into the Dickinson story. One of my research projects was the college bell, because I am considering reviving the hourly chiming of the bell during daylight hours and wanted to discover when and why this practice stopped. Although I did not find an answer to my original question, I learned a great deal about the bell along the way. The bell was manufactured in Philadelphia, and its purchase was authorized by the trustees in 1809 on behalf of Jeremiah Atwater, the second president of the college. He wanted a means to better regulate the students, who he claimed had grown unruly during the twilight of

Charles Nisbet's administration. The bell was stolen from Old West and eventually recovered from a steamboat in Pittsburgh in the 1850s. And, in 1905, the administration moved to Denny Hall from Old West, and the bell followed—where it remains to this day. By the way, I still have not pinned down the date when the bell stopped ringing on a regular basis. If any of you remember the occasion, please let me know.

Poking around in the archives also brought some other terrific surprises. For example, in the 1883 *Microcosm*, I found a "new-fangled" college seal that shares some design features with the new Dickinson medallion.

When I am on the road talking to alumni, many ask about our recent success in placing students in top graduate schools. Dickinson has a long and enviable record of preparing students for graduate study, and the early triumphs of members of the class of 2000 continues our tradition. Among the law schools to which they were admitted are some of the very best: Harvard, Penn, New York University, George Washington University, the University of Virginia, Georgetown, and (of course) the Dickinson School of Law. Our students also continue to gain admission to fine medical schools and to Ph.D. programs in the sciences, including: Johns Hopkins, Brandeis, Brown, Penn, Dartmouth and the University of Virginia. In other fields, our most recent graduates have been accepted at a number of excellent programs, including Fordham, the Monterey Institute, the University of Michigan, the University of Durham, the University of East Anglia, and Peking University. We know that this is just the first wave from the class of 2000—that many more will attend top graduate schools in the future. But this is already a strong showing, and they deserve our thanks for affirming Dickinson's reputation for preparing students for rigorous graduate and professional study.

Here in Old West and across campus, the summer was busy as we planned for the next few years. I am happy to report that the Board of Trustees approved the Strategic Plan at their meeting in June. Our task for this year is to flesh out the current goals and objectives with effective implementation strategies, ambitious deadlines and appropriate benchmarks. We also need to determine how much all of this is going to cost and to establish critical priorities. This process will take place all across the college—in every academic and administrative department.

As always, if you have feedback for me, please be in touch. The regular mail still works, or you may reach me by e-mail at billd@ dickinson.edu.

———————————

Winter 2001

As I write to you again from these grounds, I realize I have thought a lot lately about spheres of association and consequence. Dickinson College is rapidly establishing itself permanently in an appropriate sphere that includes some of America's best independent, residential liberal-arts colleges.

When we drafted the Strategic Plan last year, we articulated this goal: to position the college in its appropriate sphere of association and consequence. Some signs already point in this direction. For instance, the Massachusetts Institute of Technology invited us to join a group of institutions—including Stanford, Wellesley and Vassar— on a project in Web-based instructional technology. We do not yet know where this might lead, but it is significant and encouraging to be included with institutions of this caliber. More recently, I was invited by Middlebury College to participate on a panel entitled "The Selling of the Ivory Tower: The Liberal Arts College Confronts the Challenge of Market and Media" as part of Middlebury's bicentennial celebration. The panel was chaired by finance columnist Jane Bryant Quinn, and my fellow panelists included G. Dennis O'Brien, president emeritus of the University of Rochester; David L. Marcus, senior writer for *U.S. News and World Report*; and Malcolm G. Scully, editor at large with *The Chronicle of Higher Education*.

Here at Dickinson we have been "turning up the volume"—with promising results. To cite just one example, journalists from *Time* magazine recently came to campus to feature Dickinson in a story on male enrollment at liberal-arts colleges.

Ultimately, our goal is to position Dickinson in a leadership role within higher education in America—by expressing opinions and by inviting conversation and sometimes, inevitably, controversy. As one of the finest colleges in the nation, Dickinson has a voice of consequence and relevance to the wider world—and we are increasingly using it for issues that matter, including the importance of the independent, residential liberal-arts college. As an alumnus and now as president, I expect Dickinson to exercise this type of visible leadership.

Dickinson is poised for its next set of challenges and opportunities. Here is some evidence of why we are ready to move forward:

- The academic program and the faculty remain of the highest quality. Our recent continued success in foundation support confirms this.

- Our enrollment data are starting to turn around after a number a years of relative stagnation.

- Financially, we are moving forward in a disciplined manner to achieve efficiencies, to find new sources of revenue and to increase outside support and our endowment.

- We have a clear plan of action for our buildings and grounds.

- We are reaching out candidly and effectively to our alumni to engage them with the Dickinson story—through this magazine, new alumni services and a revitalized network of alumni clubs.

- In student life—a critical dimension of our residential mission—new leadership and energy promise to yield improvements in the quality of life and in student satisfaction.

Again, all this evidence is pointing in the right direction—forward. We have abundant energy and a clear direction. The time is soon coming to take advantage of this momentum and to secure for Dickinson—permanently and unequivocally—its rightful and historic place as one of the finest institutions of higher learning in America.

We also wish to involve our entire community in the world beyond these limestone walls. Dickinson was founded to serve society, and we wish to rekindle this deep and abiding concern for social causes and for the needs of others. Please watch these pages (and our Web site) for a new effort to connect the college and its extended community with selected international and domestic-service projects that will allow the college to engage the world in meaningful and useful ways.

I welcome your help in these efforts, and I urge you to continue to keep your letters and e-mail messages flowing. I can be reached by regular mail or by e-mail at billd@dickinson.edu.

SPRING 2001

In this edition of "From These Grounds" I will focus on how the college engages with the world around it—especially in Carlisle. As a student, I walked the streets and back alleys of the town, and I developed a strong sense of place that I carried with me as an alumnus. When I thought of Dickinson, I thought of my favorite classes and professors, the beautiful campus and my friends. But I also thought of Carlisle—especially late nights at the Hamilton and long walks through the neighborhoods with classmates discussing life and our collective futures.

From its beginning, Dickinson was not intended to be an ivory tower set apart from the world and the surrounding community. Our founder, Benjamin Rush, intended the college—in the language of our charter of 1783—"to disseminate and promote the growth of useful knowledge" and to teach "the useful arts, sciences and literature." In curricular terms, this meant an early emphasis on modern languages (in addition to classical studies) and on "new" sciences like chemistry—fields that could unlock knowledge in other disciplines.

For Rush, education went beyond the classroom into the wider world, and he urged students to attend civil and criminal trials at the county courthouse in Carlisle to see the new American republic in action and to draw lessons about oratory, rhetoric and the use of evidence. In this light, our new program in law and public service is right in line with Rush's educational philosophy.

Today, the college has an active program of engagement with the world beyond the limestone walls of campus. Students, in fact, are now required to fulfill a community experience requirement—broadly conceived as significant exposure to the world beyond campus through study abroad, internships or another structured volunteer experience in the community that engages students and their civic disposition. We took this step not to force more students into volunteerism but to recognize the good work that so many of our students are already doing. They, in fact, led us in this direction—as is often the case with good curricular reform.

Our students undertake a wide variety of volunteer activities organized by student groups. Many first-year students set the tone for their college careers by opting for a service project during orientation. Fraternities and sororities continue their traditions of service by volunteering their time and energy on behalf of national causes and local human-services agencies. Other organizations—Alpha Phi Omega, Omicron Delta Kappa and Alpha Lambda Delta—serve in the Carlisle community and on behalf of national charities. Some campus groups are devoted to a single cause or support a particular volunteer activity. For example, there are active chapters of Amnesty International and Habitat for Humanity. Other robust student groups include a tutoring program for local students, the Big-Little Program, America Reads and Adopt-a-Grandparent.

The Women's Center gives time and energy to Domestic Violence Services and the House of Umoja conducts diversity programs in schools and raises funds for Safe Harbour (a local emergency-housing provider). The Outing Club helps to maintain the Appalachian Trail, raises money for regional conservancy projects and conducts cave cleanup trips. Several varsity teams work with local groups to tutor elementary-school students, to promote girls' wellness, to help the local food bank and a soup kitchen. And ALLARM (Alliance for Aquatic Resource Monitoring) volunteers monitor stream-water quality across Pennsylvania and recently began a major stream-restoration project in Carlisle. We are moving toward providing even more opportunities for our students to do volunteer work while they study abroad.

This habit of service is an important dimension of what our founders intended in 1783 when they established Dickinson College to provide a useful education and to strengthen the young republic by training citizen-leaders. More than 200 years later, this fundamental aspect of our mission remains unchanged. Although the challenges faced by our society are different, the ultimate solution remains constant—the goodwill and energy of active, engaged citizen-leaders who understand and embrace their civic responsibilities.

Thank you for your support of Dickinson and this vital and enduring element of our mission.

SUMMER 2002

Recently, I have taken up the game of squash again, usually playing against my classmate and the college's executive director of information technology, Paul Levit '71. When I was a student at Dickinson, I played on many intramural teams—flag football, basketball and softball—engaged in countless just-for-fun athletic contests and, during the summer, pitched for an American Legion baseball team in New York. As I headed off to the Kline Center the other day to meet Paul for our weekly match, I realized that my entire adult life has now been bookended by athletic activity at and around Dickinson.

This is, of course, as it should be. The virtues and health benefits of remaining physically active throughout one's life are widely recognized and encouraged. There is, moreover, growing acknowledgement that developing the passion and discipline for regular exercise at an early age increases the likelihood that physical activity will become a lifelong routine.

Intercollegiate athletics, however, has recently received less than glowing reports in the media. *The Game of Life* (Princeton University Press, 2001), a book by James L. Shulman and William G. Bowen, and the recent sobering conclusions of the Knight Commission, which reconvened 10 years after it issued its far-reaching recommendations, have questioned the practices of intercollegiate athletics not only at big universities but also at small colleges. Have schools, these studies ask, created a gap between the academic and athletic cultures that cannot be breached? Have universities and colleges taken the love of the game too far—at the expense of academic excellence and integrity?

At Dickinson, we are keenly aware of the delightfully delicate balance that must be maintained between academics and athletics. Although we are fully supportive of our intercollegiate teams and trust they will be competitive in their respective conferences, our students are scholars first and athletes second. For us, sport is learning, and this stance permeates our intercollegiate and our intramural programs. We also encourage individual and small-group physical training and exercise. Sport plays an integral role in developing leadership qualities, team-building skills, confidence, sense of self, character, intellectual discipline and a healthy respect for competition—attributes that will help our students become the citizen-leaders of their generation.

We estimate that a solid majority of our students participate in athletics either on one of our 23 varsity sports teams—12 female and 11 male—or through our intramural program. We also have retained the four-credit physical education requirement necessary for graduation. Students may earn two of those credits by participating in intercollegiate athletics but must pursue a different activity to earn the other two. Our offerings are broad and sometimes eclectic, as we offer our students the opportunity to explore new forms of physical activity—be it expressive, endurance building or the pursuit of pure competition. At Dickinson, in addition to the more traditional sports, you'll find an Outing Club—hiking, canoeing and rock climbing— which takes advantage of our superb geographical location, ice hockey played as a club sport, a rock-climbing wall in the Kline Center and a spacious fitness center for aerobic and strength training.

And lest you think that competition is limited to students, our faculty regularly step up to the plate as members of their own spring intramural softball team—dubbed the King Vitamin—and with their first-year seminar students during the fall intramural season. Staff (and yours truly) also participate in the demanding Cumberland County softball league during the spring and summer. Like so many other activities at Dickinson, sport is part of our sense of community. It brings us together rather than divides us.

In the following pages, you will read about several Dickinson alumni who have gone on to pursue sports-related careers. While few of us will work in the world of professional sports, the contributions, success and insights of these alumni remind us of the lifelong benefits of sport. Being physically active in college can and should be an avenue to a life that is filled with healthy engagement in service and the pursuit of accomplishment. It is that perspective that will help Dickinson maintain the appropriate balance between academics and athletics. It is also that perspective that will keep me—but maybe not Paul—looking forward to our weekly squash game.

Enjoy your summer and remember to take some time to "play ball."

FALL 2002

You have no doubt heard in recent months from the college about a new term—"Distinctively Dickinson." We use this term with considerable pride and base it upon our founder's intention to define a new, pioneering direction for undergraduate education in the United States. Lest you think these words are mere trumpery, I offer in this column an explanation of why we can be so bold and outspoken about the ambition and distinction of our alma mater—an institution that some of us have traditionally thought about far too modestly. Let me discuss the conceptual justification of the term, "Distinctively Dickinson."

The evolution of American higher education has been marked, periodically, by a significant contribution from a single college or university. Johns Hopkins University, for example, takes credit for introducing to the United States the German ("Heidelberg") model of graduate doctoral study with its focus on the pursuit of new knowledge. Similarly, the University of Chicago stakes its claim as the first institution to employ a distinctive "Great Books" core curriculum focusing on Western civilization and culture.

Dickinson College made an equally distinctive contribution to the development of American higher education that is squarely at the undergraduate level. From the outset, a Dickinson education, like that offered at other 18th-century colleges, drew heavily upon the classics and a knowledge of the past. What made Dickinson's approach distinctive, however, was that past knowledge would be joined with emerging knowledge, positioning Dickinson graduates to be useful in creating a just, compassionate democratic society, one with political, social, spiritual and financial strength. A Dickinson education was intellectually comprehensive and rigorous as well as ultimately useful.

Dickinson's contribution comes directly from our founder, Dr. Benjamin Rush, signer of the Declaration of Independence and America's foremost physician of the period. His experience at the University of Edinburgh during the height of the Scottish Enlightenment profoundly influenced his views on education. This Scottish intellectual movement differed from those elsewhere because the university was at its center. Scottish universities were part of an educational tradition designed to reach all classes of society, not merely the privileged. At its core, the Scottish Enlightenment explored the interaction between individuals and their external environment, seeking the fundamental principles and discernible patterns underpinning societal change. The curriculum was progressive and reform-minded, and it placed a high premium on serving society.

Rush returned from Edinburgh in 1774 determined to introduce to America the best of Scottish Enlightenment thought and practice. With an almost missionary zeal, Rush threw himself into the revolutionary cause and, then, into shaping the newly emerging republic into a nation. For Rush, America's colleges and universities should be an integral component of this process and the best foundation for introducing Scottish Enlightenment thought to the young country.

As Arthur Herman noted in *How the Scots Invented the Modern World,* (New York, 2001), our college was the direct object of Rush's obsession. Dickinson College "became the vehicle for Rush's vision of a new kind of non-denominational education institution ... The university should be a place that pushed forward the frontiers of knowledge in all areas, Rush believed, through research and innovation, as well as a center of instruction." For Rush, education was to serve a profound purpose. In coining the motto for the American Philosophical Society, Rush succinctly asserted his conviction that "knowledge is of little use, when confined to mere speculation."

Rush's legacy to American higher education—Dickinson College—was an ambitious new type of college for a new nation born directly out of the American Revolution but influenced greatly by the Scottish Enlightenment. What defining characteristics and operative guidelines did Rush envision? From my now-extensive reading of Rush's works, I believe the following points marked his revolutionary conception of American undergraduate education. These guidelines, offered up to us from history, serve as a measure for our contemporary work.

> *Useful education accompanied by progressively enlightened instruction:* The curriculum was to be relevant, enabling students to meet the challenges and obligations they would face in the future. Their instruction was to be progressive, enlivening and adaptable, with professors imparting knowledge in the most effective way possible.

> *Modern languages to engage the world:* Latin and Greek—pillars of the 18th-century liberal-arts curriculum—should continue to be taught, but they were not to be the exclusive languages of study. Liberal education, to Rush, should be a living enterprise with an immediate application. Modern languages were to play a key role in the new curriculum since students would converse and interact with people from other nations as they embarked upon the world after graduation.

Intimate knowledge of American democracy: Universities were to acquaint students with American government and with the many national obligations that are integral to American democracy. Dickinson students must graduate prepared to be the citizen-leaders of this democracy, and they must observe and engage America as it develops. (For example, Rush intended Dickinson students to spend afternoons in the Cumberland County courthouse as keen observers of the political and judicial process.)

Science and interdisciplinarity: Science was to play a central, organizing role in the new curriculum. The sciences—especially chemistry—would help students to see the interconnectedness of all knowledge and would be useful upon graduation. Equally important, Rush viewed the sciences, of all the disciplines, as the exemplars for how to gain new knowledge through research. Providing students with access to the latest discoveries and scientific instruments would position them as leaders in the emerging fields of science and medicine.

Study of the great people of history and those who are often overlooked: Through study, travel and observation, students were to acquaint themselves with the most distinguished individuals of their times, but just as importantly, with the customs, dress and speech of those who are often disregarded. Students should, as Rush himself wrote, "converse freely with quacks of every class and sex."

Spirituality, ethics and character: Connecting with a nondenominational spirituality and pursuing ethical behavior and firm character were paramount. According to Rush, learning was incomplete without exploring questions of faith. These explorations were critical for the emerging democracy. It is important for a nation, Rush wrote, "to promote through its students knowledge in religion rather than ignorance."

Globalism—Engage the World: For Rush, all knowledge was best grasped in a global context. Students should travel the world and acquire the best practices and knowledge. Rush believed that his professional medical study in Edinburgh was the most influential period in his life, and he even once recommended that all Philadelphians should travel abroad.

Community service and social engagement: "The social spirit is the true selfish spirit," Rush wrote. Caring for the social condition of other human beings and community involvement were to be important aspects of the curriculum. Rush's open hostility to slavery, advocacy for the education of women and commitment to caring for the mentally ill—all path breaking for his time—underline his commitment to the community and his openness to all of its members.

Commitment to the wealth of the nation: Referring to universities as "true nurseries of power and influence," Rush believed that a liberal education should prepare students to gain material influence. Upon graduation, students should join enthusiastically in the commerce and industry of the emerging nation.

Here, then, is the conceptual basis of "Distinctively Dickinson"—a college intended to introduce to America a new, active, practical form of undergraduate liberal education and, in so doing, to become, in Rush's words, "First in America." Born from the contrarian spirit of the American Revolution with roots in the Scottish Enlightenment, Dickinson College was to have a distinctive personality and purpose. Dickinson was intended to pioneer for America a new direction in undergraduate education, a direction that would respect the past but push forward enthusiastically at the frontiers of useful knowledge, research and instruction. Calling the college his "petulant brat," Rush expected its students and graduates to nurture a feisty, revolutionary disposition, to adopt a strong, clear voice on the most pressing issues of the day and to take fearless and appropriate action whenever necessary.

Benjamin Rush's mandate for a useful education demands direct engagement with a growing American society and economy. His vision for Dickinson was a direct departure from the more ornamental and aristocratic liberal education he found in England. There, education was viewed as a luxury reserved for the privileged few. To Rush, this approach was inappropriate for an aggressively emerging new democracy.

Regrettably, today many higher-education institutions that advance a liberal education deny vigorously, if unknowingly, Rush's important legacy. These institutions instead assert and defend the "purity" of disengaged academic enterprise and disregard the concrete usefulness of education. By doing so, they reject the very distinctiveness of liberal education in America and, ironically, reassert the 18th-century view that a university education is for the elite.

By remaining true to Rush's vision, Dickinson College distinguishes itself—and its graduates—from other institutions. Through a firm commitment to prepare students to lead compassionately—tempered by spirituality and ethical knowledge—and comprehensively, Dickinson is providing our nation, our communities and our world with individuals who can tackle the responsibilities of an increasingly complex, challenging and global society. It is because of the defining assets we inherited from Dr. Benjamin Rush and their evolving interpretation and application that we are known proudly as "Distinctively Dickinson."

It has become almost trite to say, "everything changed after Sept. 11." And yet, as with so many clichés, there is more than an element of truth within it. The cover story of this issue of *Dickinson Magazine* explores some of the more subtle and perhaps enduring ways the terrorist attacks have changed the way we live. As standard bearers for a liberal-arts college, we have a responsibility to examine and debate these broader repercussions. And, as heirs to a revolutionary legacy, Dickinsonians must ensure that the fundamental freedoms of a democratic society remain protected.

An equally unsettling development has been unfolding since the fall of 2001. A spate of revelations, and now indictments, of those engaged in ethical wrongdoing, sheer arrogance, greed and financial fabrication in corporate America have shaken our confidence in Wall Street and cost millions of investors significant sums. These events, too, have changed the way we lead our daily lives.

These financial crises beg for corrections. As in other past instances of fallen virtue, there are those who are calling for the enlightened force of higher education to step to the fore. While I have no doubt that higher education will rise to the challenge eventually, a relationship currently exists between business and higher education—especially the traditional academy with liberal arts as its core—that is akin to oil and water.

During my 25 years in higher education, I have encountered countless liberal-arts graduates who have chosen careers in the business sector. They express consternation that their undergraduate professors view their entry into the business world as a Faustian bargain that leads only to a tarnished life. It is not so unthinkable that some business professionals would exhibit a lack of ethics after being condemned by their respected mentors. Prejudgment exerts a powerful influence on a young mind.

This tension between the academy and business wasn't part of the plan in our nation's infancy. In fact, Dickinson's founder, Benjamin Rush, promoted the notion of a distinctively American liberal-arts education that would be useful and applicable for all graduates and that was meant to advance the business and commerce of the new nation. In proposing this approach to liberal education, Rush rejected the model that was then prevalent throughout England—a model in which students and faculty prided themselves on remaining aloof from the pressures and problems of society, including and especially activities that involved the making and exchanging of money. This ivory-tower mentality discouraged involvement in commerce, a mindset that was ultimately elitist. Regrettably, many institutions today still ascribe "purity" to a liberal education. These institutions scorn publicly any activity or inquiry that encourages students to pursue a fair, balanced relationship with business.

It is time for liberal education to give business and commerce shared intellectual space again. Many colleges and universities offer a distinctly separate undergraduate business program, frequently in a separate building, that insulates business students from the broader curriculum. This approach isolates commerce from the core of intellectual activity—the sciences, the humanities, the arts and the social sciences that constitute the liberal arts. A separatist strategy does not provide an educational antidote to corporate greed. Exposure to the liberal arts, which expresses the fullest range of human thought, action, emotion and character, certainly would do no one harm. Business must be meaningfully integrated into the core of liberal education as a legitimate subject of study without apology or prejudice.

As in so many other areas, Dickinson is paving the way. Our new international business and management major, for example, balances the liberal arts and business by requiring students to take core business courses, such as financial accounting and marketing, as well as two years of a foreign language beyond the intermediate level and a full range of courses in the humanities, sciences, arts and social sciences. This is precisely the type of preparation our graduates will need to navigate the complex cultural matrix of an international economy.

Our ultimate responsibility at Dickinson is to prepare the next generation of citizen-leaders to tackle the complex challenges of a global society. Many of our graduates will undoubtedly go on to assume positions of corporate leadership. A fully integrated business dimension within the liberal-arts framework will equip them to apply to business and life lessons in accountability, legitimate creativity, citizenship and ethics. It is, of course, what Benjamin Rush intended all along.

SPRING 2003

Once again, America's colleges and universities find themselves at the center of a debate that will greatly affect the way our nation and our communities perceive and interact with people from many different backgrounds, races, ethnicities and religions. The pivotal pending U.S. Supreme Court case brought by unsuccessful applicants to the University of Michigan has refocused our attention on the merits of affirmative action. The nation's colleges and universities have long served as the lightning rod for crucial discussions and decisions about diversity. Frequently, the standards, policies and attitudes that are developed at these institutions presage those that ultimately percolate through society.

While there is general agreement that colleges and universities should strive to attract a student population that mirrors the diversity of our society, there is a wide philosophical breach over how to accomplish this end. I also would argue that the dialogue surrounding this issue reveals that there is a lack of general agreement over the scope and meaning of the term "diversity." The outcome of this court case will, at least, promote a fuller exploration of what we mean when we talk about promoting a diversity that will extend beyond the campuses and into the communities.

A recent exchange in the Carlisle *Sentinel* demonstrates that Dickinson's commitment to diversity is sparking interest and reflection within the surrounding community. On Jan. 5, the *Sentinel* published a lengthy piece on the Posse Foundation, a program that Dickinson joined in the fall of 2001. Through this program, the college selects and provides full-tuition scholarships to a "posse" or group of about 10 students from New York City. In its 14-year history, the program has found that students are more likely to have a successful college experience, particularly in a smaller community, if they attend with a group of students from a similar area and background.

In a follow-up editorial published the next day, the *Sentinel* commended Dickinson for its costly commitment to this program. "In return for admitting 10 city students who can help each other adjust to campus life and studies, Dickinson is building up diversity and encouraging multiculturalism to flourish on campus," the editorial stated. "We'd say Dickinson is making a smart investment in youth and in creating a campus with broader horizons. This country is a melting pot. We should live as if we are and appreciate the diversity offered."

Perhaps the most telling comment in the editorial, however, came—not surprisingly—from the Posse students themselves. They, "think Dickinson now needs to take the next step in looking at cultural diversity as a lot more than different skin colors." Hear, hear!

And our Posse students are not the only Dickinson students to think more expansively about the notion of diversity. In the November-December 2002 edition of the campus publication, *Diversity in Demand,* our students looked at the issue of class in America, noting that "class is often one area that is not discussed and remains a very private matter … There are many people in our society whose socioeconomic status gives them great access to societal resources or limits their ability to provide the most basic needs of life."

As this Dickinson student publication modeled, society's discussions about diversity need to be broadened. Diversity is complex, multifaceted and, sometimes, invisible. In a letter to the editor that I wrote in response to the *Sentinel* editorial, I commended the Posse students for their insight, noting that Dickinson "has maintained for generations a distinctive diversity that goes unrecognized because it isn't immediately identifiable. I'm referring to those who are the first in their families to go to college … I know well about this type of diversity that goes beyond color, since I am a first-generation college graduate too." The percentage of our first-generation students today stands at a comparatively high 15 percent—a testament to our ongoing commitment to embracing a broadly defined diversity.

The Supreme Court's decision in the University of Michigan case will not bring an end to the debate over how to construct equitable and effective policies to achieve meaningful diversity. In the meantime, however, discussions about diversity—in all of its complexity—at the national level and within local communities are, I believe, necessary and healthy. The nation's colleges and universities—including Dickinson—are at the very center of these discussions. Once again higher-education institutions are serving as the catalysts for—and leaders of—significant societal change.

SPRING 2004

Most of you are familiar with Malcolm Gladwell's defining book, *The Tipping Point: How Little Things Can Make a Big Difference.* A "tipping point" is that magical moment "when an idea, trend, or social behavior crosses a threshold, tips and spreads like wildfire," the author writes. Gladwell explains that three types of people create tipping points: connectors, mavens and salespeople. Dickinson graduates, faculty and administrators have served prominently in all three of these roles for generations and have made a distinctive mark on the evolution and development of our country.

Let us recall an early Dickinson connector—Moncure Daniel Conway (1832-1907), a member of the class of 1849 and an 1857 graduate of Harvard Divinity School. Conway was a consummate connector—a person "with a special gift for bringing the world together," as Gladwell writes. A connector lives life to the fullest by associating with overlapping circles of fascinating people. Connectors serve as, or inspire, "tipping points" in the broadest range and at the highest levels of human endeavor. The connector participates in these circles of accomplishment *and,* through them, comes to know many critical people who transmit thoughts and ideas from one person to another. A connector "crosses borders," serving as a conduit through which human advancement ultimately is achieved.

Moncure Conway was born of a distinguished Virginia family. He entered Dickinson as a sophomore at the tender age of 15. He began his career as a writer here, founding the first student publication, a forerunner of *The Dickinsonian.* Even then, Conway was well on his way to becoming a flashpoint for communication and connectivity among people.

In 1851, he became a circuit-riding Methodist minister, requiring him to change location frequently, a defining trait of a connector—one whose persistent movement promotes networking among disparate peoples. For them the connector serves as a unifying force.

Increasingly uncomfortable with what he saw as conformity, Conway exchanged Methodism for Unitarianism and enrolled at Harvard University's Divinity School. There he met Ralph Waldo Emerson, who had provided much impetus for Conway's intellectual development at Dickinson. At Harvard, he also began a long association with Nathaniel Hawthorne and became acquainted with Andrew Carnegie, who later served on Dickinson's board of trustees and helped fund our first Conway Hall.

Conway was beginning a lifelong habit of seeking out people of ideas and ensuring that they exchanged opinions on contemporary issues that mattered. The great ethical and cultural question of his day—slavery—was an issue that already engaged Emerson and Hawthorne and one that begged for a "tipping point." Conway was emerging as an abolitionist and freethinker, stances that would make him world famous.

Enlarging his sphere of connectivity, Conway relocated to London from 1863 to 1884. There, he engaged the full range of Europe's progressive thinkers, moving from intellectual circle to intellectual circle. Those connected by Conway included the authors Thomas Carlyle, Robert Browning and Christina and Dante Rossetti as well as labor activist Annie Bezant. Conway returned to the United States only to move to Paris at the end of his life.

Moncure Daniel Conway was a connector for ideas that mattered. With his energy and ideas, this connector—and his fellow travelers—achieved a "tipping point." The seminal idea for Conway, our fellow Dickinsonian, was an immensely important one in the evolution of humankind—the elimination of slavery. It was also an idea consistent with the aspirations of our founder, Dr. Benjamin Rush, who more than 50 years earlier had been one of the nation's earliest abolitionists. For his efforts on behalf of humankind, Moncure Conway received an honorary doctoral degree from Dickinson and was invited to join the board of trustees—despite the fact that the college was, back then, conservative and cautious, unlike the ideas that Conway espoused.

Conway should serve as an inspiration to all of us. He was an individual who stood for what he knew was right for his country and for all peoples. Through his tenacity and intellect he made a difference. He was a true Dickinsonian—a citizen-leader who set out to make the world and our democracy a more just and compassionate one. As I reflect upon Conway's accomplishments, I find myself wondering, as you may wonder, too, who the connectors are among us today and what the "tipping points" of the future will be. Only time will tell.

Associate Professor of History John Osborne and Archivist James Gerencser '93 provided background on the life of Moncure Conway for this essay.

FALL 2004

In June, my wife, Elke, and I spent a delightful two weeks in Germany during which time I delivered an address at the University of Bremen titled, "The Mysteries of American Education: Bowling Alone." This visit allowed me to probe some of the fundamental differences between German and American higher education—particularly the relationships that institutions develop with their alumni.

As dedicated readers of this column know, I have become increasingly appreciative of the vision that our founder, Dr. Benjamin Rush, had of a distinctively American education. Rush insisted that Dickinson offer an education that was predicated not simply on the study of known facts and past knowledge, as was the case in Europe, but which also sought to connect emerging knowledge to the broader, contemporary society. This approach, he believed, would foster character development in Dickinson students, essential for future citizen-leaders of a new democracy.

This distinctive approach was personal and nurturing, and it has helped to foster, perhaps unwittingly, another unique characteristic in American higher education—the affinity between a student—later the graduate—and an institution.

This relationship rarely exists at European universities, where students often consider education to be a mere entitlement. Attendance at any particular university is of little personal consequence. This difference in perspective reflects the disparate academic philosophies and ways of funding higher education. In Europe, universities are almost solely financed by governments. In the United States, students may receive financial aid from the state or federal government, and institutions rely on multiple revenue streams, including tuition and philanthropic support. (Private colleges and universities are almost totally dependent on extra-governmental revenues—hence, the origin of my subtitle, "Bowling Alone.") Students and alumni, therefore, become stakeholders in their educations, further strengthening their bond with their college or university.

The European model works well enough—as long as the government is willing to continue funding the universities. Recently, however, due to stagnating or even declining support, European universities, like the University of Bremen, have tried to "Americanize" their enterprises by establishing alumni associations and development offices to increase the flow of private funding. It was this topic that most interested my German colleagues.

As I prepared to give my remarks, I considered what effect these differences might have on access and attendance. Coincidentally, the morning of my presentation, a copy of the German newspaper *Die Welt* carried an article citing attendance rates at German universities, ranked by socioeconomic strata. (My ability to use this timely information is, of course, yet another argument for becoming fluent in another language!) The attendance rates, especially for lower- and middle-income students, seemed quite low—especially since German students pay little or no tuition.

I immediately contacted Patty Murphy, our director of institutional research, to see if she could acquire comparable American statistics. The data she provided me—in time for my speech—were striking. Despite markedly higher tuitions, American students from lower- and middle-income families attend college in much higher numbers than do their German counterparts. Access, it seems, may have very little to do with tuition levels but may be rooted deeply in cultural attitudes and different philosophies of higher education.

My recent trip has prompted me to explore more deeply those factors that distinguish American higher education from education in other parts of the world. My discussions with my colleagues in Bremen reinforced how much we should value the distinctiveness of American higher education and why Dickinson's legacy continues to position us as a leader among liberal-arts colleges.

As I watch European universities begin to develop relationships with their alumni, I have gained new perspective on the importance of building a close bond between the college and its students—its soon-to-be alumni. By nurturing these affinities, we create a vast network of individuals who share a commitment to the mission of the college as well as a personal stake in its future—creating a perpetual foundation for stability and growth that is not heavily dependent on the government or other sources. At Dickinson our future is defined by the responsibility we have to prepare the next generation of citizen-leaders who will be drawn from many and varied backgrounds. It is an endeavor of the highest purpose and one that I am pleased to undertake with my fellow alumni.

WINTER 2005

If you follow the dissensions that periodically rock higher education, you will notice that college and university administrators are being accused of making the academy corporative. While the precise meaning of this accusation is a bit unclear—more on that later—what is noteworthy is that Dickinson College is figuring prominently in this national dialogue. As I have often said, increased prestige brings increased visibility. It is the price—and the benefit—of being "out there."

What do these decriers mean when they bemoan the "corporatization" of higher education? Some criticize the adoption of "corporate" practices—professional fundraising, marketing, branding and enrollment management. Others refer to a dumbing down of content to meet consumer satisfaction. Still others assert that corporatization has led to the sundering of the traditional curriculum. And some claim that the humanities are threatened because the academy places a priority on pursuing funding for scientific research.

The faculty, the critics maintain, have passively permitted administrators to bring corporative concepts to the leafy, collegial grove to wreak havoc. I simply don't buy it. These are merely word politics of the most predictable variety. Increasingly, critics of administrative action utter the term "corporate," expecting the word to be so abhorrent to faculty that most will join the hue and cry without reflection.

A corporate mentality, in fact, was a distinct characteristic of early American higher education. Lacking the luxury of a supportive, moneyed patronage, as existed in England, early American educators had to be resourceful fundraisers, marketers and admissions recruiters. Our own founder, Dr. Benjamin Rush, embraced these corporate practices with vigor and humor.

In a 1784 letter to a friend who helped him raise funds for the college, he urged, "Go on with your collections. Get money—get it honestly if you can. But get money for our College." Rush also joyfully engaged in entrepreneurial strategies to attract students, incurring debt to procure the most advanced scientific equipment so that Dickinson would possess what other colleges did not. And as for branding, Rush knew that his own name did not have sufficient cachet to recruit students, so he asked if he could use that of his good friend, John Dickinson, who had far greater name recognition.

Similarly, the changes in the curriculum—now deemed so objectionable—were not the brainchildren of entrepreneurial administrators. Often, faculty initiated these improvements to make the academic program more relevant to students' lives.

As for the fate of the humanities, I, as a German literature scholar, am ready to throw the "umlaut" into the fight against the "corporate." Rather than looking to misguided administrators as culprits, this trend toward research productivity was begun in the mid-19th century, again, by the academy. In the face of an increasingly competitive global order driven by invention and innovation, American educators sought to replace the gentlemanly approach to higher education with the German model that valued research, productivity and the deliberate, ceaseless creation of new knowledge.

Many of the corporate traits that have "invaded" higher education are, in fact, the conscious result of internal discussions within the academy. As Pogo once astutely said, "We have met the enemy and he is us." What is criticized as corporate behavior often results from good administrative leadership and accountability to a broad constituency.

Dickinson's recent momentum has propelled us to the center of this national debate. We have been widely recognized for our path-breaking efforts in marketing and enrollment management. Our approach, for example, was the subject of a separate chapter in David Kirp's controversial look at academic corporatization, *Shakespeare, Einstein and the Bottom Line*. We continue to garner wide recognition for the excellence of our academic program, as witnessed by our receipt of numerous prestigious awards and scholarships, our steady rise in the national rankings and the growing acknowledgement of our pre-eminence in global education.

It is possible to achieve an appropriate balance between the supposedly competing forces of the corporate and the Academy. It is a balance that we, at Dickinson, strive hard to maintain—one that is attracting recognition for our college. A recent article in the September issue of *University Business* put it this way, "our challenge as university businesspeople and marketers: to find a way to reconcile the 'values of the marketplace' with the 'values of the commons.' The few who can, like Dickinson College (PA) and NYU, survive as winners. The rest of us lose spectacularly."

Now *that* is the kind of visibility—corporate and academic—that is becoming the hallmark of Dickinson's distinctive approach to a liberal-arts education. I rest my case.

A strong focus on the sciences always has been a Dickinson hallmark. This issue of *Dickinson Magazine* highlights the college's growing reputation for research and teaching in these disciplines. Our founder, Dr. Benjamin Rush, a physician and professor of chemistry, viewed the sciences as linchpins of a Dickinson useful liberal-arts education. Rush emphasized this when he selected the telescope as one of three symbols on the college seal.

Rush believed the sciences would be the engines of innovation for the new nation's economy and would provide connections among disparate disciplines that would fuel the discovery of new knowledge and bring pre-eminence to America. His 18th-century vision, of course, was right on target. In short order, the young country began to display an uncanny ability to combine an inherent, pragmatic spirit of invention with emerging knowledge. This potent combination ultimately made the United States the most advanced nation in the world in terms of scientific research and advancement.

Rush's faith in the power of science is, perhaps, more valid today than it was nearly 225 years ago. What may be in doubt, however, is America's unquestioned dominance. Thomas L. Friedman's provocative book, *The World is Flat: A Brief History of the 21st Century*, outlines the rapid changes that have occurred in the last 10 years, made possible by the ability to instantly transmit knowledge around the world.

This new world order depends less on relations among nations and more on the empowerment of hundreds of thousands of individuals—particularly in the emerging economies of India and China—who are eager to compete.

This new form of globalization could have major repercussions for American students who will soon enter a workforce crowded with bright, energetic international scientists eager to participate in the prosperity of the 21st century. Friedman worries that American students have developed a sense of entitlement and complacency about the future and may have a rude awakening when they encounter aggressive and ambitious international competitors who are flattening our globe.

Another of Friedman's concerns is that American undergraduates' interest in the sciences is waning. His troubling explanation concurs with that of Richard A. Rashid, director of research for Microsoft.

Rashid laments, "We have done a very poor job of conveying to [students] the value of science and technology as a career choice that will make the world a better place ... Science is what led to so many improvements in our lives." As we move further into this intensely competitive era of globalization, it is our responsibility as educators— and particularly as heirs to the legacy of Dr. Rush—to instill in our students a full comprehension of the important and exciting impact science will have on our collective future.

To that end, Dickinson has redoubled its efforts to provide our science majors with opportunities to explore connections between science and society and to experience science at work in the broader world. Since 2001, for example, more than 50 Dickinson students have received Howard Hughes Medical Institute-sponsored research internships, spending their summers working alongside top scientists at the nation's most prestigious research universities and in the most advanced pharmaceutical labs.

Last spring, Associate Professor of Physics Hans Pfister and his students previewed a model of a solar-powered engine at Innoventure, a conference that attracted hundreds of scientists and high-tech businesses in central Pennsylvania. Our students also have joined physicians and scientists at the University of Pennsylvania and Cheyney University in a multi-year research project to reduce hypertension in targeted populations in Pennsylvania.

Finally, for the last few years, the generosity of trustee emeritus Otto Roethenmund has enabled two recent graduates to attend a meeting of Nobel Prize-winners in Lindau, Germany. This year's conference, described as "the Olympics of worldwide research, attracted 700 outstanding young scientists from more than 54 countries, a group referred to as "the top 10 percent of their generation." This event epitomizes our aspirations for all of our emerging Dickinson scientists.

At Dickinson, we remain committed to the vision of our founder, Dr. Benjamin Rush, to provide a science education that is renowned for its excellence and fully integrated into a liberal-arts education that seeks to instill a global sensitivity in *all* of our students.

We expect our graduates to be prepared through a "useful" liberal-arts education to become the citizen-leaders of their generation and to use their knowledge to create a more just and compassionate society. The 21st century will pose endless possibilities and challenges for our science students. They are Dickinsonians, and therefore, I know they will succeed.

FALL 2006

"If Dickinson College were a corporation, Wall Street would view it as a classic turnaround story." So began a recent feature article in *The Chronicle of Higher Education*. The operational management of colleges and universities is not always headline-grabbing material. But at Dickinson, we have quite a story to tell.

Administrative effectiveness is a critical component for academic excellence. A well-run institution maximizes its assets to attract the very best students and faculty and then allocates available resources to create an on-campus environment that values and stimulates intellectual discovery.

At Dickinson, we have had the good fortune to assemble an administrative team whose recent accomplishments on virtually every front are nothing short of astonishing. Let's begin with the endowment—the fiscal foundation that feeds our operating budget and secures our future. Eight years ago, our endowment stood at a modest $150 million. Today, it is rapidly approaching $300 million. In fiscal year 2004-05 alone, the endowment rose by nearly 30 percent, a performance that placed us 16th among 746 higher-education institutions.

Our graduates have played a major role in the endowment's growth. A select group of alumni financial wizards has worked with our treasurer and the board's Committee on Investments to broaden our portfolio, realign asset allocation and think strategically about our investment approach. Equally important is the substantial increase in alumni contributions—large and small. While we have celebrated 21 leadership gifts of more than $1 million since 2000, alumni gifts of less than $100 totaled a whopping $174,000 last year—a testament to the hard work of our development staff and a clear indication that many of our alumni are seizing ownership of their college.

The progress on the admissions front is equally impressive. This year applications topped 5,000 for the first time—a benchmark that places us among the most competitive liberal-arts colleges in the country. The quality of our applicants continues to rise, and our list of "overlap" schools—those institutions with which we compete most aggressively for students—reveals that we are increasingly seen by applicants as a top-tier national liberal-arts college.

While our long-standing regional competitors—Gettysburg, Franklin & Marshall and Bucknell—still make the list of our top 10 overlap schools, our roster now includes Hamilton, Colby, Kenyon and Lafayette colleges, and for the first time, Georgetown, a major research university.

Providing our faculty and students with facilities that advance their academic interests has also been a recent priority. In May, we broke ground for the Keystone Phase of the Rector Science Campus—the most ambitious construction project in our history. With occupancy slated for 2008, this state-of-the-art facility will position Dickinson as a leader in undergraduate science pedagogy and research in the 21st century. We also are constructing a new Sustainable Living (or "Tree") House, among many other campus improvements. It is no small achievement that, in an era of unpredictable and rising construction costs, all projects are coming in on time and on budget.

But there's more. Earlier this year, Dickinson received solid acknowledgement of its managerial competency when Standard & Poor's upgraded the college bond rating by two notches—the highest rating in Dickinson's history.

While we are proud that we are receiving attention for being an exceptionally well-run institution, we know that the real measure of our excellence lies with our academic program and the accomplishments of our faculty, students and alumni.

Just as we can measure the increase in our endowment, we are able to gauge our rising prestige by tracking our media visibility. In

1999-2000, stories about Dickinson reached approximately 1.5 million readers. Last year, media impressions rose to a remarkable 239 million—a testament to the college's ascending reputation *and* the effectiveness of our college relations staff in propelling the Dickinson story into the wider world.

Watch those headlines! I am confident that this powerful combination of academic accomplishment and managerial effectiveness will continue to put Dickinson on front pages for years to come.

WINTER 2007

With this issue, we celebrate the launching of the most ambitious capital campaign in Dickinson's history. It is a historic turning point for our college that builds on our extraordinary recent momentum and promises to propel us into an even more impressive future. The success of this campaign will bring us closer to the highest aspiration of our founder, Dr. Benjamin Rush—to be considered permanently among the nation's premier liberal-arts colleges; to be, in his words, "First in America."

By definition, capital campaigns focus on raising resources for specific purposes—in this case, for faculty development, scholarship support, a new science facility and augmentation of the annual fund. Our capital campaign is a strategic means to reclaim, through our own personal investment, our connection with our alma mater and to remind ourselves of what it means to be a Dickinsonian.

As alumni, we have experienced a distinctive liberal-arts education that has allowed us to develop a set of shared dispositions that will forever characterize us as true Dickinsonians. Handed down to us by Dr. Rush, these five dispositions are the habits of mind that distinguish us among our peers; they are the qualities we strive to instill in our current and future students, enabling them to perpetuate the Dickinson tradition.

What are these Dickinson dispositions?

- As Dickinsonians, we possess an acute global sensibility grounded in a deep appreciation of languages and cultures. We operate confidently in unfamiliar environments as we pursue intellectual interests in the context of global affairs. We demonstrate a strong commitment to inclusiveness, pluralism and democracy as we seek to build bridges of communication with the amazing variety of people we encounter.

- We possess an intellectual flexibility that allows us to make meaningful connections among people, ideas and disciplines. Where others see only disparate dots, we see the value in connecting those dots. We eagerly seek the intersections of seemingly incongruent ideas, recognizing that these interdisciplinary crossroads spawn new discoveries, knowledge and paradigms that will shape our future.

- Our Dickinson experience has also taught us what it means to "engage the world" in every conceivable sense of the phrase. We move easily beyond that which is comfortable to embrace intellectual risk and gain self-knowledge and, by practicing leadership in useful service to society, we work constantly to build a just, compassionate and economically viable society.

- As Dickinsonians, we assume a responsibility to speak out on issues of importance to us and to society, arriving at our position through informed and reasoned reflection. Although our ideas may sometimes be unpopular, we have the courage to wield tenacity in the face of adversity, exercising respect, civility and a sense of humor when communicating with those whose views may differ from our own.

- Finally, as Dickinsonians, we understand the importance of accountability and sustainability. Driven by integrity and modesty, our personal achievements are informed by our sense of responsibility to the greater good and the ecological, financial and social consequences of even our smallest actions.

These five dispositions, introduced on campus this fall, have now become common topics of discussion. It is no accident that our more purposeful articulation of Dickinson's defining principles accompanied the kickoff of our capital campaign, for campaigns should engender a good deal of institutional soul-searching to ensure that our compass is accurate and our trajectory secure.

Lengthy conversations with key constituents about needed resources invariably led us to specify the ultimate purpose of our endeavor, and that is the responsibility we have: to give future students every opportunity to develop these dispositions to prepare them to lead in the complex, contemporary world.

Your accomplishments as alumni already have made these dispositions reality for so many of our students. This capital campaign gives you yet another opportunity to lead by example.

As you join with us to move our college forward, always remember that an investment in specific campaign priorities, ultimately, is an investment in our students—the very essence of Dickinson. It is an investment that is destined to bring us closer to Dr. Rush's goal, to be "First in America."

Spring 2007

An op-ed piece by David Brooks in the Feb. 4 *New York Times* caused me to reflect on the state of mind of students nationwide and the role a liberal-arts education should play in our increasingly complex world.

Referring to the current generation of collegians as "children of polarization," Brooks has observed a striking tendency among today's students to avoid broad philosophical arguments, drifting instead toward centrist positions in a valiant effort to balance idealism and realism. Highly suspicious of "sweepingly idealistic political ventures," students tend to pick and choose arguments from both sides of an issue to arrive at a decidedly pragmatic and anti-ideological center.

Brooks's observation stands in striking contrast to the orientation presented by students who, just a few years ago, were arriving on our doorstep with well-developed and often extremely ideological positions. Far from embracing thoughtful challenges to their views, they believed that a college education should merely affirm the validity of their ideas. Our challenge with these students was to encourage them to acknowledge and, at the very least, respect a difference of opinion.

The new pragmatic students appear to be sifting through both sides of issues, but I wonder if we should be endorsing this inclination to cobble together modest, middle-of-the-road positions that are merely transactional—like an exchange of business information—and not reached after thoughtful and extensive investigation.

All too often, pragmatic—or transactional—thinkers design their stances to achieve immediate results but lack a true understanding of the depth and complexity that characterize our global society's most nettlesome challenges.

Picking and choosing those elements of arguments that, perhaps, are safest and easiest allows one to avoid the intellectual and scientific rigor needed to develop a well-researched position that fits into a larger, comprehensive vision. Equally troubling, this transactional approach is not driven by inspiration. It lacks the intensity and passion that motivates those who adhere to a broader idealism and who are ethically and morally committed to making the world a better place—not only today but well into the future.

Brooks' article led me to revisit a recent book by Harold T. Shapiro, former president of the University of Michigan and Princeton University. In *A Larger Sense of Purpose: Higher Education and Society* Shapiro asserts that the prototypical liberal-arts education serves "society as both a responsive servant and a thoughtful critic." A liberal institution's defining charge is to act as the enduring critic of the status quo, always attempting to be "a force for change, playing a significant role in society's critical self-examination, helping to allow a shift in the allocation of resources and power" and, perhaps most important, to believe that the world and its inhabitants can achieve "a better set of arrangements."

I am not certain that one can serve as an "enduring critic" while at the same time opting for the middle-of-the-road path of transactional positions. At Dickinson, we maintain that a liberal-arts education must be useful to society. But this usefulness—infused with a healthy dose of pragmatism—must be defined by something bigger than achieving immediate results. It is a usefulness that results in sustained and meaningful progress toward a greater good, underscored by a sense of purpose and a commitment to broader ideals.

Our immediate challenge, it seems to me, is to capitalize on our students' willingness to evaluate both sides of an issue and to provide them with the intellectual tools they need to lead in an increasingly polarized world.

We need to encourage them to resist the urge to confront only the immediate and instill in them the intellectual curiosity and dedication to weave disparate strands of various arguments into a conceptual framework that provides sustained guidance beyond the issue at hand. The positions and courses of action that follow will, I am confident, rise above the purely transactional to reflect a passionate commitment to achieve "a better set of arrangements," which is the hallmark of a successful liberal-arts education.

SPRING 2008

This issue of the magazine explores Dickinson's rich, evolving and multidimensional relationship with China. Recognizing the central role China will play on the global stage of the 21st century, Dickinson is once again leading the way in forging important and enduring partnerships with this emerging giant.

The depth of our involvement with China is one more indication of the pre-eminence of our global-education program. Our China connection began more than a century ago, when Robert Samuel Maclay arrived in Fuzhou, two years after his 1845 graduation, as part of the first wave of American missionaries.

Nearly a half-century ago, Dickinson blazed a new trail as one of the first liberal-arts colleges to establish its own study-abroad programs in Western Europe. As international and geopolitical dynamics shifted, we responded by developing a network of centers and exchange programs in other critical parts of the world. Today, our reach is truly global as our students embark to immerse themselves in the cultures of India, Africa, Latin America, Western Europe, Eastern Europe—and, of course, China. This year, we have 19 students in Beijing at Peking University, with which we became affiliated in 1998.

Dickinson's position as *the* leader in study abroad was further solidified when we became the home to the Forum on Education Abroad in 2006. Under the leadership of the executive director of Dickinson's global-education program, Brian Whalen, the Forum is composed of more than 300 institutions and organizations that, together, represent more than 80 percent of U.S students who study abroad. It also is recognized by the U.S. Department of Justice as the Standards Development Organization for Study Abroad.

Most recently, and in response to heightened scrutiny of the education-abroad industry, the Forum sponsored a meeting on our campus to draft a Code of Ethics, which will become part of its highly regarded *Standards of Good Practice for Education Abroad.* These standards have now been widely disseminated and establish best practices relating to study-abroad mission, policies and procedures, resources, and ethics and integrity. It is, of course, no coincidence that the bar for excellence in global education was recently raised even higher on Dickinson's campus.

Dickinson is now poised to push the frontiers of global education in yet another critical and timely way. The college was recently awarded a $1.4 million grant from the Andrew Mellon Foundation to develop a comprehensive environmental-sustainability initiative that will engage most, if not all, academic departments. Just as a grant from the National Endowment for the Humanities laid the foundation for our global-education program 25 years ago, we envision the Mellon grant as the bedrock of a focus on environmental sustainability that will become infused throughout our curriculum and our day-to-day operations. We anticipate that environmental sustainability will become—along with excellence in global education—a defining characteristic of a Dickinson liberal-arts education.

Even more exciting will be the convergence of these two defining initiatives. We fully intend for environmental sustainability to become an integral component of the student experience on all of our campuses and in all of our study-abroad programs. The opportunities and possibilities that could emerge from an intersection of our focus on global study and environmental sustainability are breathtaking and extraordinarily important.

We have already begun, for example, substantive discussions with our partner institution, the University of East Anglia in Norwich, England, which is a world leader in environmental science and management. Dickinson's Australian site at the University of Queensland also has extensive environmental course offerings, and our program in Costa Rica specializes in sustainable agriculture and tropical ecology. As our focus on environmental sustainability takes root, we will explore similar connections with our partner institutions in Cameroon, France, Germany, India, Italy, Japan, Mexico, Russia, Spain—and, of course, China.

The environmental challenges created by the world's emerging economies, such as China's, are among the most serious our global society will face in the 21st century. By infusing our students' experience with both global and environmental-sustainability perspectives, we intend to prepare our students to confront these challenges from the global, multicultural and sociopolitically complex vantage point they deserve. As *the* leader in global education, Dickinson must expect no less.

FALL 2008

On Sept. 9, Dickinson College celebrated the 225th anniversary of the enactment of its charter. On that date, the commonwealth of Pennsylvania established "in the borough of Carlisle, in the county of Cumberland ... a college ... forever hereafter called and known by the name of 'Dickinson College.' "

It is both interesting and enlightening to revisit the first several sections of this act that so succinctly and clearly lay out the purpose for which our college was formed:

> *Whereas, the happiness and prosperity of every community ... depends much on the right education of youth, who must succeed the aged in the important offices of society, and the most exalted nations have acquired their preeminence, by the virtuous principle and liberal knowledge instilled into the minds of the rising generation:*

> *And whereas, after a long and bloody contest with a great and powerful kingdom ... [we] are placed in a condition to attend to the useful arts, sciences and literature, and it is the evident duty and interest of all ranks of people to promote and encourage ... every attempt to disseminate and promote the growth of useful knowledge.*

In these two brief paragraphs, one can see the persuasive, guiding hand of our founder, Dr. Benjamin Rush. There is the strong emphasis on the "usefulness" of a liberal-arts education. There is the firm acknowledgement that education and the dissemination of knowledge must be indispensable foundations of the emerging democracy. And there is the explicit expectation that those who are to be educated at Dickinson College will become the leaders of their generation. It is, of course, the timelessness of these directives that is most impressive.

This lively presidential election year provides us with a particularly good opportunity to think about and reframe these expectations for the contemporary world. Regardless of one's political leanings, it is fair to say that we are seeing a resurgent interest in the electoral process—particularly among younger voters—and that the outcome of the election will shift and shape our nation's future. Benjamin Rush would have relished the chance to participate in such momentous change.

For Rush, preparing students for civic participation went well beyond mere voting. Always an expansive thinker, Rush thought in terms of a broad national educational system that began with public elementary school and culminated in a national university that would provide graduate training for those who would serve in the most responsible public positions. Arriving at the national university with college degree in hand, these students would, Rush wrote, "acquire those branches of knowledge, which will increase the conveniences of life, lessen human misery, improve our country, promote population, exalt the human understanding, and establish domestic, social and political happiness." Although Rush's idea of a federal university never came to pass, these remain expansive and daunting expectations for those of us educated in the liberal arts at Dickinson College.

The mandates of our charter, coupled with Rush's call for a federal university to train public servants, are all the more interesting given recent congressional interest in establishing a National Public Service Academy. This proposed legislation complements other national efforts to revive a strong sense of civic engagement and commitment among college students.

Dickinson, not surprisingly, is at the forefront of some of these discussions. Later this year, we will join in partnership with the University of Maine and other institutions to explore the advisability of a public-service academy, especially since liberal-arts schools like Dickinson have been advancing these responsibilities for generations. It is time to debate rigorously and seriously the proper relationship between institutions of higher education and public service in the 21st century.

And so, 225 years after the enactment of our charter, we find ourselves still guided by its sage and timeless mandates—and still challenged as to the best way to fulfill our historical responsibilities. I invite you to reflect deeply upon our charter's fundamental premises. (If you wish to read the full charter you may find it at http://chronicles.dickinson.edu/archives/charter_orig/.) More than mere words on an ancient document, the charter's precepts still provide Dickinson College—our students, faculty and alumni—with remarkably wise guidance and an impressive sense of purpose.

On March 22, I received a visit from Lockwood Rush—a direct descendant of our founder, Dr. Benjamin Rush, and his wife, Jackie. Over the last several years, Elke and I have enjoyed getting to know Lockwood, an accomplished individual whose own life mirrors closely that of his famous ancestor—Princetonian, doctorate in psychology and longtime Philadelphia resident.

This particular visit, however, proved to be an exceptional one, as Lockwood presented me with Dr. Rush's personal Bible. This well-worn volume—complete with Rush's notations in the margins—leaves no doubt that religion was important in Rush's life. As Charles Coleman Sellers so accurately observed in his history of Dickinson College, Rush "acknowledged no segments or boundaries to Christian duty—medicine, politics, social reform, education, all were one."

And so, in Rush's underlining and handwritten marginalia sprinkled throughout his Bible we find the collision of various aspects of his life. Take Luke 4:6, for example (with underlining by Rush): "And the devil said unto him, All this power I will give thee, and the glory of them; for *that is delivered unto me*, and to whomsoever I will, I give it." And Rush's wry, handwritten commentary in the margin: "The bad characteristics of kings, and the misery of kingdoms, make this truth."

If Rush sought guidance from the Bible to explain his position against the crown, it also propelled him to take progressive and often controversial positions as he advocated for the abolition of slavery, penal reform, better public-health policies and—as the foundation of it all—access to education. Consistent with Rush's overarching philosophy about a liberal-arts education, action motivated by Christian principle was to be above all useful.

As in so many aspects of his life, Rush's religion was ecumenical, fluid and, ultimately, so very American. Born and raised a Presbyterian, Rush readily accepted those whose faith differed from his own, and he was intrigued intellectually and culturally with the Islamic and Jewish religions. Over time, Rush's own commitment to Presbyterianism shifted as he became a Universalist. And while he remained a devout Christian, Rush joined the other Founding Fathers in their adamant opposition to comingling of church and state, emphatically rejecting calls to make the new government a Christian nation.

Pragmatic to the core, Rush originally sought an affiliation between Dickinson and the Presbyterian Church, believing that such a relationship would result in a constant source of students and financial support for the new college. When it became apparent that he would have to seek public funding for Dickinson, however, Rush quickly saw the advantages of establishing a college that was technically "nondenominational."

Rush's Christian faith, his ecumenicalism and his passion to leave the world a better place than he found it have left their mark on Dickinson. Dr. Rush's Bible—which I encourage you to view in our Archives & Special Collections—provides a tangible link between our founder's historic vision and our contemporary values and mission. Our heartfelt gratitude goes out to Lockwood and Jackie Rush for their generosity and for understanding how much this extraordinary gift means to Dickinsonians.

FALL 2009

Although the rising cost of higher education has been a national issue for several decades, the collapse of the economy last fall has given it heightened visibility and made it an urgent concern for many prospective students. Tightening student loan options, employment uncertainty and continuing market volatility have caused many families to question seriously their ability to pay for a college education—particularly at prestigious residential liberal-arts colleges.

Dickinson has responded quickly and creatively to the current crisis. Maintaining access for all qualified students has been—and remains—a core element of our mission. Our founder, Dr. Benjamin Rush, intentionally established our college on what was then the nation's Western frontier to broaden access to higher education among the citizens of the new democracy. In an effort to fulfill this responsibility under these singular 21st-century circumstances, we have taken several significant and innovative steps.

First, even though Dickinson has experienced a significant drop in endowment and other revenue since last fall, we made the decision early on to increase need-based financial aid by 12 percent above that expended last year. This means that, this academic year, we anticipate allocating $31.5 million to give worthy and qualified students the opportunity to receive a Dickinson liberal-arts education.

Our second step occurred earlier this spring, when we launched an extremely creative partnership with five community colleges that are within 100 miles of Carlisle. Recognizing that community colleges are increasingly the entry point to higher education for many students, we established the Community College Partnership Program to provide a structured pathway for students to transfer to Dickinson after their first two years.

The program ensures that the selected first-year students—all of whom will be enrolled in community-college honors programs—will receive the support, coaching and coursework necessary to eventually transfer and be successful at Dickinson. The college also will offer financial incentives—a community-college scholarship and financial aid—to enable students to complete their education here.

Giving returning military veterans easier access to a liberal-arts education by participating in the Department of Veterans Affairs (VA) Yellow Ribbon GI Education Enhancement Program is a third step in our new affordability outreach. Eligible veterans will receive course grants and scholarships which, when coupled with educational grants from the VA and other sources, will allow them to attend Dickinson tuition free.

Dr. Rush equated patriotism not only with military duty but with community and public service—defined most broadly. "Patriots … come forward!" he wrote. "Your country demands your success … in her governments, in her finances, in her trade, in her manufactures, in her morals and in her manners."

To acknowledge the enormous role public service plays in our society and to encourage prospective students to embrace this form of patriotism, we have established a fourth new college access and affordability option, the Dickinson College Public Service Fellowship.

This program accommodates those students who may wish to take a "gap" year—or years—after high school before matriculating. Participants will earn a $10,000 tuition credit per year for up to four years by engaging in meaningful public service devoted to improving the human condition or the natural environment. Upon matriculation, participants will be eligible for additional financial assistance and receive priority consideration for positions such as residential and community advisors.

These new programs acknowledge the shifting higher-education landscape within which we now must operate. They demonstrate that we remain adamantly committed to providing a first-rate education and firmly convinced that our nation and our global society desperately require the talents and leadership of those who have received a "useful" and distinctive Dickinson liberal-arts education. Our ongoing challenge will be to continue to find innovative ways to maintain affordability and offer access to students who demonstrate the promise of becoming true Dickinsonians.

WINTER 2010

This academic year, Dickinson celebrates the 125th anniversary of the matriculation of women. We mark this milestone from the arrival of Zatae Longsdorff in 1884 as a transfer student from Wellesley College.

Zatae, of course, proved to be a most remarkable woman. After graduating from Dickinson, she went on to earn a medical degree, serve as a doctor on an Indian reservation, win election to the New Hampshire legislature and become the first woman elected president of the American Medical Society.

Zatae's accomplishments not only heralded the value of a Dickinson education for women as well as men, but they also confirmed the convictions of our founder, Dr. Benjamin Rush. As on so many issues, Rush was far ahead of his time in his views on the role of women in American society. He was an early advocate for giving women access to public education, primarily because he believed educated mothers would be better able to prepare their children—especially, their sons—for lives of engaged citizenship in the new democracy.

Although this emphasis on women as mothers reflects the prevailing 18th-century perspective, Rush clearly valued the contributions a learned woman could bring to the pressing issues of the day. We see this in the company he kept. He was, for example, a very close friend of the magnificent and powerful Abigail Adams. He also was extremely supportive of Elizabeth Graeme Fergusson, about whom he eventually penned a biography. Ferguson established what may have been the first literary salon in America; it became the intellectual center for a firestorm of revolutionary ideas. A frequent visitor to her parlor, Rush once wrote that she "appeared to be all mind."

Today we continue to find inspiration in the accomplishments of Zatae and in Dr. Rush's progressive views about women. Last year, with the generous assistance of Raphael Hays '56 and Linda Goodridge Steckley '63, Dickinson was able to hire a full-time director for the Women's Center.

And at the recent opening of an exhibit celebrating the 125th anniversary of women at Dickinson, I announced that Landis House located at the corner of College and Pomfret streets would become the permanent home of the center, providing a dedicated space in which issues related to women and gender can be addressed to enhance our campus culture.

It is fitting that Landis House has its own special history that celebrates the accomplishments of women. The house was once the home of Lois Lowry, a granddaughter of its former owner, Merkel Landis, class of 1896. Lois became a noted young-adult author and a recipient of the Newbery Medal.

During World War II, she and her mother returned to Carlisle to live in the family house. Her memories of those years later served as the basis of her popular book, *Autumn Street*. For a college that reveres its past, we are now appropriate stewards of this little piece of history.

As we celebrate the past 125 years of women at Dickinson, it is equally important that we look to the future. We have a powerful legacy to uphold as we seek to provide opportunities for our women students—who now constitute 55 percent of our enrollment—to contribute to the advancement of our 21st-century global society. I am confident that the new Women's Center, coupled with our strong curricular offerings in women's & gender studies, will open new doors for our current students that will allow them to set an example for future generations of Dickinsonians.

SPRING 2010

Environmental sustainability has become a defining characteristic of a Dickinson education. While our nation and its colleges and universities come to grips with the sustainability issues that must become global priorities in the 21st century, Dickinson is maintaining and accelerating a focus on the environment that dates back to our founder, Dr. Benjamin Rush.

As a physician, Rush understood the interplay between the environment and public health. He specifically rejected one proposed site for Dickinson College because he believed the swampy environment would lead to unhealthful conditions for the campus community.

While arguably behind the advance of medicine in his advocacy of practices such as bleeding, Dr. Rush was more characteristically ahead of his peers in the medical community when he hypothesized that the 1793 yellow fever epidemic in Philadelphia was somehow tied to the stagnant water that existed in the city. Although Rush neglected to identify the mosquitoes that bred in the stagnant pools as the ultimate cause, his assertion that the disease was linked to natural environmental conditions rather than imported from abroad was path breaking and bold for its time.

Dickinson has continued to be a leader in the exploration of the impact that environmental factors have on quality of life. More than a quarter century ago, we were one of the first institutions of higher education to establish programs in environmental science and environmental studies. These programs, in turn, spawned the highly regarded ALLARM (Alliance for Aquatic Resource Monitoring) initiative that helps central Pennsylvania communities monitor the quality of their water.

Our efforts to promote sustainability through sound operational practices are no less impressive. Since September, 100 percent of the college's electricity consumption has been now offset through the use of wind power.

Our utility trucks run on vegetable oil recycled from our dining services, and most of our fleet vehicles are gas/electric hybrids. Our new facilities and renovation construction projects are earning LEED (Leadership in Energy and Environmental Design) certification, while the College Farm supplies dining services with locally grown produce.

All of these efforts contribute to our pledge to the American College and University President's Climate Commitment to become carbon neutral by 2020. Our historic focus on environmental sustainability was sharpened two years ago when we received a $1.4 million grant from the Mellon Foundation. This funding allowed us to bring Neil Leary, a national leader in the study of climate change, to campus as the director of the Center for Environmental and Sustainability Education. Through his leadership, Dickinson is infusing creative concepts about sustainability and the natural world throughout the curriculum, and the center has become a central, integrative hub for all of our sustainability initiatives.

Our comprehensive approach to sustainability reflects our belief that issues related to the environment will be absolutely critical in the 21st century. Irrespective of one's political point of view, our students must be prepared to address these global issues knowledgably, constructively and critically when they depart these limestone walls for the wider world.

Dickinson's leadership in this key area is gaining considerable national attention. In the last year alone, Dickinson was:

- given an A- on the 2010 Sustainable Endowments Institute Green Report Card, the highest overall grade given by the institute

- listed as a "cool school" by the Sierra Club and as one of the top-20 greenest colleges in America

* placed on The Princeton Review's Green Honor Roll

* listed by *Forbes* magazine as one of America's top-10 greenest colleges

* and awarded the 2009 Pennsylvania Governor's Award for Environmental Excellence.

Although many colleges and universities now tout a commitment to environmental sustainability, Dickinson's focus is genuine and deeply rooted in our history. As Neil Leary notes, we're not just following the pack, "We're the real deal." We are, in short, renewing and refining our historic commitment to a useful liberal-arts education and, in so doing, positioning Dickinson College and its graduates for global leadership as we confront the pressing environmental challenges of the 21st century.

Summer 2011

Upon learning that animals would be the theme for this issue of *Dickinson Magazine,* I immediately knew what I wanted to focus on—Mabel. It probably comes as no surprise to learn that, as a college president, I am often asked to speak to groups of young people about what it means to be a leader and to comment on my own leadership journey. On such occasions, people often are surprised to learn that my experience raising chickens as a boy in upstate New York provided me with several life lessons that I continue to draw upon. Mabel, my prized, winged friend, was at the heart of it.

The groundwork—if not the first egg—was laid in 1958 in Rensselaer County, N.Y., when I joined my local 4-H chapter, the Happy Clovers. I began growing vegetables—not knowing there were such varieties as pencil pod wax beans, honeycross sweet corn, Kennebec potatoes and Chontenay carrots, until I cultivated them for entry at the nearby Schaghticoke Fair. I learned one significant lesson during that first year concerning the dangers of procrastination. As I noted on my official notes for the '58 season, "failure to plough early this spring almost resulted in my not having a garden!"

As I grew older and assumed more responsibility, I learned first-hand about raising animals—this is where Mabel enters the story. The local Kiwanis Club gave me Mabel when she was a chick. To ensure that I was raising her properly, a Kiwanian—the first of several mentors in my life—would come to our house periodically to see how Mabel and I were doing. I also had to bring her to a Kiwanis meeting and report to the group on our progress. Of course, as all good farmers know, the hardest part of the job is realizing that one day you must bid farewell to your livestock.

So what did I take away from my experience with Mabel? First, I learned about responsibility by working with my Kiwanis mentor and ensuring that Mabel was well cared for. Second, as I acquired more chickens, I developed entrepreneurial skills, creating my own egg-selling business and making cold calls to customers—my neighbors. This latter skill would translate into my development/fundraising work later in life. Third, what better way to develop public-speaking skills than to have to make a presentation to a club while holding a clucking, flapping chicken under your arm?

However, the most important lesson did not occur to me until much later in life, when I was working for Johns Hopkins University and meeting with leaders of a prominent Los Angeles-based foundation to whom I was making a fundraising pitch.

The meeting was not going too well, until I noticed an image of a chicken hanging on the office wall. I immediately asked about its origin and discovered that the foundation officer and I shared a common bond of raising chickens as youngsters. My discovery of that commonality brought the meeting to a successful conclusion that included a significant gift for the university. And most strikingly, I came away realizing that no one should ever underestimate or belittle any life experience, no matter how seemingly trivial—you never know when that knowledge and skill may come in handy.

When I arrived at Dickinson in 1999, I had several ambitions for the college, which the leadership team and Board of Trustees quickly embraced. They were: to elevate Dickinson's name recognition and prestige as a top-tier national, liberal-arts college; to recapture its history and intrinsic strengths and make them known internally and externally; to develop a strong institutional identity and an accompanying leadership narrative; to strengthen the operating budget; and to increase the endowment considerably.

We also knew that achieving these ambitions would require bolstering significantly Dickinson's culture of philanthropy by expanding the circle of engaged and committed alumni, parents and friends. To achieve this aim, I vowed that Dickinson would never be out of "campaign mode," as a more-robust fundraising program would be critical to achieving our strategic goals and fulfilling the still very relevant guideposts set forth by our founder, Dr. Benjamin Rush.

In October 2006, the college kicked off the $150 million *First in America: Fulfilling Our Destiny* campaign under the incredible leadership of George and Jennifer Ward Reynolds '77. The college community came together at Alumni Weekend this June to celebrate the successful conclusion of the campaign.

Even with the added challenge of weathering a global financial crisis and the country's most challenging economic times since the Great Depression, the *First in America* campaign inspired many Dickinsonians to make the college a significant beneficiary of their philanthropic investments—and we reached our goal six months early!

If we consider just the last 10 years, the college has raised nearly $200 million—three times more than in any other decade in the college's history. At a time when many organizations faced shrinking budgets and vanishing contributions, our community stepped forward to make the goals of this campaign a reality.

The impact of the *First in America* campaign is evident across the campus. It includes the creation of the Rector Science Complex, renovations to Biddle Field, an additional $80 million for the endowment, 70 endowed scholarships, 16 endowed chairs and two directorships,

$25 million to support academic programs and student life, and funds to launch the Center for Sustainability Education.

These are incredible advances that directly benefit today's students. In addition, we have enrolled more highly qualified and diverse students than in the past, and we have made headway in growing the endowment which, even with the additional campaign gifts, remains undersized compared to the endowments of our peer and aspirant institutions. As you may know, a robust endowment ensures future financial stability for the college—through good times and bad—permitting more resources to be directed to our students' education, thus amplifying the college's distinction and prestige.

The overwhelming response to the *First in America* campaign confirmed what our senior leadership and the Board of Trustees suspected all along—that this college was ready to advance again to ensure a more financially sound future. Therefore, I am pleased to share that the trustees voted in May to extend the *First in America* campaign with the goal of raising an additional $150 million during the next six years for a total of $300 million.

Much like the initial phase of the *First in America* campaign, the projects and initiatives identified as priorities for the second phase have been developed with our undergraduates in mind.

We will continue to focus on enhancing the academic experience by improving not only the quality of a student's experience inside the classroom, but also a critical and complementary element—the environment outside the classroom. To solidify our place among the college's most competitive liberal-arts colleges, with which we now compete directly for students, these are essential ambitions.

While we celebrate the success of the most recent campaign, we also pragmatically acknowledge that Dickinson remains one generation behind its aspirants, many of which in the last two years have initiated campaigns of $400 million to $500 million. But we are rapidly closing the gap.

We enter this next campaign with a new confidence and proven track record, demonstrating that our alumni, parents and friends are determined to make this college one of their top philanthropic interests. They recognize that with a Dickinson diploma comes an obligation—to give back through volunteer efforts, to promote Dickinson through personal networks and to make meaningful financial contributions. Serving as co-chairs of this new phase of *First in America* are college trustee Amy Nauiokas '94 and her husband, Harry Harrison.

With renewed enthusiasm and the confidence that our constituents are dedicated and committed, I anticipate the new aspirations we will achieve by continuing *First in America*.

SPRING 2012

The subject of this issue—technology—can be at once disturbing and welcome in the liberal-arts setting. While liberal-arts colleges permit technologically delivered syllabi and electronically submitted exams and papers, few give credit for a course taken online. Of course, there are some outstanding liberal-arts colleges that are venturing into uncharted territory. Wesleyan, Bryn Mawr and Dickinson are developing course segments that treat online what is considered necessary but not worthy of precious class time. Many colleges see technology as an inevitable development in undergraduate education, as it can deliver increased access, convenience and scope of information.

Dickinson is engaging technology in many positive ways, as you will read in this issue. However, having received a liberal-arts education at Dickinson and respecting the necessity to question what it all means, I will share a few thoughts that I have not fully processed. You might simply say that I am using this space to think out loud (remember those wonderful late night "bull sessions"?)

I recently read in *The Economist* that our ongoing global economic crisis can be attributed, in part, to a delivery cycle of new technological products that is so short and includes so many products that the consumer simply can't keep up. The only form of self-protection is to retreat and avoid or delay consuming. But markets are not designed for hesitancy. There can be no slippage; there can be no pause. If the consumer does not respond as the markets expect, the economy becomes a train wreck. Technology meets an immutable force—the human mind's capacity for innovation and tolerance for distraction.

I relate this technology-human collision to undergraduate education via an article I read in the winter 2011 *Johns Hopkins Magazine*. "Paying Attention to Distraction: Why is something as vital as attentiveness so hard to achieve?" by Dale Keiger begins with a vignette that many of us might appreciate. An iPhone user exchanges his smartphone for one without e-mail, GPS or fun apps. "The manager of the AT&T store said that a striking number of his customers were doing the same thing—and so had he. He was fed up with the distraction," wrote Keiger.

Keiger then correlates this distraction with undergraduate education, citing P.M. Forni, a JHU professor of romance languages who published a book, *The Thinking Life*, on the topic. Forni "worries that reliance on the Internet, plus the distractions inherent in constantly being connected to digital information streams—Facebook, texting—has begun to undermine deep reading, serious thought, and the ethical engagement of one person with another."

Keiger also cites Nicholas Carr, author of *The Shallows: What The Internet Is Doing To Our Brains*, linking rapid technological change to consumer resistance. "Carr … calls working memory 'the mind's scratch pad,' and it is essential to the formation of long-term memory and higher intellectual ability like reasoning and creating knowledge. The amount of information following into working memory, known as cognitive load, can exceed working memory's capacity for storing and processing it. Whenever this happens it impairs learning, knowledge, and deeper thinking."

Keiger also invokes JHU history professor Gabrielle Spiegel, who "has noticed [that students] are used to really small chunks of things. … A noticeable consequence is they now have greater difficulty in building a long logical argument, [understanding] what should be subordinate, etc."

Forni's worries about what is lost when one succumbs to the distractions inherent in the Internet and Carr's desire to preserve long-term memory and higher intellectual ability, like reasoning and creating knowledge, sound a lot like a defense of the very purpose of a liberal-arts education. And Spiegel's observation resonates with a judgment about the quality of theological reasoning that I read recently in *Bonhoeffer: Pastor, Martyr, Prophet, Spy*, a new biography about the late German theologian.

According to author Eric Metaxas, Dietrich Bonhoeffer distinguished between Karl Barth and Adolf von Harnack, saying that von Harnack's theology was "like Archilochus's proverbial fox, knowing many little things, while Barth's theology was like a hedgehog, knowing one big thing." Bonhoeffer "learned how to think like a fox and respect the way the foxes thought, even though he was in the camp of the hedgehogs."

Seems to me that we who believe in the liberal arts are on the side of the hedgehog, but when it comes to rapid and dizzying technological innovation on campus and in the world around us, it remains to be seen if we can also dance with the foxes.

FALL 2012

In my final year as Dickinson's president, I have been prompted to reflect on a number of topics, including what makes a Dickinson education so valuable and distinctive in today's 21st-century society. Some of my thoughts on this, which were included in my August Convocation address when I welcomed the incoming students, are relevant for alumni and parents as well.

In my remarks, I related that last summer I read in the *International Herald Tribune* about the "exploding" audience for original works of art. The head of the venerable auction house, Christie's in London, Steven P. Murphy, explained the increased appeal: "I think that the virtual world, the ease of access to images in high definition, the total availability of art online—all those things have increased the value of the object itself." The role of an institution like Christie's, he said, is that of "honoring the object."

Well, in a strange way, Dickinson is like Christie's—our primary mission is to "honor the object itself." Those who choose to come to

Dickinson realize just how precious and ultimately useful the pursuit of the object itself is, as opposed to its mere image—a facsimile—even if it "costs" more. Of course, it has to cost more: It is the "object itself." It is created by high-labor intensity and unfolds in intricate precision.

Undergraduate research universities, and increasingly many colleges, are filled with exceedingly large classes, radically diminished in- and out-of-class resources, graduate-student and adjunct instructors, professors obsessed with their own research agendas, online-virtual courses and degree programs that often extend over six or more years because of the unavailability of required courses. Instead, Dickinson students have chosen to experience a premier undergraduate education—direct interaction in a physically and emotionally safe 24/7 residential setting with a small group of similarly motivated learners. They have chosen to be among dedicated professors who are committed solely to their students and their intellectual development, with sustained focus on original texts and artifacts and engagement in those skills and experiences in and out of the classroom that mature a student's mind and emotion—and all of this in an efficient four years of study.

This costs a considerable amount to honor. And like the "object itself"—the original work of art—it only continues to increase in value as its scarcity becomes apparent in a broader world where a mere reflection of the original undergraduate education seemingly suffices.

I, along with all Dickinson alumni, students and their families, have demonstrated that we collectively desire the real thing—the "object itself" in higher education and will not suffer a substitute.

WINTER 2013

Some within the academy might consider an issue of *Dickinson Magazine* highlighting popular culture and celebrity to be trivial and wasteful. Yet, is not a healthy and broad-based intellectual curiosity encompassed in a *useful* liberal education? My position is enforced strongly by Dickinson's founder, Benjamin Rush, who, in a letter to a young man preparing to study medicine abroad, urged him to seek the company not just of the intellectually serious, but also the "wisdom" of all the characters within society, including the cobbler and street sweeper.

As a Dickinsonian, I have taken such advice to heart. My life of "indiscriminate, yet disciplined outreach" was reinforced by a mentor, the esteemed 20th-century English literature scholar Hugh Kenner while I was at Johns Hopkins University. Kenner urged my wife and me to approach people whom we might otherwise hesitate to bring into conversation, observing that you will be surprised how much insight and opportunity they can offer. He gave us the example of his trip to Paris as a graduate student hoping to interact with a radical dramatist to complete his dissertation. Night after night he sent a message to this gentleman's flat seeking a meeting. No answer. Then on the night that he was to sail back to the U.S., he received a note: "Dear Mr. Kenner, of course, I would be delighted to meet. Please come over now. Bring some wine, bread or cheese and we can talk. Samuel Beckett." That meeting was formative in Kenner's career, leading him to meet also Erza Pound, W.H. Auden and others who defined 20th-century English literature.

An example from my own life: On my many flights about the world, I would read all magazines provided on the airplane, to include *People* and *US Weekly*. You might think that as a purported scholar, I would avoid such reading. Oh, no! After one such flight I arrived in London to give a keynote speech at a conference. At the banquet I was seated between the CEO of EMI Records and the head of Prime Minister Tony Blair's Domestic Policy Unit at 10 Downing Street. The gregarious CEO asked if I had heard of the Spice Girls (he signed them). I said I had. He was astonished, asking, "Can you name them?" I said, of course, and proceeded to do so, as I had read an article about them in *People* the night before on my flight. He was so tickled that I as an academic appreciated his entertainment world that he facilitated my conversation with Blair's policy head. At the dinner's conclusion, Blair's representative asked if my wife and I would like to come by 10 Downing Street the next day for tea and conversation about American and English culture. After a quick but profoundly deliberate scan of our agenda, we said we were indeed free (actually, we had nothing on the schedule that day!) and would love to have tea. That meeting led to an introduction to Blair and the beginnings of an advising role for myself.

Also, decades ago I read an op-ed in *The New York Times* on education by Adm. Hyman Rickover, founder of the nuclear Navy, and wrote to him commenting upon the piece. I heard nothing for months but then received an invitation to the admiral's 80th birthday party hosted by presidents Jimmy Carter, Richard Nixon and Gerald Ford. The invitation was marked by the words "Compliments of the Admiral." My wife and I attended and met an array of Washington notables including the presidents. The admiral followed by asking that I arrange a lunch at Johns Hopkins (where I was then working in my late 20s) with his old friend Milton S. Eisenhower, former president of the university, and the then president, Steven Muller. What an incredible experience listening to Rickover and Eisenhower talk about working for President Dwight Eisenhower, the end of World War II and the beginning of the Cold War. I remained connected with Rickover and his work in education reform and had the pleasure of being mentored by Milton Eisenhower (who was also president of Penn State and Kansas State universities) in higher-education leadership.

Finally, my pop-culture curiosity led to one of the most sentimental moments in my life. Always interested in baseball and growing up in upstate New York and born in the city, I cheered for the Yankees as a child and read everything about them and their historical giants. One evening many decades later I was taking a red-eye flight from San Francisco to New York City. At midnight the lounge area was somewhat dark and oddly empty. I was looking down reading and saw traces of formal dark shoes and elegant black pants appear across from me. Most folks then did not travel on a red-eye in such a formal way. We were the only presence in the waiting area. The person was quiet—not a sound—but I perceived a formidable but gentle person across from me. Gradually I raised my eyes and saw who was sitting there looking right at me. It was one of those Yankee giants—one from an earlier generation, but who was without question a massive celebrity as a ballplayer and as a husband to Marilyn Monroe—Joe DiMaggio. I did not speak, but merely nodded in appreciation for all that he had done for baseball and as a hero for me growing up. He simply nodded. I shall never forget that encounter. I saw before me the elegance and graciousness of a person truly accomplished in his field. I experienced the power of not speaking, yet profoundly communicating. Were it not for my youthful obsession with baseball, I would not have recognized Mr. DiMaggio.

As detailed in my "Notes to a 21st-Century Student," never belittle any area of knowledge or experience. You never know when it will come in handy. I rest my case. Engage the world—all of it.

SPRING 2013

One of the highlights of serving as president of Dickinson for the past 14 years has been to engage with the college community in multiple ways—whether it be on campus, at off-campus alumni and parent gatherings around the globe, through phone and e-mail exchanges, through my writings in the national media or through this column. Throughout all of these exchanges, my goal has been to inform, to inspire, to speak out on issues that matter and to position Dickinson appropriately as a top national liberal-arts college.

As I pen my final column for this magazine, I can't help but reflect on these aspirations and how the hard work and determination of the entire community has built a platform of accomplishment upon which the college can continue to build well into the future. And with the help of the many talented individuals who have made up my leadership team over the years, we have worked with great purpose to achieve an evolving and broad-based set of key performance indicators that have taken Dickinson to the next level.

A snapshot of those accomplishments from 1998 to 2012 demonstrates the results of this extraordinary effort:

- First-year applications rose from 3,030 to 5,844 (with an all-time high in 2011 of 6,067).

- The average SAT scores for incoming students went from 1189 to 1293.

- The percentage of domestic students of color increased from 5.4 percent to 13.8 percent.

- The amount of gifted scholarship/institutional grant monies offered rose from $18.5 million to $39.2 million.

- Total endowment monies increased from $151.7 million to $355.8 million.

- Campus wireless infrastructure grew from a single connection in 1998 to a completely wired campus with close to 900 connections.

- Likewise, we started with one technology-equipped classroom and now have 114 across campus.

- Prior to 1999 the college received only three gifts of $1 million or more from individuals; during the past 14 years, the college received 33 such gifts.

- Prior to 1999 there were no faculty positions supported by gifts of $1 million or more; today, 17 faculty positions are supported by gifts at this level.

- Last, the college's visibility through the media grew exponentially, with the number of news stories rising from 56 to 3,584 and a corresponding increase in impressions from 10.3 million to 904.9 million.

In terms of the less-quantifiable changes, I look to the new campus signage, and in particular, the beautiful "Dickinson" arches around the academic quad that were generously contributed by the class of 1960. We have the red Adirondack chairs, the organic farm, the many new construction and renovation projects across campus and the collaboration with the Borough of Carlisle that led to the reduction of High Street from four to two traffic lanes through town and the campus, plus the addition of bike lanes. Last, I note the significant increase in Dickinson's nationwide name recognition (as opposed to confusion with another school in northern New Jersey).

These markers *never* could have been reached without the hard work of the entire faculty, administration and staff, as well as the financial support and volunteer efforts of the alumni, parents and students. I am indebted to each member of this community for the determination and perseverance it required to make these accomplishments a reality. Your efforts have put Dickinson in the spotlight as a true leader in the higher-education landscape.

While my time as president comes to a conclusion on June 30, I look forward to returning to my alumni roots. In essence I think of myself as an alumnus who did what he could for the college when he could with what he could. And I realized something defining about myself as a person while at Dickinson: I like to build things. I like to take—with the significant help of others—an institution from one level of achievement to another. I like to think that my colleagues and I did that at the Johns Hopkins University with the Center for Talented Youth over a 16-year period, and it is still going strong and helping hundreds of thousands of children and youth around the world. I like to think that we did that here at Dickinson. That we built a platform that will educate our future students extremely well, that is rich material for our next president, Nancy Roseman, and her team to advance even further, and that will continue to make us alumni proud of our association.

Elke and I leave Carlisle with a wonderful feeling of community effort and achievement. And I like the way that we are leaving town: understated, low key and in the same car in which we arrived—a 1999 Audi with but 28,000 miles on it and symbolically, I like to think, in good shape and with miles to go. That continuity and momentum are comforting. Thank you, each and every one.